The Art
of
John Fowles

Katherine Tarbox

The University of Georgia Press

Athens and London

© 1988 by the University of Georgia Press
Athens, Georgia 30602   All rights reserved
Designed by Mary Mendell   Set in Trump Medieval
The paper in this book meets the guidelines for
permanence and durability of the Committee on
Production Guidelines for Book Longevity of the
Council on Library Resources.
Printed in the United States of America
92 91 90 89 88   5 4 3 2 1

Library of Congress Cataloging in Publication Data
Tarbox, Katherine.
The art of John Fowles.
Bibliography: p.
Includes index.
1. Fowles, John, 1926–
—Criticism and interpretation.   I. Title.
PR6056.O85Z85   1988   823'.914   83-4809
ISBN 0-8203-1043-3 (alk. paper)

British Library Cataloging in Publication Data
available

For J.T.

Contents

Acknowledgments   *ix*

Introduction   *1*

1   *The Magus*   *11*

2   *The Collector*   *39*

3   *The French Lieutenant's Woman*   *59*

4   *Daniel Martin*   *87*

5   *Mantissa*   *119*

6   *A Maggot*   *135*

Appendix. Interview with John Fowles   *169*

Notes   *193*

Bibliography   *201*

Index   *209*

Acknowledgments

I would like to thank some of the many people and institutions who have seen me through this wonderful project. The University of New Hampshire has been extremely generous in its financial support of parts of this work. The Goodall Library in my own town of Sanford, Maine, has been as useful to me as a big city library, and the staff has unfalteringly filled one zany request after another.

I extend warm thanks to Pat Vasalle, who transcribed the very difficult tapes of my interview with Fowles while her tomatoes were dropping off the vines; to Wilma Rollins, a gifted mathematics teacher, who helped me with some of the arcana in *A Maggot*; to Caroline Lumbard, for giving me access to her excellent Jung library; to Father Linton Studdiford for his erudition and patience in going over with me some of the most difficult parts of the Bible; to Al Bashian for helping me find, at least for a moment, the line between physics and metaphysics.

The editors at the University of Georgia Press have made the publication of this book a joy for me. I thank Melinda Conner for her unfailing vigilance, Debra Winter for her efficiency and expertise, and Elizabeth Makowski for being warm, wise, and full of the love of books. She has been my spiritual ally throughout the process.

Three friends, teachers, and colleagues have been of inestimable help to me. The late Gary Lindberg will always be for me the bearer of the standards against which I measure my own work. Michael DePorte really gave me the first flush of excitement about this book. He read it in several of its drafts and inspired me with his warm praise. Carl Dawson read the manuscript several times and each time, by his shrewd, astute comments, pushed me toward a new level of achievement.

And Jack: there's the man for it.

The Art of John Fowles

Introduction

The following project on the novels of John Fowles (b. March 31, 1926) came about for several reasons, not the least of which is my profound and long-standing regard for his work. Fowles is only now beginning to get the critical attention he deserves with the publication of special issues on his works in two major scholarly journals. It is gratifying to see that he is finally being recognized as a major talent, his dizzying successes with the booksellers notwithstanding. But there is still much work to be done.

In this book I have written an essay on six of Fowles's novels. In my analyses of the novels I have been guided by one light alone: Fowles's implicit demand that the reader of his works "see whole." Seeing whole means diving bravely into the teeming substance of each Fowles text, into the glut of detail, the language play, the eccentric modes of narration, the bizarre events, the dislocations of time, the distinctive use of history, the structural architecture of patterning and counterpoint, the deviations from genre, the flagrant use of cinematic, novel-defeating conventions, the metafictional concerns, and so on. But seeing whole is a skill each reader must learn, and Fowles teaches his reader *how* to see whole by using the education of his protagonist as an example. Thus, each Fowles novel is about learning to see, but also about its own relation to that learning. In my essays I have, in effect, shown how Fowles teaches us how to read his books.

I have not examined *The Ebony Tower* because it is, in intent, theme, and technique, so similar to *The Magus*. In both novels an unsettled man invades the private domain of a much older man, a mentor or hierophantic figure. In each case the young man becomes involved in an elaborate game with two women—one wanton, one demure—in which sex plays a major part. Even the motifs of the novels—art, music, swimming, drinking—are the same. At the end of the game they disgorge their victim back into his ordinary life a changed man, not immediately understanding what has happened to him.

All the novels are the same story at bottom, and we shall soon see why. They begin with a protagonist who suffers some degree of narcissism. He (or in the case of *The Collector* and *A Maggot*, she) has been living an inauthentic life and playing roles that substitute for true identity. He lives, as Nicholas might say, as though someone were looking over his shoulder. Nicholas Urfe sees himself as the *homme revolté*, while Miranda sees herself as the *femme revoltée*. Charles Smithson tries to be a proper Victorian gentleman, Rebecca Hocknell tries to be the most depraved of whores, and Daniel Martin has simply forgotten who he really is. The protagonists are, however, always in a state of disequilibrium. They feel nebulously ill at ease in their inauthentic lives, but do not know why; in fact, they are not even aware that they are playing roles. They are, to use one of Fowles's favorite metaphors, schizophrenic—torn between what they perceive is expected of them and what they dimly intuit they need to be. Nicholas confesses, "I was not the person I wanted to be"; and Rebecca echoes his dilemma: "I would not be what I am, sir."

This statement of desire to escape a false identity, to shed one's self-imposed mask, seals the protagonist's election; and to be elect in Fowles's terms means to be poised on a fulcrum, prepared to change one's wayward course even though the personal risks involved are significant. Charles showed great courage in setting off on an irreversible course that would expose him to ridicule and loss. Victorian society was safe and predictable, while the freedom Sarah offered was decidedly dangerous. Dan needed a similar courage to divest himself of his easy, glib, but superficial life. He took a path that led him to the terrors of self-confrontation.

The elect individual is swept up by a benevolent magus who has already attained selfhood through some personal trial. This mentor draws the protagonist into what Fowles calls the godgame, a complex production designed to upset, disorient, and in all ways distress the "initiate." In the first phase of the godgame the magus takes the protagonist away from his familiar surroundings and thereby disturbs his tired habits of perception. Nick goes to Bourani, Miranda goes to her cell, Charles goes to the infamous Ware Cliffs, Dan goes up the Nile, and Rebecca journeys to Cleave Wood. Once the game is under way the protagonist becomes bereft of ordinary frames of reference. He will have to see with new eyes and use new standards of judgment.

The main strategy of the godgame is metatheater (though the metatheater is less overt in *The Collector* and *Daniel Martin*), a kind of living drama performed for and with the protagonist, without his knowledge of the artifice. The magus involves the protagonist in many layers of illusion by playing out, in metaphorical form, aspects of the protagonist's inauthenticity. Conchis dramatizes many of Nicholas's failings, such as his compulsive abstraction of women and his failure to understand his own nature. Sarah dramatizes, in her bizarre charade involving the French Lieutenant, Charles's struggling will to be free of Victorian restraints. Bartholomew shows Rebecca, in the extraordinary maggot vision, her own longing for peace, sanity, and "more love." The masque is meant to be a mirror in which one sees the reflection of one's self. The various anima figures throughout the novels also act as mirrors for the male initiates. June and Julie, for example, exist in their masque only to receive the projections of Nicholas; they will be whatever he wants them to be. Similarly, Sarah acts as the embodiment of everything Charles secretly wishes he were, just as Jane becomes the eyes through which Dan eventually sees himself.

Sex is always a significant part of the masque because the erotic element functions as a symbol for the ways in which human relationships are deformed by the protagonist's habit of games playing. Sex within the masque is virtually always masturbatory, voyeuristic, or pornographic, suggesting physical analogues to existential conditions. Nicholas is narcissistic and Fowles reveals him masturbating often. Charles is afraid to leap into selfhood, but he enjoys being on the fringe of Sarah's rich life; hence, she makes him the voyeur to her affair with Varguennes. Rebecca debases herself in prostitution, so Bartholomew contrives to involve her in a degrading threesome.

As the protagonist becomes enmeshed in story upon story and endeavors to make sense of the chameleon players he is involved with, he has increasing difficulty in discerning what is real and what is not. The protagonist's habitual approaches to life are unworkable, and slowly the cyclone of appearances works to deconstruct him. This is the ultimate point of the game—to make of the elect what Nicholas calls "a litter of parts." The game works to stress and ultimately break down the protagonist's false identity. The last act of the magus and his players is to abscond; they leave the protagonist alone, in exile, thereby forcing him to put himself back together again in a new way. Each godgame illustrates the lines from "Little Gidding" that Conchis leaves for Nicholas to find:

> The end of all our exploring
> Will be to arrive where we started
> And know the place for the first time.

The major lesson of the godgame is that individual existential freedom, the insistence upon one's right to an authentic personal destiny, is the highest human good. Each protagonist learns that he must see through the roles we all play in ordinary life. The one who is elect must make a conscious choice to live his real life in the world, but choosing once is not enough. Charles, for example, has to suffer anew each day for the freedom he stole and therefore must be willing to be perpetually crucified. Rebecca Lee must suffer poverty, ridicule, and persecution to be true to her vision. Thus, the protagonist who sets himself against the conforming, role-playing masses must be willing to suffer exile for his dissent.

In the journey toward self-awareness Fowles asserts the primacy of intuition, what Dan calls "right feeling," as the vehicle for knowledge. The very point of the godgame is that it cannot be understood by science or logic. It resists rational scrutiny. Appearances are always deceptive, as the numerous spy-narrators prove. The narrators of both *A Maggot* and *The French Lieutenant's Woman* are consistently deceived by the evidence of their senses. Nicholas is deceived by the glut of "proof" that Conchis offers him: the photos, letters, newspaper clippings, and so on. The use of language to deceive is a major theme in all the novels. Fowles shows that in ordinary life we interpret our surroundings according to established codes. We tend to put experience in categories, interpret new material by received ideas, to see with others' eyes, and this epistemological habit is what Fowles calls collector-consciousness. The magus thwarts the protagonist's collector tendencies by giving him an experience that goes far beyond his ability to categorize it. There is, for example, no code that will help Rebecca understand her flying maggot, as there is no easy way for Nicholas to interpret his fantastic trial. The protagonist finds himself by looking inside rather than outside for explanations. Each must "turn in," as Anthony warns Dan, to find the "right feeling" that both reason and language are inadequate to convey.

Fowles uses characteristic metaphors and motifs throughout his novels to express his themes. He uses cinematic techniques (most notably the narrator, who rolls the story before us like a kind of living movie camera) to parallel the way in which we ordinarily perceive life. That is, we are all victims of the tyranny of a present tense that drags us on, treadmill style. We tend to see life as a progress from a beginning to an end, and as a result exclude the sense of "whole sight." Certainly Dan's problem is that he literally perceives his life as a film because films can only work in one tense at a time—the present. Fowles believes that linear time is an artificial measuring device imposed upon experience, that real time is nebulous, and that all time lies parallel. He believes in what he calls a "spinning top" model of history and holds as ideal vision the perception of all three tenses at once. This ideal is fully expressed in *A Maggot* when the silver woman first splinters into her three ages, then merges again.

The typical Fowles protagonist is temporarily blinded by the customs and fashions of his own time, and thus looks upon life with tunnel vision. A major characteristic of each godgame is that it takes the protagonist not only out of his physical space but out of his own time as well. All the elect become time travelers. Conchis throws Nicholas into a whirlwind of myth and archetype, and in his masque he meets Diana, Ashtaroth, Desdemona, a dead Edwardian girl, and so on. Dan's journey represents a going back in time, as he visits first the ancient ruins of Egypt, then, finally, the very roots of human civilization in Mesopotamia. Rebecca journeys into the future of the human race, and when she returns she finds she can also communicate with dead spirits. Of all Fowles's protagonists, she achieves what is perhaps the most nearly complete whole sight. Because Fowles believes in quantum time rather than linear time, he eschews the notion of endings. The godgame always leaves its subject in a quandary because the magus denies him a neat conclusion to his ordeal. The protagonist is a "litter of parts" adrift in a sea of mysteries. But it is the existence of mystery, the denial of an artificial ending, that gives the protagonist the energy to quest on, to reconstruct himself and his perception of the world. His new life feeds on mystery.

The themes of time and perception are conveyed through different narratorial strategies in each novel, but Fowles always uses the motif of doors, rooms, and windows to express the difference between tunnel vision and whole sight. In these novels crucial discoveries take place outdoors. Nicholas has penetrating insights into his predicament when he awakes on a hillside after his trial. Charles finds himself on the Ware Cliffs, as Rebecca finds what she is looking for in Cleave Wood. Dan understands most about himself as he surveys the dismal waste of desert at Palmyra. Indoors, characters are confined and confused, and rooms, as well as closed doors, become a metaphor for lack of personal freedom. In his "stage-settings," in which he plays much with the physical structure of buildings, Fowles examines the ways in which humans enclose, confine, and limit space. The brain in *Mantissa* has a door but no apparent means of egress for Miles. The drawing rooms of *The French Lieutenant's Woman* are an appropriate counterpoint to the open spaces Sarah inhabits. Nicholas moves through the warren-like hallways and bedrooms of Bourani and ends in the trial cell before he earns his meeting with Alison, out of doors, in London. Ayscough's quarters are much like a prison, and in fact he often keeps his deponents under arrest. Miranda's prison is, of course, the ultimate metaphor for lack of freedom. Inside rooms people are confused and unreal. In each of the novels Fowles is looking for the door that leads out of the prison.

If the protagonist learns that all time is one, he also learns that he has a "linked destiny" with the rest of his human fellows. The protagonist who begins as *Homo solitarus* ends, as a result of his trial, with a sense of empathy. The godgame breaks down the walls he builds, the arbitrary categories he puts between himself and others. Nicholas, Charles, and Miranda all experience the deflation of their pretensions, the sense that they are somehow better, smarter, more astute than their fellows. Dan and Rebecca, both of whom had been exiled from friends and family, find their way back into the human fold and "the warm web of kin."

Thus the characters undergo complete metamorphosis. They begin with false, provisional identities and end as freer, more authentic beings. The metamorphosis encompasses the journey from narcissism to humanism, from games playing and artifice to a respect for decency, moderation, sanity, feeling, and caring. The Fowles protagonist comes to honor "the elementary decencies of existence—method, habit, routine . . . continuity." The orderly life is reflected in our last glimpse of Dan, who is standing beside Jane in her kitchen. It is also expressed in Rebecca's vision of the Shaker community.

Of course the most obvious question about any Fowles text is, why does there have to be a godgame at all? Through his various unusual technical strategies Fowles shows in each novel how limited our seeing is in everyday life, how time bound and tradition bound we are, how accustomed we are to looking at the world with collector-consciousness, and how sullied are our true natures. In our everyday lives we train ourselves to ignore and to conform. As Fowles said to me in conversation, "Life does condition us so frightfully, that it's terribly difficult to sense . . . the underlying nature of existence. You know, we are caged more and more by present society in roles, and I think being able to see through the roles is most important. . . . Most people like to be conditioned; unfortunately, it's a fallacy that everybody wants to be freer in the sense we're talking about. They're much happier I think, having fixed routines and a limited way of life." We need to be awakened from this existential torpor and, in his extravagant metaphor of the godgame, Fowles proposes that fiction itself is the great awakener, the great teacher. The maguses involve their subjects in fictions to teach them how to see. Thus the godgame is heuristic. The logic of the godgame is identical to Hamlet's logic when he says, "The play's the thing wherein I'll catch the conscience of the king." Fiction teaches by the method of metaphor because to interpret the difficult material of the story, material that always suggests and never assigns meaning, one must "turn in" to process the information. In this way fiction is a reflection of the protagonist. It illuminates what everything else in ordinary life conspires to hide: what is already there inside him. Because stories lead to self-understanding, fiction is the great existential adventure.

But Fowles always takes the godgame one step further. Through narrative technique he deconstructs the reader as well as the protagonist, and each reader is in turn the elect. Each novel is a parallel godgame in which both the protagonist and the reader grope through the multiple deceptions and illusions of the text. The same operations the protagonist performs, the reader must perform as well. Each novel itself is a dense tapestry of allusiveness, studied confusion, moral quandary, myth, archetype, symbol, and motif. The reader struggles with this polysemy as well as with the substance and mechanics of the protagonist's masque. This density mirrors the complexity of life and if the reader would see the text whole, he must undergo the same sort of reconstruction as the protagonist.

Like the protagonist, the reader must cast off his collector-consciousness and, in terms of the novel, that means he must give up certain generic expectations. He must not expect endings because endings, as Fowles shows us, are arbitrary and artificial. He must also, like the protagonist, not expect to have the mysteries solved for him. The traditional model of the novel's author is the fight fixer as Fowles describes him in *The French Lieutenant's Woman*: "Fiction usually pretends to conform to reality: the writer puts the conflicting wants in the ring and then describes the fight—but in fact fixes the fight, letting that want he himself favors win." Fowles consistently repudiates the notion of an author-god, and he assiduously avoids fight fixing. He refuses, in effect, to collect his readers. He desires in his fiction to allow the reader the same psychoanalytic, reconstructive experience as the protagonist, with its attendant, sometimes uneasy freedoms.

Each novel ultimately tells the same story, and the story of the survival of individual freedom is the *only* story. Upon it are contingent all other human stories, such as history and evolution, because, as both Fowles and Jung affirm, the survival of the race depends upon the salvation of each individual soul. In *The Magus* Fowles uses Hitler to illustrate this idea. Conchis asserts that the real tragedy of Nazi Germany was not that one man had the courage to be evil, but that the millions who followed him, and who were basically sensible, decent people, had not the courage to be good.

In telling his urgent story again and again, Fowles is really conveying his sense that the process of understanding is what he considers important. The real art of John Fowles lies in his showing us the different ways by which we can come to know and be ourselves, despite formidable handicaps and pressures to conform. Always in his novels he compares the art of reading well with the art of living well. Both require considerable perceptual acuity, indeed whole sight. We transfer the methods by which we come to understand his texts onto the plots of our everyday lives. To study the art of Fowles is to study how fiction humanizes us.

I approach the novels on Fowles's own terms, which demand that the reader first submit to the godgame, then step back and see the experience whole. I have tried to communicate the real pleasure of coming to understand his work, a kind of *jouissance* that matches

1 The Magus

The pearly west glowed golden charms

While I held Julia in my arms,

Sweet Julia with the eye of dew,

The heath-bell hasn't one so blue.

Her neck, the lily of the Vale

Is not so fair and sweetly pale,

Her cheek—the rose cropt in the dew

Is not so blushing in its hue.

JOHN CLARE

"Honey Dew Falls from the Tree"

T*he Magus*[1] is actually the first novel Fowles wrote, though he published *The Collector* first, in 1963, and *The Aristos*, his "self-portrait in ideas," second, in 1964. He began working on *The Magus* in the early 1950s as a result of his experiences on the Greek Island of Spetsai, where he was teaching English. Fowles continued to work on his recalcitrant novel for many years, finally allowing it to be published in 1965 after his literary confidence was secured by the great success of *The Collector*. But Fowles continued to be disturbed by the flaws and excesses in his novel and he persevered with its revision over the next twelve years. In 1977 he published a revised version of *The Magus* with which, he says, he is pleased. The new version is not substantially different from the first, though the prose is cleaner, the dialogue less cumbersome, and the supernatural element virtually effaced.[2]

This essay on *The Magus* is divided into two parts which, when taken together, will aim to see the novel whole. The first part deals with the abundant and extravagant material of the masque. Because there is so much minutiae—so many stories within stories (Seidevarre, DeDeukans, Neuve Chapelle, Wimmel), maskings and unmaskings (Lily-Julie, Rose-June, the trial doctors), plays and subplays (Lily Montgomery, the German soldiers, the stench in the night, the trial), symbols, motifs, and allusions—many critics find the novel overwhelming. Ralph Berets epitomizes this attitude: "Fowles has made it difficult for the reader to follow the novel's many digressions and diverse patterns. The reader is sometimes bored and frequently frustrated by Nicholas's opacity and the novel's deliberate complexity. Consequently, much material flows over into the novel's margins never to be put to thematic or structural use. Only by a careful process of selection by the reader does the intriguing material take on the coherence and form demanded of a major artistic creation."[3]

Part I of this chapter is a prismatic look at this intriguing material and an assertion that there is coherence in the apparent chaos. Part II is a stepping back from that material (much like Nicholas's own stepping back from the masque) to consider its implications as they relate to the whole notion of fiction, the relationship of reading to living, and the evolutionary importance of self-knowledge. In effect, this essay tries to accomplish what the book demands: to understand, along with Nicholas, the meaning of the masque and its reason for being.

I

Nicholas's ordeal begins when, after abandoning his girlfriend, Alison, he accepts a teaching position on the Greek Island of Phraxos. There he falls in with the magus, Conchis, who involves Nicholas in an extraordinary "godgame" designed to teach the irresponsible young man about the consequences of his dissolute past. Conchis disorients his pupil by entangling him in a real-life masque and manipulating his affections with siren-like twin sisters. After Nicholas succumbs completely to the magic of the game the magus abruptly abandons him, leaving him to put his life back together. When Nicholas slaps Alison at the end of *The Magus* the masque is finally over. He has been changed from the "débauché de profession" to a man on his knees, enjoying the possibility that tomorrow he may (and probably will) know love. We may rightfully wonder how the bizarre events manufactured by Conchis have produced this change in him. Does Nicholas understand? And if so, how and when did understanding come to him? In short, what has it all been for, why has it been so extreme, and, more important, why has it been at all?

To begin we must look at the mechanics of the masque. The most obvious feature of the godgame is that it takes place on a remote and relatively deserted Greek island. The setting facilitates the abandon-

ment of the familiar to the possibilities of mystery, which Nicholas
feels at once: "When that ultimate Mediterranean light fell on the
world around me, I could see it was supremely beautiful; but when
it touched me I felt it was hostile. It seemed to corrode, not cleanse.
It was like being at the beginning of an interrogation under arc-
lights . . . already my old self began to know that it wouldn't be able
to hold out. It was partly the terror, the stripping-to-essentials of
love" (49). Greece, with its associations of myth and archetype, is a
projection of everything Nicholas is afraid of—the going back, the
going deep, the excavation of frightening, hidden things—and an
evocation of the real human condition where nothing is absolute.
Phraxos's identification with the mind is further stressed when we
learn that Bourani means "skull." Fowles speaks many times of the
"island of the self."[4] Thus, the physical situation of the events assumes many associations with a psychological experience. Fowles
also slants Conchis's physical appearance toward the metaphorical:
"He had a bizarre family resemblance to Picasso; saurian as well as
simian . . . the quintessential Mediterranean man" (81). The lizard,
the monkey, the man, and the artist represent the stages of man's
evolution and suggest unpleasant depths that Nicholas must con-
front.

The game becomes "an extraordinary voyage into the human unconscious," designed to unravel Nicholas's mind, and it has the desired effect: "The masque, the masque: it fascinated me and irritated
me, like an obscure poem . . . he must want me to flounder; flounder indeed, since the curious books and objects he put in my way,
Lily herself, and now the myth figures in the night, with all their
abnormal undertones had to be seen as a hook, and I couldn't pretend that it had not sunk home" (192). Conchis willingly confesses
the artifice of his "meta-theatre": "We are all actors here, my friend.
None of us is what we really are. We all lie some of the time, and
some of us all the time" (404). Conchis puts on a show that Nicholas
must realize is a show, yet he adds enough ambiguous material to
confuse thoroughly his willing subject. Frederick M. Holmes says:
"The blatantly fabricated character of the godgame functions not as
an invitation to take a holiday from life's important concerns but as
a challenge to penetrate beyond the artifice and as a reminder that

one should not completely assume the existence of an accessible core of reality."[5] Toward the end of the masque Nicholas is nearly hysterical, maddened by his failing defenses against the chaos of appearances: "For weeks I had had a sense of being taken apart, disconnected from a previous self . . . and now it was like lying on a workshop bench, a litter of parts . . . and not quite being sure how to put oneself together again" (386).

The analyst-patient relationship between Conchis and Nicholas indicates that the game has therapeutic intentions. Nicholas feels this clinical reserve at their first meeting: "Outwardly he seemed to have very little interest in me, yet he watched me; even when he was looking away he watched me; and he waited. Right from the beginning I had this: he was indifferent to me, yet he watched and he waited" (85). Yet traditional therapy is reversed in that all the telling, the confessing, the reaching into the past is done by the analyst. Conchis (and Lily, who is coanalyst) becomes an interminable teller, creating his past, suggesting its meaning as he goes, leaving all for Nicholas to understand or not, as he is capable. The episodic nature of the telling compares with the session theory of psychiatry. Naturally the doctor never explains the meaning of his stories. He works by innuendo alone, like the Delphic oracle Fowles mentions in *The Aristos*, who "neither hides nor states, but gives signs."[6]

As with any other drama, Conchis's production is attentive to the symbolic possibilities of stage properties, timing, pace, and lighting. The luxurious minutiae of the masque are calculated to shed light on various aspects of the drama: the priapus in the garden reflecting Nicholas's deformed sexuality; the Bonnards that "give the whole of existence a reason"—an illumination of a kind of love Nicholas knows nothing about; the biographies that line Conchis's shelves, betokening his obsessive interest in others' lives; the portrait of Conchis's mother, expressing a filial bond, a sense of family, which Nicholas has never known. The events are carefully timed to affect Nicholas in specific ways, as when Conchis produces the sound effects of an airliner (to remind Nicholas of Alison) in the middle of his story about his lost love. Pace is also important in this play, becoming more and more frenetic in time with Nicholas's increasing disorientation. As Nicholas says after his scuffle with the German soldiers, "The masque was running out of control" (374). The dominant lighting effect might best be described as the elements of chiaroscuro, the events taking place in either brilliant sunlight or blackest night. Conchis's fiddling with the brightness of the lamp during his stories becomes a motif. Fowles creates a moody canvas, suggesting themes of illumination and benightedness.

This, then, is the face of the masque, a game of disorientation and sometimes violent manipulation, an ambitious piece of symbolic metatheater whose director is an unorthodox doctor of the mind. There can be no doubt that Nicholas, for all his frustrations, loves the game. Yet, as he is aware, it all seems designed to teach him a lesson. The main problem Nicholas has throughout is trying to understand what the lesson is and how the strange happenings relate to him. The understanding is a little easier for us because we possess the script.

The major lesson Nicholas must learn from the masque is that he is leading an inauthentic life. He has established a persona for himself that he tries to project to the world. We see this in the first paragraph of the novel when he blandly states, "I was not the person I wanted to be" (15). What he wanted to be was the angst-ridden romantic: the *homme révolté*. What he thought he was revolting against was the heritage of his father, who was motivated by Discipline, Responsibility, and Tradition, the long shadows of Queen Victoria. For all his pseudorebellious spirit, he has simply rejected one role in favor of another. A good part of Nicholas's problem is his middle-class Englishness: the English, as he says, are "born with masks and bred to lie" (372). Alison, with her un-English perspicacity (she is Australian), realizes this immediately: "I offend you and I don't know why. I please you and I don't know why. It's because you are English. You couldn't ever understand that" (33). So Nicholas, as heir to a heritage of falseness, to a moral system based on catchwords, and to an obsessive need to present a front to the world, is doomed to be untrue even in his revolt against untruth.

Nicholas plays many roles in his dealings with Alison. Fowles plays her authenticity, her real love, against Nicholas's equivocation. At their first meeting Nicholas tries a line with her, and in her usual manner she replies, "Let's cut corners. To hell with literature.

You're clever and I'm beautiful. Now let's talk about who we really are" (26). She could not have answered better had she been schooled by Conchis; in fact, this meeting is much like the first one between Nicholas and Conchis, who also rebuffs Nicholas's line: "You come here to meet me. Please. Life is short" (80). Alison has always a remarkable affinity to Conchis's group of elect. Lily de Seitas tells Nicholas this at the end: "You are really the luckiest and blindest young man. Lucky because you are born with some charm for women. . . . Blind because you have had a little piece of pure womanhood in your hands. Do you not realize that Alison possessed the one great quality our sex has to contribute to life? Beside which things like education, class, background, are nothing. And you've let it slip" (601). Nicholas is eager to enjoy Alison's complexity, as long as she stays in the closet. He is openly embarrassed that an old classmate has seen him with her, and makes a tasteless machismo joke about it, "Cheaper than central heating" (36). Alison *is* crude; her language is tough, she sleeps around, her whole aspect is blatantly sexual. What Nicholas wants is for her to turn into an angel in public.

Nicholas ultimately rejects Alison (in a highly orchestrated farewell scene) because she does not harmonize with the role he has cast for himself. In their early days together he never realizes that he loves her. The irony and the tyranny of his posture is that it is so convincing that he can ignore even the most patent truths, a trait that becomes very important in the masque. His curious system of logic suggests that he should not love Alison; he believes, therefore, that he does not love Alison. Always life must conform to his personal fiction. And that does not apply only to Alison.

Part of his role is to play the esthete. He imagines himself a great poet but he can never see the real relationships between real things, a fundamental requirement of the poet. Again, he has not the calling of the true poet, but the desire to attain the trappings of poethood, the facade: "I had begun to write poems about the island, about Greece, that seemed to me philosophically profound and technically exciting. I dreamt more and more of literary success. I spent hours staring at the wall of my room, imagining reviews, letters written to me by celebrated fellow-poets, fame and praise and still more fame"

(57). When he finally realizes that he is no poet he does the proper thing, the thing that brilliant temperamental people are supposed to do: he tries to kill himself. As he sits with the gun pointed at his head he knows he has gone too far: "I was putting on an act for the benefit of someone. . . . I was trying to commit not a moral action, but a fundamentally aesthetic one. . . . It was a Mercutio death I was looking for, not a real one. A death to be remembered" (62). After Alison's alleged suicide (which is intended partly to shed light on his own histrionic one), he is capable of making of her death a literary experience: "I had begun to absorb the fact of Alison's death; that is, had begun to edge it out of the moral world into the aesthetic. . . . By this characteristic twentieth century retreat from content into form, from meaning into appearance, from ethics into aesthetics. . . . I dulled the pain of that accusing death" (401–2). When Nicholas and Alison make love by the waterfall they achieve one of their purest and most authentic moments together. Yet Nicholas appreciates the experience not for its reality, but for its symbolism. As she weaves flowers in her hair he perceives her as an archetype: "Eve glimpsed again through ten thousand generations . . . an intense literary moment" (269). The literary always rules Nicholas's consciousness. To him, people are never people but characters; incidents are always familiar scenes in some familiar drama. He variously casts himself as Robinson Crusoe, Alice in Wonderland, Pip, Joseph K., Caliban, Hamlet, Orpheus, and so forth. Nicholas's greatest problem is his inability to see the distinctions between fiction and reality, real feelings and posturings, identity and persona.

As therapy Conchis offers a lavishly produced dramatization of Nicholas's shortcomings, designed to show Nicholas the truth about himself. Many times the magus insists that it is Nicholas who makes the masque (in the same way that Joseph K. makes his own trial). Conchis simply provides the wherewithal; it is up to Nicholas whether to play or not. His reaction to the events determines the future of the events, and the game may be stopped when Nicholas discovers its meaning. As Conchis explains it, "The object of the meta-theatre is . . . to allow the participants to see through their first roles in it. But that is only the catastasis. It is what precedes the final act, or catastrophe, in classical tragedy. Or comedy. As the case may be . . . [depending upon] whether we learn to see through the roles we give ourselves in ordinary life" (408–9). Conchis's fiction has therapeutic—even humanizing—value because it asserts that illusion and subsequent disillusion are stages we pass through on the way to the truth about ourselves.

The first of Conchis's strategies is to induct Nicholas into the domain, recalling severally the *domaine sans nom* of Alain-Fournier, the untouched and untouchable Garden of Eden, the kingdom of Prospero, and the enchanted isle. The notion of the domain appeals to Nicholas because he feels that any world fit for him to inhabit must be a world outside dull, bourgeois reality. He is in self-imposed exile from what he sees as "mass-produced middle-class" England. At Bourani Conchis simply literalizes Nicholas's escape fantasy.

He brings Lily in to be both dramatic catalyst and coanalyst. In her first incarnation she is Lily Montgomery, the lovely (but dead) and long-lost love of Conchis's youth. The story Conchis spins around Lily is basically a story about two lovers who cannot get together because their situation seems hopelessly complicated. The story has its desired effect on Nicholas: "Conchis paused. There was no emotion in his voice; but I was thinking of Alison, of that last look she had given me" (152). Conchis goes on to say that Lily died in his absence (foreshadowing the "death" of Alison) and then adds cryptically, "The dead live." Nicholas asks, "How do they live?" Conchis replies, "By love" (153). This is the entire story of Nicholas and Alison in microcosm, from the beginning of the novel to the end. The masque could end here if Nicholas were able to see himself in the fiction, but he is preoccupied by the astonishing events.

Lily plays the schizophrenic to show Nicholas how the mind is able to put on and take off different identities. Conchis explains to Nicholas: "I am sure you can see where I am driving. I wish to bring the poor child to a realization of her own true problem by forcing her to recognize the true nature of the artificial situation we are creating together here. She will make her first valid step back towards reality when one day she stops and says, This is not the real world. These are not real relationships" (282). Conchis's diagnosis of Lily is a covert description of the masque, as well as an explanation to Nicholas of his own problem. It is Nicholas who is the split personality, the one who presents well-rehearsed masks to the world, the un-Nicholas. But Nicholas cannot read Conchis's symbolism because he is deeply involved in yet another self-delusion—that Lily (Julie) is his ideal woman.

As Julie Holmes, the budding actress cum damsel in distress, she is more tantalizing because she is approachable. Julie is everything Alison is not: flawlessly beautiful, intellectually inclined, well-bred, dignified, well educated, only latently sexual. Nicholas is all but bludgeoned with clues that Julie is not what she seems. She shifts not only her roles but her demeanor toward him with accomplished dexterity. In the beginning, when Conchis throws the two together for a day, Nicholas believes he has made great advances with his mysterious lady. After she leaves, Maria brings him a telegram from Alison, saying that she wants to meet him in Athens. Nicholas turns and sees Rose standing next to Anubis. The timing and the symbolism of both the intrusive telegram from another world and the vision are studied. Anubis is the Egyptian god of the tombs, the weigher of hearts. Nicholas is having his heart weighed, though he does not understand it at the time. When Lily next sees Nicholas she announces cryptically, "I am Astarte, mother of mystery" (205). In other words, she is personifying an archetype, becoming a projection of what Nicholas wants in a woman. But he is deaf to the truth of her words: "There was no one in the world I wanted to be with now that I had found my Ariadne, and held her by the hand" (210).

Lily's clothes signify the metaphorical role she is playing. She is nearly always dressed in white, to suggest that she is impossibly rarefied. We remember the whiteness of Lily's clothes when Conchis takes Nicholas octopus fishing. Conchis rips a piece of white sheeting to use as bait and catches his prey: "The octopus came reluctantly but inevitably . . . its suckered arms stretching, reaching, searching. Conchis suddenly gaffed it into the boat, slashed its sac with a knife, turned it inside out. 'You notice reality is not necessary . . . even the octopus prefers the ideal' " (138). Considering what eventually happens to Nicholas, this scene is heavy with symbolism. Conchis associates Nicholas with the octopus: both are enticed by lethal bait, both are symbolically castrated, and both are, in their own ways, turned inside out. White cloth appears later to

Nicholas in the "hanging dolls in a sacred wood." One effigy is a skull, the other is a black doll with "two wisps of white rag" around its ankles. He sees these talismans just before his consummation with Lily, and they constitute one final warning: Nicholas will die (the skull speaks of his metaphorical death) if he continues to pursue this ideal woman. When he gets to her bedroom he finds that, like the doll, she is dressed in black and white. Conchis says unabashedly at one point, "Guai a chi la tocca [woe to him who touches her]. . . . Go to Athens, my friend" (233). The incident in the "Earth" also illustrates the penalties for trafficking with illusions. Nicholas follows Lily into this underworld; she escapes and he remains trapped in hell. Nicholas never does see through Lily's role, which is ultimately why he goes on trial. Like Narcissus, he figuratively drowns chasing a reflection of himself. The love he feels is really transference, a reflexive love one feels for teachers and analysts. She is enchanting but unreal, and Nicholas must pass through this mock love before he can truly love.

Alison's arrival in Athens presents Nicholas with a heavy burden since her quotidian reality compares so unfavorably with the magical company at Bourani. Conchis wants Nicholas to go to meet her so that he might have some insight into the game of ideals they have been playing. Their ascent of Mount Parnassus comes at the exact midpoint of the chapters, suggesting, in this symbolic novel, the possibility of a turning point. The mountain itself has many associations with inspiration, and Fowles leads the reader to expect that great things are going to happen, great insights will be achieved. But no Muses dash about and no one has visions. Instead, Nicholas lights the fire and Alison makes dinner in what is an absurdly domestic scene. This vignette is more important for what does not happen than for what does. It has the feel of reality, not archetype. Nicholas should see that there really are no Muses and magic mountains, but he sulks single-mindedly because Alison is not Lily. In other words, Nicholas does not see the lesson of the masque: that islands are beautiful but unreal, and princesses are unreal but beautiful.

Nicholas always has difficulty understanding the complex relationship between sex and love. He divides women into two classes:

those who are meant to be loved and those who are meant to be used. Consequently, his affairs with women are deformed by his inability to see beyond arbitrary categories. Of his Oxford days he says, "I found my sexual success and the apparently ephemeral nature of love equally pleasing" (21). He has a well-rehearsed line and a pat approach: "My 'technique' was to make a show of unpredictability, cynicism, and indifference. Then, like a conjuror with his white rabbit, I produced the solitary heart" (21). The facade of *homme révolté* is useful as well as philosophically pleasing. He leaves his East Anglian public school because "there was also a girl I was tired of" (18). He treats Alison in much the same way. With her one day at the Tate he experiences a tremendous rush of feeling: "I suddenly had the feeling that we were one body, one person, even there; that if she had disappeared it would have been as if I had lost half of myself. . . . I thought it was desire. I drove her straight home and tore her clothes off" (35). To Nicholas it is very simple; Alison is the kind of woman you abandon to go to Greece. And you leave her £50 to smooth things over.

He insists on this separation between her body and her self throughout. When she asks to meet him in Athens he says, "I began to think erotically of Alison again; of the dirty week-end pleasures of having her in some Athens hotel bedroom; of birds in the hand being worth more than birds in the bush" (159). When they do get together "sex with her was unthinkable" (245) because of his romantic fidelity to the chaste Lily. The excuse he offers to Alison for his celibacy is his syphilis, a highly ironic lie. Conchis has arranged for him to be diagnosed as syphilitic so that Nicholas might be forced to evaluate the injustice of the double standard; it is now he who is the whore. As usual, he fails to recognize Conchis's metaphor. When the syphilis ploy doesn't work with Alison, Nicholas tries to explain to her the curious nature of his Petrarchan constancy; but she sees through his posturing and deflates his pretensions: "All that mystery balls. You think I fall for that? There's some girl on your island and you want to lay her. That's all. But of course that's nasty, that's crude. So you tart it up. As usual. Tart it up so it makes you seem the innocent one, the great intellectual who must have his experience. Always both ways. Always cake and eat it" (274). In view of Nicholas's self-serving and licentious conduct with women, it is ironic that he sees Lily's final treachery as the worst of crimes: "How could any girl do what she had done?" Even at the end of the masque he does not perceive that her actions are projections of his own attitudes.

This novel contains a most masterful sex tease, and of all the waiting that goes on in this book the waiting for sex seems to Nicholas the most interminable. At every encounter with Lily all Nicholas gets is reluctance and pulling away. Her behavior is meant to signal that her role is symbolic, and therefore impersonal. But every time she pulls away Nicholas interprets her reticence in a way that is consistent with his idealization of her: "I sensed . . . a delicious ghost of innocence, perhaps even of virginity; a ghost I felt peculiarly well equipped to exorcize, just as soon as time allowed" (210). Lily tries to train his thoughts onto his real love by mentioning Alison in the middle of an embrace: "She ran fingers through my shirt. 'Was she nice in bed? Your Australian friend?' " (455). Or during their final love scene, "Tell me what you liked her doing best to you" (485). She gives him every chance to feel guilty, but he tosses her indelicacy off with a cliché: "girls possess sexual tact in inverse proportion to their standard of education" (485).

Fowles skillfully dramatizes Nicholas's ill-inspired lust by one of Conchis's playlets within the play. On one of the rare days when Lily and Rose are allowed to be together with Nicholas they entice him into sunbathing. Rose is nearly naked (her bikini shocks him) and Lily is dressed in her white one-piece bathing suit. The twin sisters in this case are employed to personify Nicholas's schizophrenic attitude toward women—that is, that there are only virgins and whores. Rose teases him unmercifully, allowing him to see her breasts and adopting seductive poses, while Lily remains prim. Nicholas becomes furiously excited, and Lily manages to take him to the chapel alone, where they are fortuitously interrupted. It is Rose who arouses him but Lily to whom he turns for relief. Thus his lust has nothing to do with Lily or his love for her. His lust is bound up purely in himself, disconnected from the object, hence masturbatory. Lily's masturbation of him later at Moutsa serves as the logical conclusion of this scene.

Conchis leaves pornographic material about to suggest to Nicholas the sordid consequences of dislocating love and sex. The book Conchis leaves on his bedside table shows breasts disconnected from bodies. Lily Montgomery's photograph is surrounded by pornography, suggesting that the adoration of ideal ladies is closely related, in origin, to the titillation produced by pornography. The pornographic automata kept by DeDeukans suggest the mechanical, rather than human and emotional nature of the voyeur's obsession. At the end of the masque Lily becomes Maîtresse Mirabelle. Fantasy (such as Nicholas fabricates around Lily) is essentially autoerotic, as is pornography, and both close him off from the reality of the exciting subject. The point of pornography is to allow one the impulse to make love to oneself. In this light it is easier to see why, in the revised edition, Fowles gives so much more weight to the "erotic element," and why he allows Nicholas to masturbate in front of us so many times: Nicholas is essentially a masturbatory personality.

The same sexual lessons figure heavily at the trial. Nicholas is strapped to the flogging frame, literalizing his penchant for voyeurism, and made to watch a blue movie starring Lady Jane (Lily) and the Black Bull (Joe). The Victorian ambiance of the film suggests Nicholas's love for having dirty things kept behind closed doors. This fantasy sex is then followed by the real copulation of Lily and Joe before his eyes. The juxtaposition suggests a contrast between the way Nicholas views sex and the way Conchis feels sex should be regarded: as "two people who were in love making love." Nicholas thinks, "What they did was in itself without obscenity, merely private" (529). The overtones of *Othello* in this scene inform Nicholas's situation: Nicholas is cast as Iago, a miserable creature who has loved neither wisely nor well. Desdemona (Lily) and Othello (Joe) represent the real love from which Nicholas is excluded. Like Iago, he is doomed to cause the ruin of others (such as Alison) through his vanity and compulsive fantasizing. Even now Nicholas misconstrues the lesson: "I suddenly knew. . . . We have no choice of play or role. It is always *Othello*. To be is, immutably, to be Iago" (530). What he doesn't understand is that these visions are not things that have to be.

Nicholas's unhealthy attitude toward women and sex remains only one part of what Conchis sees to be Nicholas's "collector-consciousness." A collector categorizes and dehumanizes life and people. As we have seen, Conchis uses the twin sisters to personify Nicholas's tendency to categorize. Nicholas is disturbed that Alison does not slip without a fight into the role he casts for her: "She stood there in her white dress, small, innocent-corrupt, coarse-fine, an expert novice" (28); "She was bizarre, a kind of human oxymoron" (24). At the trial Nicholas is presented with the suggestion that inside an empty "coffin box" (suggesting Alison, whom Nicholas thinks to be dead) resides the goddess Ashtaroth, who is Ishtar in Babylonia, Astarte in Greece, and Ashtareth to the Jews. She is also related to Isis, Aphrodite, Venus, and Demeter; she is the goddess of love, beauty, motherhood, vegetable fertility, creativity, war, virginity, and prostitution. The goddess, in whom the trial doctors say reside their meaning, is the culmination of all goddesses. She is the extracted essence of a real woman—a harmony of contradictions—like Alison. She cannot be pinned down, hence her absence.

Conchis offers the DeDeukans story as a parable of the consequences of collector-consciousness. DeDeukans had "devoted his life to the collecting of collections" (177). As a result, he became lifeless, depraved, a fanatic misogynist. What Conchis says of DeDeukans might easily be applied to Nicholas: "Self-denial was incomprehensible to him . . . for him even the most painful social confrontations and contrasts . . . were stingless. Without significance except as vignettes, as interesting discords, as pleasurable because vivid examples of the algedonic polarity of existence" (178). The logical extension of DeDeukans is Wimmel, whose similar attitudes assume extraordinary social and historical significance: "He had eyes like razors . . . without a grain of sympathy for what they saw. Nothing but assessment and calculation . . . they were the eyes of a machine" (418). Wimmel says to Conchis, "I have only one supreme purpose in my life, the German historical purpose—to bring order into the chaos that is Europe" (428). The compulsion to collect is malignant. In personal relationships it destroys love; in political situations it breeds fascism and destroys humanity. Conchis says of his war experience, "I saw that the attempt to scientize reality, to name it and categorize it and vivisect it out of existence, was like trying to remove the air from the atmosphere" (410).

The same attitudes that shape the collector breed overintellectualization. We have seen how the primacy of Nicholas's intellect fosters his literary view of life, and how Alison's spontaneity compares favorably with his studied posing. Part of Conchis's purpose in the masque is to obliterate Nicholas's power to reason. The many plays within the play (the stench after the Neuve Chapelle story, the apparition of Robert Foulkes, the tussle with the German soldiers, etc.) are designed to estrange Nicholas from the safe ground of logic. The drama of Apollo, Diana, and the satyr, for example, takes place in the middle of Conchis's DeDeukans story, during which Nicholas is having dinner with a dead Edwardian girl. The moral of both the story and the play is that seeking pure pleasure is foolish. Nicholas tries desperately to see the connection between crazy old DeDeukans and this theater of the gods, but he flounders: "I'd enjoy it more if I knew what it meant." Conchis replies, "My dear Nicholas, man has been saying what you have just said for the last ten thousand years. And the one common feature of all the gods he has said it to is that not one of them has ever returned an answer" (185). Conchis's strategy is to destroy Nicholas's ability to use reason alone as a means of understanding his bizarre predicament. Conchis disorients Nicholas to stimulate his intuitive faculties. The speciousness of pure reason is illustrated by a motif, or ritual, in the novel: the bringing forth of proof or evidence such as photographs, newspaper clippings, letters, documents, and pamphlets. All are used to confirm or validate assertions of fact, but are really lies that lead to more lies.

Nicholas's overuse of intellect causes the atrophy of his more affective powers, and inevitably leads him into exile from his fellow humans. Nicholas feels alone from the start. He is indeed the *Homo solitarus* the trial doctors accuse him of being. What Conchis offers as a corrective is to be elect; and to be elect means to be "one of us" in the Conradian sense. Conchis and his proselytes form a group who represent sympathy, loyalty, integrity, and humanism. Nicholas feels that they are a "deeper, wiser, esoteric society" than the masses at large. Thus, Conchis is calling Nicholas into the family, showing him the possibilities of a brotherhood of true minds. He offers Nicholas a kind of sanity and stability, represented by his ritualistic playing of Bach and Telemann, whose regular music signals harmony, order, and the resolution of discord. The trisyllabic bell that always calls Nicholas at Bourani is the symbol of this larger calling. It also recalls a conversation between Nicholas and Conchis about Donne's conception of men and islands; the bell is a literalization of "it tolls for thee."

The secret knowledge shared by the elect, and promulgated by Conchis, is that self-knowledge and authenticity are the keys to personal freedom. Existentialist studies have dominated criticism of Fowles's work because Fowles so often presses this idea.[7] Conchis couches this lesson in the Neuve Chapelle story: "What I thought was fever was the fire of existence, the passion to exist. I know that now. A *delirium vivens.* . . . Try to imagine that one day you discover you have a sixth, a till then unimagined new sense—something not comprehended in feeling, seeing, the conventional five. But a far profounder sense, the source from which all others spring. The word 'being' no longer passive and descriptive, but active . . . almost imperative" (129). Beside pure being, education, science, valor, and intellect are meaningless. When Conchis says he is "psychic" and can travel to other worlds, he means that he is able to put aside the artifices everyday living requires of him, and turn inward to find his constants. This metaphor also informs Nicholas's hypnosis, during which he is manipulated to become aware of his sixth sense: "It dawned on me that this [experience] was something intensely true and revealing; this being something deeply significant about being; I was aware of existing, and this being aware of existing became more significant than the light" (238).

The vision that ends Nicholas's hypnosis is the lesson of the god-game: "The endless solitude of the one, its total inter-relationship to all" (239). For a few moments Nicholas understands the basic Heraclitean paradox of life, the secret of the elect. The smile, which is a code in Conchis's secret society, is the symbolic expression of this understanding.

The narrative structure of this novel (with all its twistings, digressions, narrative hooks and baits, interruptions, and frustrations) is based on the verb "to wait"; and under hypnosis Nicholas realizes that "the waiting was a waiting for" (238). Avrom Fleishman has done extensive work on the relationship of the *The Magus* to the ancient Eleusinian mysteries. At Eleusis initiates were taken to a waiting room and shown a reenactment of the Persephone myth.[8] In this case it is Conchis who waits for Nicholas to come to understanding by himself. Conchis says of his first coming to Bourani: "I had immediately the sensation that I was expected. Something had been waiting there all my life. I stood there, and I knew who waited, who expected. It was myself. . . . There comes a time in each life like a point of fulcrum. . . . You are too young to know this. You are still becoming" (408–9). The players of the masque await the moment when Nicholas will stop the masque and decide what fabric he will make out of the loose threads of his being.

The notions of pure being and pure selfhood bring up some difficult moral problems. Assertions of personal freedom raise the specters of egotism and anarchy. In a sense Lily de Seitas imposes the limit on selfhood with her eleventh commandment: "Thou shalt not commit unnecessary pain." But more than that, Conchis and his family (and Fowles himself) believe in the essential goodness of men and women; the self is, for them, the only source of integrity. Conchis explains, "It is the self that must not be betrayed." Nicholas retorts, "I suppose one could say that Hitler didn't betray his self." Conchis: "You are right. He did not. But millions of Germans did betray their selves. That was the tragedy. Not that one man had the courage to be evil. But that millions had not the courage to be good" (132). Conchis enacts a strategy of proselytization that has far-reaching social effects. Lily de Seitas explains, "We are rich and we are intelligent. . . . And we accept the responsibility that our good luck in the lottery of existence puts upon us. . . . Do you really think we do this just for you? Do you really believe we are not . . . charting the voyage?" (604) "Charting the voyage" refers to the moral evolution of the species, the goal of which is a society of self-aware individuals whose confidence and strength will subdue evil.

The awareness of being imposes the responsibility of freedom, the lesson of the "eleutheria" story. This story is the true climax of the

What troubles Nicholas most about the masque is that he cannot solve all its mysteries. Conchis has tried to teach him that the nature of the mind, the self, is basically incomprehensible by ordinary means. He says, "The human mind is more a universe than the universe itself" (131). Fowles creates in this book a sustained motif of windows and doorways, of people peeking and disappearing, of glimpsing something partially concealed and then losing it: Alison is viewed through a window and then lost, twice (her disappearance from the Russell Square flat and her reappearance in Athens); Lily Montgomery first appears through a cracked door, which she hurriedly closes; as Nicholas pursues Lily out of the Earth she slams the door in his face; Lily de Seitas shows Nicholas a painting of herself peeking from behind a door; mysterious figures are always just disappearing behind doors; and there are divers locked doors. The motif suggests that at best Nicholas will only receive partial answers and that a good part of what he tries to understand will always resist the assault of logic. Conchis consistently cautions Nicholas against trying too hard to find all the answers to all his questions. Mystery, he says, "has energy. It pours energy into whoever seeks an answer to it. . . . I am talking about the general psychological health of the species, man. He needs the existence of mysteries. Not their solution" (235). Lily de Seitas adds, "An answer is always a form of death" (626). That mystery should be respected is the point of the Seidevarre story, which is a grotesque parody of science's inability to deal with the mind, of trying to reduce this complex man to a classic Freudian case of anal overtraining. The same idea is brought up in all the unmaskings at the trial. A concatenation of hobgoblins enters, all from different countries and different eras, all of whom represent man's projections of the mysterious forces in life. Nicholas expects some sort of explanation of this smorgasbord of the occult. They unmask and are introduced as eminent doctors whose duty it is to dispel bugaboos; they in turn are revealed as frauds. Nicholas never does hit bottom because there is no bottom. Part of truth will always defy explanation, which is a cause for celebration, not dejection, as Lily says: "I think God must be very intelligent to be so much more intelligent than I am. To give me no clues. No certainties. No sights. No reasons. No motives. . . . If I prayed, I'd ask God never to reveal himself to me. Because if he did I should know that he was not God but a liar" (296). In effect, "there is no truth beyond magic."

II

John Fowles is the true magus of this novel. Because he has Nicholas tell the story as it happened to him, without an intervening hindsight, he allows Conchis to perform the same operations upon the reader that he does upon Nicholas. Fowles makes the reader Nicholas's fellow initiate and tests the perception and understanding of both equally. Therefore, just as Fowles asks the reader, along with Nicholas, to translate the arcane language of the masque, he further asks that he question why there has been a masque, and why it has taken such an extreme form. At the end of the trial the reader shares this quandary with Nicholas. But it is Fowles's hope that, by watching Nicholas struggle and err, the reader will supersede him in understanding. The protagonist is also the reader's foil.

Nicholas has consistently failed to see the flaws in his character that Conchis projected in his fictions. At every junction in the plot Nicholas thinks he understands the masque, but Conchis proves him wrong at the plot's next divagation. What he does learn he forgets immediately. At the trial he had accurately perceived that the masque was a test of his selfhood. But by the next day he forgets his insight and assesses the masque as "evil fantasies sent to test my normality, and my normality had triumphed" (533). Yet, for all his obtuseness, he has moments of Orphic illumination (as signaled by the epigraph to the third book).[9] It appears that he has learned something. He awakes from his drugging (fittingly) amid ruins. His descent of the cliff is attended by birth symbolism. Back in Athens he is appalled by the masks he sees at the English embassy party: "They were all the same. . . . Nobody said what they really wanted, what they really thought. Nobody behaved with breadth, with warmth, with naturalness. . . . The solemn figures of the Old Country, the Queen, the Public School, Oxbridge, the Right Accent, People Like Us, stood around the table like secret police, ready to crush down in an instant on any attempt at an intelligent European humanity" (560). Nicholas's insight into Englishness shows that he has grown out of that mold he was in at the beginning of the novel. He later feels a similar scorn for Mitford's chauvinism and public school mentality. (Mitford never did understand the masque, and he became one of Conchis's dropouts; he is later shown to be a "forger.") Immediately after his unsavory interview with Mitford, Nicholas phones Lily de Seitas, whom, he protests, he hates. Nicholas begins to feel displaced in his old life and turns to his new family for help.

As if to refute the label *Homo solitarus*, Nicholas begins to show humanity toward others. He gives money to a needy peasant family aboard a steamer. He befriends Kemp, "a sluggish, battered . . . Charlotte Street bohemian," with real feeling, not condescension. His charitable impulses backfire in his affair with the "poor mongrel," Jojo. But he is finally able to grieve genuinely for inflicting pain upon another. Though he blunders in his attempts to understand and rectify his past errors in love, he has some moments of genuine insight into Alison: "Her special genius, or uniqueness, was her normality, her reality, her predictability; her crystal core of non-betrayal; her attachment to all that Lily was not" (533). And, "a new feeling [about Alison] had seeded and was growing inside me, a feeling that haunted me day and night, that I despised, disproved, dismissed, and still it grew, as the embryo grows in the reluctant mother's womb, sweeping her with rage, then in green moments melting her with . . . but I couldn't say the word" (577). This reference to birth prefigures the ending, where Nicholas finally understands the anagram of the one body. At the beginning of the book Nicholas thought the one body meant lust. Nicholas finds at the end that Alison is "mysterious, almost a new woman. As if what had once been free in her, as accessible as a pot of salt on the table, was now held in a phial, sacrosanct" (650). As Lily de Seitas argued, Alison was always precious; it is Nicholas's perception that is different.

Nicholas begins to discard his old pose of romantic angst and substitutes for it a healthy and seminal self-doubt:

> What was I after all? . . . Nothing but the net sum of countless wrong turnings. . . . All my life I had tried to turn life into fiction, to hold reality away; always I had acted as if a third person

was watching and listening and giving me marks for good or bad
behavior . . . a god like a novelist, to whom I turned, like a character with the power to please, the sensitivity to feel slighted,
the ability to adapt himself to whatever he believed the novelist-god wanted. (538)

Nicholas realizes what he has been, but he does not realize that he
has discovered Conchis's method. Conchis has played the paternalistic author-god to literalize Nicholas's metaphor.

At the end of the novel Nicholas feels nothing but scorn for Conchis and all the players. So these illuminations happen virtually
against his will and not as a result of his conscious endeavor or his
desire to flaunt his insights to Conchis. The question that arises
from this paradox is, how does Nicholas change if he understands
nothing of the machinations that were used to bring about that
change? How is it that he begins to emulate the values of the elect
even as he continues to misconstrue the lessons of the masque?

To answer these questions it is necessary to consider Fowles's
macrocosmic godgame with this novel. The book through which the
reader gropes, as well as Nicholas's personally tailored masque, represent strategies designed to belie the expectations of their subjects
and therefore stimulate their perceptiveness. Fowles's position is
that everyday life teaches us to ignore and to interpret the material
of life according to conventions. His book deals with seeing beyond
conventions and fixed ideas into the truth of matters. Fowles, like
Conchis, seeks to teach his subjects to notice.

Part of Fowles's strategy of disorientation comes through the confusion of genre. Throughout the book the reader is manipulated to
expect possible outcomes as a result of generic conventions. It begins as a traditional confessional novel, and the narrator adopts an
ironic stance of the older, sadder, wiser man toward the events of his
early life. But that perspective is abruptly changed early on as the
novel slips into another genre, the bildungsroman, where the narrator gives an unimpassioned account of his growth toward maturity. That category cannot contain the narrative for long, as Fowles
makes it clear to the reader that Nicholas does not understand how

his present life has been shaped. The novel then becomes a mystery story, but the conventions of that genre are not observed because the mystery is never solved. Through most of the novel Fowles leads the reader to believe that he is reading a romance, with its familiar conventions: the clash of the real with the ideal, the familiar imposed upon by the bizarre, the shifts in expectation, the appeal to the reader's intuition. Many critics acknowledge that Fowles is part romancer but that, as Ronald Binns says, he manipulates "the romance form to effect . . . a sceptical examination of the romance experience."[10] The romantic element of the novel compares with the Conradian impressionistic novel, in which an effort to deal with experience is recorded by a thousand discoveries, interpretations, and misinterpretations. The sense of genre is further confused because while the reader interprets the material as a romance (with its quest, the enduring of rituals, the achievement of the quested object), the protagonist feels himself to be in a satire (the labyrinth that has no exit, the angst, the meaningless, the eternal struggle). The romance does not end conventionally, as Fowles forces his hero to quest on: "The maze has no centre. An ending is no more than a point in sequence, a snip of the cutting shears. . . . What happened in the following years shall be silence" (645). To end the book Fowles would have to belie one of its premises: that every answer is a death. The satire does not end traditionally, either, because Nicholas's struggle has not been meaningless. *The Magus* is a profoundly optimistic novel, though some still persist in calling it nihilistic.[11] Fowles sets many generic conventions in motion and then stops them. The novel is, finally, nongeneric; or one might say, it creates its own genre and makes sense only on its own terms. The form of the novel ultimately mirrors its theme: the praise of individuality, the skepticism of convention.

The strategy of disorientation works by disturbing the reader's complacency about his ability to process information. *The Magus* is, essentially, an epistemology; Fowles places a great deal of emphasis on what one should know, but he places much more emphasis on how one comes to know it. Fowles deliberately tries to overwhelm the reader with material, actually to preclude any possibility of immediate understanding. A thought from Martin Price applies:

Once its premises are given, the world of a novel becomes the stage of an action, and our commitment to the narrative movement tends to absorb our attention. Narrative may be said to depress the metaphorical status of character and setting; it gives a coherence to all the elements on the level of action that deflects attention from their meaning and from their position in the structure. . . . Narrative movement, with its strong temporal flow and its stress upon causal sequence, may compel full attention to itself.[12]

The perception of meaning clearly occurs on a different level. Once the reader (and Nicholas) are thoroughly disoriented, certain operations, which are implicitly defined in the novel, must be performed to attain reorientation.

The construction of meaning is a reconstruction, a return to the difficult material of the text. The reconstruction is bound up with the operations of time. Conchis deliberately sets Nicholas adrift for a time so that his memory can begin to examine, organize, and synthesize his weird ordeal. Because he writes the book from a time future to the masque, and because he wishes to share this method of disorientation with the reader, he must have achieved understanding, become one of the family. His aim must be, like Conchis's to proselytize. Nicholas struggles with the masque in his memory. The reader exercises the freedom of consecutive readings. The operation performed is deconstruction, which entails a return to what one had erroneously believed to be true meanings, and a substitution of other possible meanings. It is the method of metaphor (Conchis has said many times that "the masque is only a metaphor") in that metaphor forces us to reevaluate our notions of reality; it exploits the distance between belonging and disorientation.

In the novel Fowles uses psychoanalysis as a metaphor for rethinking. As many critics have shown, Nicholas's quest is synonymous with the process of individuation through archetype that Jung described.[13] But this kind of reading, though helpful, too narrowly literalizes Fowles's metaphor. Interpreting Nicholas according to Jung is not substantially different from interpreting Henrik Nygaard according to Freud. Nicholas uses the method of deconstruction at the end of the novel when he seeks frantically to understand the truth behind all the fictions, and when he tries to synthesize a catalog of details from the masque. He has not achieved selfhood by the end, but the existence of his memoir suggests that he did quest on and come to some understanding.

Reading itself is a form of deconstruction, and Fowles consistently draws parallels between Nicholas's groping and the act of reading. Competent and perceptive reading is a process of seeing through and assimilating the many layers of deception in fiction. Both Fowles and Conchis assert that one may solve existential problems by learning how to understand metaphor. One reads and one lives in motion, trying to arrive at something. He must lose his way, find it again, and find it in a new world. The stanza from "Little Gidding" that Conchis leaves for Nicholas to find defines Fowles's feelings about the value of fiction:

> We shall not cease from exploration
> And the end of all our exploring
> Will be to arrive where we started
> And know the place for the first time.
>
> (69)

The masque and the novel, then, are seductive and enchanting adventures; but they are merely tools that teach us who we are.

The psychological operations Conchis performs on Nicholas are the same operations Wimmel performed on Conchis. Wimmel makes Conchis participate in many fictions: that they are good friends, that they are both civilized, educated men, that the guerrillas are still at large when he knows they have been caught, that the gun is loaded, when it is not. When he realizes that logic can no longer sustain him in this situation he turns inward to draw upon his intuitive powers. In effect, he reads his situation; he reads perceptively the symbolism of the guerrilla's burned mouth, and has a penetrating insight into the meaning of personal freedom. *The Magus*, then, is a self-conscious novel. It is about being and knowing, and also about itself in relation to being and knowing.

If Fowles praises perception, he also defines the limits of perception. His notion of reality is that the real is constituted by both the revealed and the concealed. Some of that part of truth that is concealed will always be concealed, always resist understanding. Henry James says, "The real represents to my perception the things we cannot possibly not know, sooner or later . . . the romantic stands, on the other hand, for the things that, with all the facilities in the world, all the wealth and all the courage and all the wit, and all the adventure, we can never directly know."[14] Fowles echoes this notion of a bifurcated reality in *The Aristos*: "We are in the best possible situation because everywhere, below the surface, we do not know; we shall never know why; we shall never know tomorrow; we shall never know a god, or if there is a god. . . . This mysterious wall around our world and our perception of it is not there to frustrate us, but to train us back to the now, to life, to our time being."[15] Because there are mysteries that cannot be solved, Conchis never reveals his identity, and the gods (including the novelist-god) abscond at the end of the novel. It is also the reason that the symbolism in the book is so calculatedly polysemous. My explanation of the masque is not so much a definition of meaning as a conviction that it is both possible and necessary to find meaning. Fowles calls this book a "Rorschach test." We can understand both the microstructure (Conchis's masque) and the macrostructure (Fowles's book) by methods of deconstruction, using the recalcitrant conventions of language. But Fowles has also succeeded in giving us an "experience beyond the literary."

2 The Collector

To have and to hold,

till death do us part.

If Fowles gives the reader expansiveness, sunshine, passion, and the glow of humanity in *The Magus*, he gives him darkness, pain, despair, and death in *The Collector*.[1] The reader of *The Magus* turns pages eagerly because, like Nicholas, he is made hungry for the magic. The reader of *The Collector* is required to hope that Miranda will escape, though he knows almost from the beginning of the novel that she will not. There is hope that somewhere Fowles will reveal some justification (as in classical tragedy) for the torments to which he subjects the reader. No amount of critical surgery on this book will reveal any brightness or hope beneath the bleak facade. As a sad, black, and wrathful diatribe against the abuses of freedom, *The Collector* earned for Fowles a place in Britain's gallery of angry young men.

In this chapter I have tried to offer some new thoughts on the novel. In his introduction to the Fowles special issue of *Modern Fiction Studies*, William Palmer offers an explanation of why there are no entries on *The Collector*: "Crickets seem hard pressed to say anything new about it."[2] Indeed there has been little critical activity on the novel. I have considered two main aspects of the book. The first is Fowles's skilled handling of the double point of view, which he uses both to contrast and compare the two tellers. The second is an examination of Fowles's extreme distance from the text and the implications that distance has for the moral resolution of the novel.

A good deal of the malaise created by the novel comes from several kinds of claustrophobia, the most obvious of which is the confinedness of Miranda's cell. Virtually the entire story takes place behind bolted doors and shuttered windows, or in the hideous cellar that recalls so strongly Poe's tales of buried madness and walled-in tragedy. Clegg systematically sends away the outside world, creating an airtight environment, a perverted domain.[3] Fowles invites the reader to feel a sense of imprisonment in the two monologues. For roughly half the book the reader is trapped inside an appallingly sick mind, made to witness the workings and effects of depraved logic. For the second half of the book the reader is inside Miranda's mind, unpleasantly burdened with dramatic irony, frustration, and a sense of helplessness. The story itself is a kind of imprisonment because it has no plot. Frank Kermode says that in reading novels, "we concern ourselves with the conflict between the deterministic pattern any plot suggests, and the freedom of persons within the plot to choose and so alter the structure, the relations of beginning, middle, and end."[4] Rarely has there been, even in the darkest of naturalistic novels, a character more literally and utterly without power to affect events than Miranda Grey. The beginning of this novel is its end; Miranda is doomed from the moment Clegg decides to make her his "guest." No action that she takes can produce any result. Every encounter between her and Clegg ends the same way—with her seeking freedom and him locking the door. The series of nonproductive events in the novel are so many flutterings against the glass of the killing jar. The movement of the book is circular rather than linear. The same things happen again and again until the situation runs out of energy. The plot, then, is not progressive, but entropic.

The feeling of confinement is what thrilled the millions of readers who bought this novel. But, like Hitchcock, Poe, James, and Hawthorne, Fowles treats many serious subjects beneath the thrills, subjects that come to light through his delicate handling of the double point of view. Most obviously he uses this narrative technique to contrast his characters and their perceptions of the situation. Further, the adjacent narrations would seem to reveal the stock gothic types of villain and heroine. But Fowles undermines the reader's desire to categorize the characters by making them "grey." As Jeff Rackham says of Clegg, "The chilling intensity of the story arises from the ambiguous response to him which both Miranda and the reader share."[5] Miranda is too often priggish and petulant, undercutting her status as romantic heroine.[6] Clegg has in his favor his supremely reliable narration; he may lie to everyone else but he does not lie to his diary. Miranda misinterprets much of what she sees, both in her life and in her imprisonment, because of her obsessive intellectualizing. She turns encounters with Clegg into battles of ideas, when in fact she is engaged in a no-nonsense life-and-death struggle. Clegg is right when he tells us so many times, "She never understood." One of Clegg's endearing features is his maniacal cleverness. His "precautions" are so ingenious that even Miranda admires his work, against her will. Fowles exploits the universal fascination with the perfect crime. The characters are neither uniformly good nor uniformly evil because Fowles refuses to collect them by slipping them into categories.

If we first look at the differences between the tellers we note that while Miranda is all energy and vitality, Clegg approximates that state of nothingness, of sheer negation, that Fowles calls the nemo.[7] Miranda says, "He's not human; he's an empty space disguised as a human" (240). The most striking feature of Clegg's logic is its consistent and complacent negation of the ordinary materials of normal existence. He borrows positive community values and twists them to suit his destruction mania. He turns the notion of "guest," for example, into "prisoner." The "snug and cosy home" for Miranda becomes both prison and crypt. "A good day's work" for Clegg is finding where Miranda lives so he can kidnap her on her way home. Courtesy and thoughtfulness in Calibanese mean not raping Miranda when "not many would have kept control of themselves" (92). Clegg construes his abduction of Miranda to be an extraordinary feat of bravery, "like climbing Everest or doing something in enemy territory" (28). And, of course, he turns love into suffocation. Michael Bellamy demonstrates that Clegg perverts nature in many ways, such as by exploiting natural solitude for his depraved purposes.[8] Clegg systematically takes every healthy and noble human virtue and destroys it.

Clegg's contorted sense of the real community is matched by his twisted sense of self. He is dominated by unrecognized desires, such as when he finds his dream house: "I saw an advert in capitals in a page of houses for sale. I wasn't looking for them, this just seemed to catch my eye" (15). He succeeds in hiding his depraved nature from himself by putting his actions under the protective blanket of "pretending." So completely confused are his conscious and unconscious minds that he displaces the act of dreaming from the night to the daytime world: "I lay there thinking of her below, lying awake too. I had nice dreams, dreams where I went down and comforted her; I was excited, perhaps I went a bit far in what I gave myself to dream. . . . Then I went to sleep" (27). The materials of Clegg's dreams define the substance of the real Clegg—the maniacal abductor, the "dirty little masturbating worm"; and when he makes his fantasies come true he complains, "I felt like in a dream" (18). Clegg fully accepts the facade he has erected for the world's sake. Miranda observes that "he's what people call a 'nice young man' " (128). His entire monologue, in fact, shows an extraordinary vacancy of thought or reflection about himself and his crime. The phrase "I don't know why" is the refrain that follows each mad action: "I still say I didn't go down there with the intention of seeing whether there was anywhere to have a secret guest. I can't really say what intention I had. I just don't know" (15). Clegg has never applied serious thought to any subject, as we see when Miranda asks him if he believes in God: "I don't think about it. Don't see that it matters" (59). All his thoughts descend to the cellar and alight on Miranda. What energy he has is spent in describing everything she does and says. He figures very little in his own monologue. He seldom speaks, and when he does, he does not dignify his words with quotation marks. He is nothing but turnkey and observer and is therefore of such little account as a human being that he appears with surprising infrequency even in Miranda's diary. Clegg's telling is a masterwork of self-delusion and self-effacement.

Miranda, on the other hand, shuns neither community nor self. Her diary contains a refreshingly large cast of characters whom she looks upon with warmth. While Clegg's thoughts sink, hers soar. She compensates for her confinement by imagining and remembering. Seclusion teaches her that she has a bond with "the people on the Tube," whom before she had always treated with condescension. Her intense need for companionship and humanity drives her into a relationship with Clegg that she neither welcomes nor understands:

It's weird. Uncanny. But there is a sort of relationship between us. . . . It can't be friendship, I loathe him. . . . Perhaps it's just knowledge. Just knowing a lot about him. And knowing someone automatically makes you feel close to him. . . . He sits by the door and I read in my chair, and we're like two people who've been married years. . . . The only real person in my world is Caliban. It can't be understood. It just *is*. (148)

Miranda, who has always been a snob, learns what Lily de Seitas taught Nicholas, that "love may really be more a capacity for love in oneself than anything very lovable in the other person" (*The Magus*, 601). Deprivation teaches her that she has a "linked destiny" with all humans. She reaches even through the centuries to be touched by Bach's spirit: "I always used to think Bach was a bore. Now he overwhelms me, he is *so* human" (258).

Clegg's portion of the novel is a recollection, which always has the potential for utilizing the reconstructive capabilities of memory. As *The Magus* suggests, one learns from remembering by a process of dismantling and reassembling oneself. But Clegg has gained no insight into his crime from the remembering of it. His monologue is a pointless ramble; like everything else in his life, it has no reason. Miranda's diary is a progress and a process. Her seclusion naturally breeds introspection, and her diary, much more than a record of passing emotions, represents real self-examination. The idea of being set apart and adrift is always important in Fowles's works. The protagonist must be allowed to struggle alone and reconstruct himself in exile and silence—as Nicholas does after Bourani and Charles Smithson does after he loses Sarah. Like Nicholas under the exigencies of his godgame, Miranda often feels that she is being disassembled:

Something I have been doing a lot these last days. Staring at myself in the mirror. Sometimes I don't seem real to myself, it suddenly seems that it isn't my reflection only a foot or two away. . . . I look all over my face, at my eyes, I try to see what my eyes say. What I am. . . . You become very real to yourself in a strange way. As you never were before. . . . I watch my face and I watch it move as if it is someone else's. I stare myself out. I sit with myself. . . . I sit down here in the absolute silence with my reflection, in a sort of state of mystery. In a trance. (242)

Unlike Clegg, she utilizes fully the deconstructive and reconstructive powers of memory in trying to understand her past; she does little else but remember. As she recalls her relationship with George Paston (GP) she realizes "everything's changing. I keep on thinking of him: of things he said and I said, and how neither of us really understood what the other meant" (165).

Her introspection leads her to reexamine her bitter relationship with her mother: "I've never really thought of M objectively before, as another person. . . . I've never given her enough sympathy. . . . I feel that I could overwhelm her with love now" (150). Her greatest emotional struggles concern GP and her difficult affair with him. Her feelings are always ambivalent, swinging from annoyance to veneration, and at each divagation of her memory she tries to reassess her love for him. Toward the end of her remembering she is able to say, "I'll marry him if he wants. I'm sick of being young. Inexperienced. . . . Clever at knowing but not at living. . . . I pick up my old self and see it's silly. A toy I've played with too often. . . . He has the secret of life in him. . . . It's as if I'd only seen him at twilight; and now suddenly I see him at dawn. He is the same, but everything else is different" (265).

Miranda's existential awareness broadens when she lets go of the notion of a paternalistic God who can intervene and help her. Her first impulse in captivity is to pray. But as time goes on, and her situation worsens, she realizes that "God can't hear." She says, "These last few days I've felt Godless. I've felt cleaner, less muddled, less blind. . . . The sky is absolutely empty. Beautifully pure and empty. . . . There *must* be a God and he *can't* know anything about us" (239). Miranda has ceased to abdicate the responsibility for her own destiny. Her personal growth leads her to see even her abduction in a new and positive light: "I would not want this not to have happened. Because if I escape I shall be a completely different and I think better person" (270). If Clegg's impulse is only for destruction, Miranda knows only growth.

Fowles uses the characters' writing to contrast their psychological states. Clegg's "filthy English" is symptomatic of a larger problem—his inability to deal with ideas. His tortured syntax in the following example, and elsewhere, reveal his vague understanding of cause and effect, of how to get from one idea to another: "I used to come on things out collecting, you'd be surprised the things couples get up to in places you think they would know better than to do it in, so I had that too" (10). He is referring to pornographic photos he took after having failed with a whore. But the undisciplined way he puts his thoughts together shows how he can also be unaware of the paradoxes and ironies he is expressing. Similarly, his pronoun referents are usually unclear, showing his carelessness with the relationships between things. His speech is cluttered with clichés and euphemisms (the most ghastly of which is calling Miranda "the deceased"), both of which deny the possibilities of language to explain and reason, and lean mindlessly on given notions. Miranda's criticism of his language is incisive: "You know how rain takes the colour out of everything? That's what you do to the English language. You blur it every time you open your mouth" (69).

Clegg's destruction of the word parallels closely his destruction of Miranda. Both have their roots in stagnation. The appeal of collecting lies in the stasis one can impose upon the collection. The serious sociological implications of Clegg's deed arises when he tells us that he learned about keeping prisoners from reading *Secrets of the Gestapo*: "One of the first things you had to put up with if you were a prisoner was the not knowing what was going on outside the prison . . . they were cut off from their old world. And that broke them down" (41). As Fowles suggests in *The Magus*, Nazi politics, like collecting, rely on isolation and the maintenance of the status quo. Clegg must have Miranda, and his having her is contingent upon her remaining unchanged: "What she never understood was that with me it was having. Having her was enough. Nothing needed doing. I just wanted to have her, and safe at last" (101). The situation recalls Browning's "Porphyria's Lover," especially in Clegg's obsessive enchantment with Miranda's hair. The night he captures her is all wind and rain, and at one point he says, "I could sit there all night watching her, just the shape of her head and the way the hair fell from it" (65). Clegg estimates perfectly the inertia he has created:

"So nothing happened really. There were just all those evenings we sat together" (65).

Fowles uses Miranda's diary as a psycholinguistic model of her growth and introspection. She always struggles with her literary chores, is always a self-conscious writer. Because many of her paragraphs are one and two sentences, and she seldom makes much transition between thoughts, it is apparent that her task is difficult. She admits to taking "hours" between sentences. She complains, "What I write isn't natural. It's like two people trying to keep up a conversation. It's the very opposite of drawing. You draw a line and you know at once whether it's a good or bad line. But you write a line and it seems true and then you read it again later" (136). Many times she is frustrated by the insufficiencies of language: "When you use words. The gaps. . . . I can draw his face and his expressions, but words are all so used. . . . Words are so crude, so terribly primitive. . . . Like trying to draw with a broken lead" (158). Her difficulties with language are compounded by the lack of communication bond to a listener, as she complains: "I can't write in a vacuum like this. To no one" (131).

Miranda's writing is more creative than her drawing because it is free from outside influences and is unbound by traditions, conventions, and expectations; it seems to spring fresh, new, from nothing. What she feels to be the inadequacy of language is really just the difficulty of using the verbal mode of reasoning. Her love of abstract art suits Miranda's compulsion to see all life metaphorically, to lift reality to a meditative level. But she finds that language is uncompromising; it is a record, a pinning down, a coming to terms that ill conceals insincerity and hedging. Thus a large part of her growth stems from her battle with language. For her, telling is creating. Her telling and her being become so closely connected that she cannot give up her writing even as she is dying. She uses the last of her energy to clutch her pad and scrawl her final invectives. Four times in her last entry she says "I can't write," even as she writes. She clings to writing as she clings to life. Both parts of this novel are full of Miranda's words. Through her constant talking and her constant writing she builds walls and walls of words, some to fence out the horror and nothingness at the center of the godgame, and some to fence in a place that is real and untouched by madness.

Each character utilizes time differently. Time is normally thought to be progressive and generative, but in his domain Clegg has made time stand still. Clegg says, "I lived from day to day really. I mean there was no plan. I just waited" (80). The waiting is not as it was in *The Magus*, a waiting for; it is a killing of time. His lack of plan is his plan. All possibilities for change are carefully contraverted, as suggested by the motif of unmailed letters and unkept promises. All potential remains unfulfilled, such as Miranda's newfound desire to have children.

While Clegg enjoys a state of perfect stagnation, Miranda is all urgency about her future. She wants to live as normal a life as possible in her prison, and she observes the outward forms of life such as exercising and bathing. Her optimism indicates the expectation of a change in fortune. As Kermode points out, "Time cannot be faced as coarse and actual. . . . One humanizes it by fictions of orderly succession and end."[9] She participates in this normal and healthy fiction making because she cannot comprehend the unmitigated ongoingness of the situation. She constructs a series of endings for herself: that she will be released in four weeks, that she will surely escape tomorrow, that she will move upstairs in a few days. She understands time to mean change and progress, because to deny time its regenerative power is to live with death, which is Clegg's disease.

The contrasts Fowles makes between the two characters, then, define their attitudes toward life: Clegg is given to destruction, Miranda to creation. The ways in which Fowles compares them, however, mitigate this polarity and draw them together in one common flaw—their lack of existential freedom. He muddies the waters partly to deny the reader a facile comprehension of his characters (to thwart the reader's own collector impulses) and partly to demonstrate that inauthenticity can dwell at the center of even the most virtuous and idealistic of us. Unfreedom, in all its many manifestations, is the great evil in this novel.

Clegg lives in fictions because he is mad. But in the novel Fowles works out his fiction making rhetorically to mirror Miranda's own. Clegg's eyes are camera eyes; he sees everything from a distance, voyeuristically. The opening paragraph might be from an Alfred Hitchcock film where a long lens sweeps high over a city and gradually lowers to pick the victim's face out of a crowd: hazard. Clegg begins by looking out his window over the city and zooms down to Miranda—down to the specifics of coiffure. Photography becomes a metaphor for distancing and taking the life out of things. Miranda realizes this as she criticizes his photographs: "They're dead. . . . Not these particularly. All photos. When you draw something it lives and when you photograph it it dies" (55). He loves the pictures of Miranda because "they don't talk back to me." He prefers the ones with her head cut off, because they further deny her individuality.

When GP criticizes Miranda's drawing he uses similar language: "A picture is like a window straight through to your inmost heart. And all you've done here is build a lot of little windows on to a heart full of other fashionable artists' paintings. . . . You're using a camera. . . . You're photographing here. That's all" (169). She admits that she spends much of her time copying other painters' works. Her aspiration is "to paint like Berthe Morisot. . . . To capture the essences. Not the things themselves" (138). Her drawing, then, is also a photographic distancing—from reality and from herself. Her unqualified enthusiasm for abstract art is consistent with her compulsion to ideate. Posed against her is GP, whose representational art she finds embarrassing. Yet while he sits and talks to her he chips the rust off old bronzes or pieces together fine old broken porcelain. He restores integrity to the things themselves.

Clegg plays out an elaborate fantasy in his patent anima worship of Miranda. When he once thinks of letting her go, he quickly checks himself: "Then I thought of her face and the way her pigtail hung down and twisted and how she stood and walked and her lovely clear eyes . . . I knew I couldn't do it" (36). He fails to individuate and humanize her. He says, "The truth was she couldn't do ugly things. She was too beautiful" (66). But Miranda does many ugly things in this book: she vomits, she menstruates, she gets dirty, she fills her "buckets" every day. She is full of animal life, but Clegg sees only the glow of the facade, the dream girl. GP, with the benefit of wisdom and experience, sees Miranda's anima qualities right away. "You've read Jung?" he says. "He's given your species of the sex a name" (187).

If Clegg sees her as anima, she, with no less intensity, sees GP as animus. She has for him a kind of veneration that stems more from his being a famous painter than from genuine love. When she takes Piers and Toinette to see him at his studio it is with the air of showing off something rare one has collected. When he becomes angry at being exhibited, she gets panicky: "I could see Antoinette and Piers looking rather amused and I was sure it was because they felt I didn't know him as well as I'd said. So I had to try to prove to them I could manage him" (176). When GP has sex with Toinette, Miranda becomes furious, even though he has no commitment to her: "I was *so* angry and *so* shocked and *so* hurt" (189). She feels she owns GP, just as Clegg feels he owns her.

GP's looks—his ugliness—prevent Miranda from relating to the real man, just as Miranda's looks—her beauty—distract Clegg from her individuality. Of GP's appearance she complains, "Short and broad and broad-faced with a hook-nose; even a bit Turkish. Not really English-looking at all. I have this silly notion about English good looks. Advertisement men" (181). His age is also a "cruel wall fate has built." When GP finally tells her to go, it is because he knows what game she is playing. He says, "You don't love me." She responds, "I can't explain it. There isn't a word for it." He: "Precisely" (231). He shoves her out the door, and she savors the drama of it, the playing-at-experience aspect of the situation: "Of course I *looked* sad. But I didn't really feel sad. Or it was a sadness that didn't hurt. . . . I rather enjoyed it. . . . The romance of it, the mystery of it" (233). As she sits in her cell she tries unsuccessfully to draw GP from memory; she finds she cannot draw an idea. Her playing with the idea of GP is so complete that one must suspect her final realization that she loves him; one must question whether it is motivated by love or simple loneliness and deprivation.

The sex taboo involved in anima-animus relationships works for both characters. Clegg scrupulously avoids any sexual contact with Miranda, and when he finally does rape her it is with a camera. Of sex he says, "I dream about it. . . . It can't ever be real" (106). It is her attempted seduction that ultimately kills the anima in her: "It was no good, she had killed all the romance, she had made herself like any other woman" (110). Miranda shies away from sex with GP in much the same way. Both characters blush furiously in front of their beloveds, betokening an obsolete Victorian reticence. When GP asks her to go to bed, she refuses, saying lamely, "I hate promiscuity." She adds (for our benefit) "I didn't mean that" (184). She uses the same excuse to him that Clegg uses to her. Both cover up the real issue by taking it into a moral sphere, hiding behind conventions. Both show a determination not to break the fairy-tale spell of these unreal relationships. When GP does become tainted with sex (after Toinette), Miranda says of their relationship, "It was never the same"—virtually the same words Clegg uses after his sexual misadventure with Miranda.

Both characters suffer from a kind of Bovaryism in regard to their "lovers." Both dream of idealized lives with the beloved that are based on the substance of sentimental romance. For Clegg it is, "I thought of her sitting on my knees, very still, with me stroking her soft, blonde hair, all out loose. . . . In my dreams it was always we looked into each other's eyes one day and then we kissed and nothing was said until after" (34). For Miranda it is, "There isn't much sex, it's just our living together. In rather romantic surroundings . . . white cottages" (253).

Clegg is an accomplished role player. He is variously spy, daredevil, chaste lover, and misunderstood guardian of morality. Because he has little experience in the real world he often relies on films and plays to suggest his next move. One day he dreams of hitting Miranda as he saw it done once "in a telly play." Another time, when he doesn't know what to do with her after he has chloroformed her, he simply puts her in her pajamas—as he saw it done once in an American movie. He desires to do the done thing, to act according to the vague standards of conformity imposed by society. When he visits a whore he says, "I suddenly felt like I'd like to have a woman, I mean to be able to know I'd had a woman" (9). Having a woman would entitle him to society's approval for manly behavior, even though the act is repulsive to him. He showers Miranda with gifts because he lives by the cliché of the devoted lover. Indeed, Clegg's life is largely facade.

Miranda plays roles as well. She tries to define herself and her situation in terms of familiar contexts, conjuring images from *Emma*, *The Tempest*, and *The Catcher in the Rye*. Similarly, she thinks that if she acts roles from "Beauty and the Beast" or "The Frog Prince" she can manipulate Clegg. Miranda is as shallow as Clegg in her own way. GP cruelly but honestly sees her hollowness in her painting: "They're teaching you to express personality at the Slade. . . . But however good you get at translating personality into line or paint it's no good if your personality isn't worth translating" (168). There is in Miranda, as there is in Clegg, a disquieting sense of emptiness behind all the poses. For example, she has the kind of studied and self-conscious idealism that suggests posturing. She tells Clegg, "Do you know I'm a Buddhist? I hate anything that takes life. Even insects' lives." Clegg shrewdly counters, "You ate the chicken." Miranda's alleged Buddhism compares with Clegg's empty pose as a nonconformist. Even her hunger strikes and silences seem more like Gandhiesque dramas than real attempts to deal with her situation. Her hypocrisy about class reveals the hollowness of her professed liberal commitment. When Clegg accuses her of being a snob she yells, "I hate snobbism. . . . Some of my best friends in London are, well, what some people call working class." Clegg: "Like Peter Catesby?" Miranda: "He's just a middle-class suburban oaf" (38). Clegg leans on his class status to explain his alienation and dejection. He says of his relationship with Miranda, "There was always class between us" (72). But it is not class that is between them, it is their inability to see beyond the blinds of class distinction.

Miranda's shallowness surfaces in her petulant breaking up of Clegg's house: the act is far more histrionic than sincere. She smashes his furniture and breaks his miserable china duck not for the reason she should; that is, not because Clegg's interior decoration demonstrates his nothingness (the place was done by decorators because he has no personality to express), but because the house is done up in "*The* most excruciating women's magazine good taste" (132). Even this concern with Clegg's taste is not so much any commitment of hers as it is something GP put in her head: "He hates 'interior decoration' and gimmicks and *Vogue*" (162). Much of what Miranda does and thinks is borrowed from others, especially GP. She says of Clegg, "He makes me want to dance round him, bewilder him, dazzle him, dumbfound him. . . . The hateful tyranny of weak people. GP said it once" (134). Her conduct toward Clegg, as well as her opinions of him, are borrowed from GP, who has taught her well to dazzle and confound by his own example. When GP brutally criticizes her work she says, "It hurt like a series of slaps across the face" (174). She uses nearly the same words ("like continually slapping someone across the face") to describe her equally harsh criticism of Clegg. As she thinks back over the teachings of GP (some of which take the form of rules to live by) she wonders, "How many times have I disagreed with him? And then a week later with someone else I find I am arguing as he would argue. Judging people by his standards" (151). Her lack of authenticity is counterpointed by the young priest-to-be she met in Spain, who had a determination to try to be a priest and to try to live in the world: "A simply colossal effort of coming to terms with oneself. . . . He had to do it every day" (213).

Pedagogy is an important notion in this book, with Miranda trying to teach Clegg about art and manners, Clegg teaching her how to behave, and then looking forward to teaching Marian. Clegg wants to teach Miranda to be a docile specimen. She feels she has a mission to instruct Clegg in the meaning of art, but fails because she is such a poor teacher. When she tries to tell him about the subtleties obtained by a modern painter she says, "There . . . he's not only saying everything there is about the apples, but everything about all apples and all form and colour" (61). These insights are in no way meaningful to Clegg; rather her criticisms are pat, full of cant, and clever academic. They are formulas, art-school catchphrases. Her desire cannot be so much to educate Clegg as to show off her false erudition, her borrowed ideas. She also tries to teach him foolish things, such as not to say "lounge." She gives him pseudolessons in modernity and refinement that say more about her trivial concerns than about anything amiss in Clegg.

Clegg and Miranda are compulsive simile makers. Both take the materials of the real world and relate them to their obsessions, establishing fraudulent points of reference for understanding experience. To Clegg all the world is like butterfly catching; he is excused because he is mad. But Miranda thinks that reality mirrors art, and in this misconception lies the reason for her inauthenticity. Miranda, despite her pretensions, is hopelessly unfree.[10] GP explains her problem to her indirectly when he describes his failures with other women: "Do you know what they always think is self-ishness? . . . Not that I will paint in my own way, live in my own way, speak in my own way. . . . What they can't stand is that I hate them when *they* don't behave in their own way" (186).

Ultimately both Miranda and Clegg are collectors. Clegg slips people into categories—the public school types, the la-di-da types, the slimy types—as does Miranda. Her long invective against Calibanity, about the battle between the Few and the Many, the New People and the established people, is a superb piece of collecting, because it puts people into categories without regard for their individuality. Similarly, she tries to square all her actions and thoughts against an abstract collection of values. She disputes whether or not she should use violence, but decides she must be true to pacifism. She fears marriage and children because she feels sure that some force inherent in domestic life will turn her into a "Great Female Cabbage." When she dreams of a future husband it is as if husbands can be bought out of catalogues. All Miranda's various dogmas show that she, like Clegg, denies the richness of existence, its contingency, its hazard.

Both characters have narrow, collector-oriented views about the age they live in. Clegg's monologue is partly a malediction against "nowadays." He disparages everything modern and considers himself a bastion of old-fashioned values. He is square. Miranda hates obsessively everything old or square or "unwithit." Both are guilty of putting time into categories. Clegg is mired in the past, unable to cope with change, progress, movement. Miranda is maniacal about the present and tries to dissociate herself from the older generation, as if the world began with her. She has no mooring in the past. Time, Fowles argues, must be understood in a Heraclitean sense: "The beginning and the end are the same."[11] But both characters think that concepts and values are contingent upon a day and age. Jung diagnosed their problem accurately: "Whoever protects himself from what is new and strange and thereby regresses to the past, falls into the same neurotic condition as the man who identifies himself with the new and runs away from the past. The only difference is that one has estranged himself from the past, and the other from the future.

In principle both are doing the same thing; they are salvaging a narrow state of consciousness."[12]

The ambiguous nature of both characters clouds the reader's understanding of many issues Fowles presents in his novel. It is not uncommon in a novel that no character speaks for the author. But Fowles has created such a complete illusion of autonomy for his characters that they seem to have no author. Wayne Booth catalogues the ways in which authors *seem* to be effaced, but in *The Collector* Fowles goes beyond these elementary techniques of deception. In *The Sound and the Fury* (also a collection of monologues), for example, Faulkner is very distant, but there is no doubt about how he means the reader to feel about everything Jason Compson says because Faulkner controls the irony, the tone, the image patterns. Faulkner is not distant at all, but in collusion with the reader behind the backs of the characters. In *The Collector* there is no such background noise coming from Fowles. He does guide the reader's feelings for the characters by rhetoric, but guides him only to qualifications and contradictions. The only truth of which Fowles assures the reader is an ironic truth: that both characters are self-deluded. No standards appear, either in the characters or from the author's manipulation, against which the reader can resolve the many peripheral questions Fowles asks in the novel.

Trust, for example, is a subject turned over and over by Clegg and Miranda. Miranda, naturally, takes up arms on behalf of trust and charity. She tries to convince Clegg to send money to various charitable organizations that, she believes, will use the money to make a better world. Clegg's response is that her idealism is unfounded because organizations abuse money and accomplish little. Miranda says, "He thinks everyone is corrupt, everyone tries to get money and keep it" (227). Her assessment of Clegg's position is correct, but what she does not realize is that she shares his cynicism, as she reveals in her bitter denouncement of the New People (in which she condemns all but a handful of elect to avarice and perversion). She adds, "Everything beyond what he pays for and sees himself get is suspicious to him" (228). Again, she is correct. But the reader must give Clegg's position some consideration because, even if he is ex-

treme in his distrust, he is at least a corrective to Miranda's pretensions to idealism. Her trusting nature is praiseworthy but Fowles
does not let the reader forget that it was trust that got her into the
back of Clegg's van. Fowles provides no solutions to the moral quandary he creates, but rather, like Conchis, leads his listeners only to
questions.

The question of the right use of violence is the most emotional
issue Fowles raises in the novel. It becomes natural for the reader to
find himself in the uncomfortable position of wishing that Miranda
would bury an axe in Clegg's skull. As in a mystery story, the reader
begins to participate in looking for ways—violent ways—out of the
cell. Miranda's opacity, her inability to see that either she must escape or die, undermines the reader's patience. When she does decide
that she must be violent, her decision may be justified by allowing
that questions of morality are contingent. But when the axe falls,
Miranda is horrified: "Violence and force are wrong. If I use violence
I descend to his level. It means that I have no real belief in the power
of reason, and sympathy, and humanity" (145). The reader is chas-
tened. Yet the issue circles on. If Clegg has no compunction about
being violent with her, does he deserve her sympathy? Should she
not be released from martyrdom and respond in kind? When the full,
dead weight of the novel's pathos hits, traditional notions of morality seem almost trifling. Again Fowles offers no answers.

The most troubling of the unresolved problems in the novel is
why Miranda dies. Her death does not serve the purifying function
of tragedy; it is not the logical conclusion to her life. Her death
serves no dark theme because *The Collector* is not a parable about
the triumph of evil over good; no such categories exist in this book.
Miranda says as she is dying, "This pain . . . that is in me now. It
wasn't necessary. It is all pain, and it buys nothing. Gives birth to
nothing. All in vain. All wasted" (274). Her death serves no purpose
but to open the subject of death to the reader's reluctant mind. In her
end each reader faces his own end. Her death is a memento mori.
Each person who witnesses Miranda's death is forced to make sense
of his own end through hers. "What has it all been for?" is a question
that applies universally, and one on which, like all other questions
in the book, Fowles offers no opinion.

The many other subjects Fowles brings up in *The Collector*—free, uninhibited sex versus commitment; the question of what constitutes real teaching; the responsibility of the moral to the degenerate; the value of art; the effects of money on human beings, and so on—circle without ever coming to rest. Fowles uses his position and his authority only to indicate that his characters are unfree. In a sense, this novel, like *The French Lieutenant's Woman*, has two endings: Miranda's utter ending and Clegg's ending, which is not an ending at all, but an ongoingness. Both endings are too painful. But Fowles uses the reader's despair to press his one clear position: that to abuse freedom is the worst crime of all.

The bewilderment Fowles creates at the end of this novel is organic to the novel in that he enacts, as he did in *The Magus*, a strategy of studied confusion. Every technique he uses serves this strategy. By putting his characters in an isolated situation he shuns reflectors (except for GP, who is very limited in that capacity). The use of a reflector assumes there is a ground of agreement between author and reader; that there are notions we all hold to be true. Fowles resolutely refuses to offer his reader such a contract because in this book, as well as in the others, he demonstrates the injurious effects of codes and norms.

Readers look for clear resolutions to complex problems because they have come to expect totality and coherence in a novel. Wayne Booth says, "From the author's viewpoint, a successful reading of his book will reduce to zero the distance between the essential norms of his implied author and the norms of the postulated reader."[13] But Fowles's determination to muddle both characters and issues represents a cutting loose of the reader from the comfortable guiding hand of the author. If Fowles plays God—as all writers do—it is a modern god, an absent god. He raises questions not to answer them, but simply to raise them. He reasserts the fundamental premise of *The Magus*, that to grow man needs the existence of questions, not answers. Fowles is absent as this implied author, "this second self [which] is usually a highly refined and selected version, wiser, more sensitive, more perceptive than any real man could be."[14] The existence of the implied author assumes that the writer is a teacher and that the reader must learn his lesson. It makes sense that Fowles does not set himself up as sage, since the one thing he clearly abhors is the human penchant to lean on borrowed ideas and behavior.

Fowles carefully maneuvers the reader into a dialectic within himself. The only standards of judgment for all the confusions in this book are within the reader. In this sense the narrative technique mirrors the theme of freedom. The reader's freedom is counterposed against Miranda's lack of freedom, and the arguments he carries on within himself parallel Miranda's thinking in her cell. The reader, like Miranda, is alone.

The end of bewilderment should be insight. Fowles is still a highly didactic writer. There can be no doubt that he is out to teach, but not in an ordinary sense. He does not desire to teach what he thinks, but what we think. He poses difficult existential problems that call forth the reader's finest powers of discernment. Each reader is forced to examine many questions and put his own feelings in order. In essence, Fowles gives what Clegg withholds.

3 The French Lieutenant's Woman

David. Have they decided how they are going to
end it?

Mike. End it?

David. I hear they keep changing the script.

Mike. Not at all. Where did you hear that?

David. Well, there are two endings in the book
aren't there? A happy ending and an unhappy
ending?

Mike. Yes. We're going for the first ending—I
mean the second ending.

David. Which one is that?

Mike. Hasn't Anna told you?

HAROLD PINTER
Screenplay of *The French Lieutenant's Woman*

As Fowles tells it, the vision of Sarah Woodruff came to him early one morning as he lay half asleep.[1] He saw her as she first appeared to Charles Smithson: at the end of the Cobb, looking accusingly into the sea. He fell in love with that face. Fowles was working on another project (several projects, as a matter of fact) at the time, but the vision was so intrusive and compelling that he was forced to lay aside his other work and follow the mysterious Sarah wherever she might lead. So into Fowles's life she came, in much the same way she came into Smithson's: commanding undivided interest and attention, and pushing rivals aside with a look. That the author and his protagonist are both in love with the heroine is one of the many eccentric features of this eccentric novel.

When Fowles first published *The French Lieutenant's Woman*,[2] critics invested a good deal of energy in trying to determine what species of novel Fowles had created. Patrick Brantlinger says that the reader must choose between seeing the novel as historical or experimental, just as he must choose an ending.[3] Walter Allen feels that it is a modern novel full of "boring red herrings," which is his term for the Victoriana.[4] Others have tried to explain the book by attempting to trace its origin and influences.[5] The temporal ambiguity, along with the glib and intrusive narrator, the triple ending, the sometimes intractable characters, and other technical filigree, present the reader with a challenge that is a mirror of the challenge Sarah offers to Charles. Fowles has constructed a unique godgame, as singular as the production at Bourani or Sarah's dramas at Lyme Regis and Exeter. This chapter will examine the mechanics of both Sarah's and

The Cobb and cliffs in Lyme Regis. This view was taken from the end of the Cobb, looking back on the village.

Fowles's godgames. It will also discuss the implications of Fowles's games playing.

At the beginning of the novel Charles Smithson is poised on an existential fulcrum. Superficially, he leads a comfortable life and seems to be at home in high Victorian society, but inside he is torn by doubt and self-reproach. On one hand, he is content to see his life as a story, a familiar plot, a neat Victorian novel, in fact. He decides to choose a wife, not because he has any of the higher yearnings associated with marriage, but because it is "time" to plug a wife into his plot. The woman he chooses is certain to play out the rest of the drama neatly. Yet even as he seeks comfort in this safe predictability, he experiences deep longings for a life that is based more on contingency: "His future had always seemed to him of vast potential; and now suddenly it was a fixed voyage to a known place" (130). When Charles imagines the first ending to this novel, a quotidian existence with Ernestina, "he felt himself coming to the end of a story" (339). One of the cornerstones of Victorian thought, as symbolized by Mrs. Poulteney, is that the status quo must be preserved. The narrator flippantly points out that "there would have been a place in the Gestapo for the lady" (20). As we saw in *The Collector* and *The Magus*, Fowles compares, both philosophically and morally, stasis and Nazism. Sarah is, of course, the breath of fresh air, the world of hazard, where books never really end. With her anything can (and does) happen.

Charles feels trapped in many ways, but he is bound most frustratingly by his language. He and Ernestina communicate by a kind of elegant badinage, teasing, punning, circumlocuting. Like Miranda, they construct barriers with their words in their adipose bantering, to keep truth or depth of feeling away. Playing with words is one way of playing with reality. The real Charles frequently gets lost in his rhetoric, as the narrator tells us: "Charles, you will have noticed, had more than one vocabulary. With Sam in the morning, with Ernestina across a gay lunch. . . . We may explain it biologically by Darwin's phrase: *cryptic coloration*, survival by learning to blend with one's surroundings" (144). Charles feels that he has an adequate vocabulary for every situation until he meets Sarah. When she pleads with Charles to hear her confession he lapses into an almost baroque Victorian indignation; he uses atrociously formal and distancing language with her. But she does not allow these rhetorical flourishes because of the capacity they hold for making the speaker dishonest. She gives him a lancing look: "Very few Victorians chose to question the virtues of cryptic coloration; but there was that in Sarah's look which did: Come clean, Charles, come clean. It took the recipient off balance" (144). Again, after they have shared an extraordinary, passionate kiss in Carslake's Barn, Charles retreats into verbiage: "You must forgive me for taking an unpardonable advantage of your unhappy situation. . ." His voice trailed off. It had become progressively more formal. He knew he must sound detestable. She turned her back to him" (257). Even after they have made love the note he writes her is wretchedly formal. Charles never does manage to shake off those protective plates of language. His eloquence falters and dies before Sarah.

Charles fails to communicate verbally with Sarah because he has no language to use with her; the vocabulary for dealing with her has, so to speak, not yet come into being. Fowles states that in this novel he is "trying to show an existential awareness before it was chronologically possible."[6] Sarah represents a different set of values based on honesty, straightforwardness, and integrity. There is, in short, no formula for dealing with her as there is for Ernestina, Sam, or Mr. Freeman. The narrator underlines this curious dichotomy in two ways. First, he makes Sarah laconic. She is mostly silent throughout the book, communicating with meaningful looks and gestures rather than words. Her answers (when she does not answer with silence) are brief and pointed, with "a substance and purity of thought and judgement"; or she will often respond with "I do not know how to explain." She only speaks at length when she is telling stories: first her story of Varguennes, then its retraction. Her verbal contribution to this book, then, is her story telling. She does not divulge her true language because it is a language Charles will have to learn on his own. Second, the narrator frequently alerts the reader that he is putting the words to Charles's thoughts, giving him a vocabulary (Sarah's vocabulary) in which to express the strange feelings she awakens in him. The strategy is much like Faulkner's when he gives eloquence to idiots, as if to say, "This is what he would think if he had the words." Both writers consistently explore the relationship between language and reality. In this case Charles is torn between the safe existence offered by irony and the glittering world he can dimly see but does not know how to name.

Just as Charles's speech is irrelevant in dealing with Sarah, so are most of his assumptions. Charles moves very competently in his own world; he handles daily life with what he would call a manly confidence, a sense of being in control. Protocol plays an important part in his life. But when it comes to handling Sarah he is at a loss. He tends to imagine each meeting with her before it happens. He habitually casts himself as condescending benefactor and her as tearful suppliant. Or he imagines her in some distress: Will she fling herself off that cliff? Will she be walking the streets, penniless? And he is always wrong in his imaginings. He is wrong because he is working with an obsolete and irrelevant set of assumptions and code of conduct. All he knows is that women are frail and ignorant and incompetent and that men exist to save them. He never does get past this powerful myth, and to the end of the novel Charles is left with his mouth agape over Sarah's nonconforming behavior, especially when he sees how happily she fits into Rosetti's exotic family circle: "He saw nothing; but only the folly of his own assumption that fallen women must continue falling—for had he not come to arrest the law of gravity? He was as shaken as a man who suddenly finds the world around him standing on its head" (443).

Charles is torn in many ways between what he is and what he feels might be wrong with himself. He is, in effect, safe and dry on the beach, but he can't help sticking a foot into that strange water. Because he is confused, he is burdened with "a general sentiment of dislocated purpose" (11). The life of idle squirearchy, for example, has its appeals for him, and he frequently thinks of Winsyatt as a "domain." But, as his guilt over the shooting of the "immortal bustard" shows, there is in him a reticence about accepting the genteel life. He is equally unable to commit himself to the real work of the world, both as a scientist (in which role he simply plays the paleontologist) and as a tradesman. He feels the same kind of tension between duty and self-interest. He abhors meeting the petty demands of Ernestina's schedule, but another part of him feels safe in routine. Charles suffers from what the narrator insists is the major infirmity of the age: schizophrenia. A civil war is taking place inside him; two people are fighting it out, and the conflict is between what Jung calls "the ego and the shadow."[7]

Sarah appears at the right time in his life, and the reader senses throughout the novel that fatedness Fowles finds so provocative. Fowles allows to exist the possibility that she has been sent to Charles, so mysteriously do some of their meetings transpire (as when she "appears" in Charles's ivy tunnel on the cliff). But Sarah's metaphysical glow is actually created by Charles's perception of her. All the reader's impressions of Sarah come either from Charles or from a narrator who looks at her only from the outside, and who stubbornly refuses to give any irrefutable information about her. While the narrator reports, insofar as he is able, Sarah's activities, it is Charles who attributes to her various emotions and intentions. If Sarah is a mystery, she is a mystery that can never be solved, because

Charles blurs both his own and the reader's perceptions of her by projecting onto her the half of him that is submerged, the rebel faction in his civil war.[8] As Jung describes it, "The individual has an ineradicable tendency to get rid of everything he does not know and does not want to know about himself by foisting it off on somebody else."[9]

Charles distorts Ernestina as well by projecting onto her his ideal of social perfection. She is the counterpart to his facade, the perfect complement to his own conventionality. They share the same characteristics. The narrator gives us long, detailed descriptions of their clothes to show how current and cryptically colored each is (though he stresses that Charles finds his clothes inhibiting). She is his equal in the game of language play. Her lack of self, the surrender of identity to wifehood (she says she must "honor and *obey* my *dearest* Charles even when my feelings would drive me to contradict him" [253]) matches his own tendency to repress personal drives. Charles eventually sees that he does not love Ernestina as Ernestina. He realizes that all along she has been for him an idea, an abstraction of Victorian respectability, in which he had believed he wanted to participate. That he sees her more as an idea than a person is underlined by the narrator, who refuses, to use one of Fowles's favorite metaphors, to collect her. He will frequently interrupt to correct some excess of Charles's. When Charles condemns her (and himself) for being shallow and vapid, the narrator steps in to show us some of her hidden depths: "an imperceptible hint of a Becky Sharp that denied . . . total obeisance to the great god Man" (25).

Fowles shows Ernestina and Sarah in apposition all through the novel. One is the fair lady, the other the dark lady. He writes many parallel scenes, even parallel paragraphs, that put the two at antipodes. Ernestina's clothes are always de rigeur, while Sarah dresses masculinely, in black, eschewing the trendy. Ernestina is mistress of the drawing room and usually presides over events indoors. She rules the world of artifice. Sarah is a creature of nature. "Woodruff" is the name of a common sweet herb, whose other name is waldmeister: master of the forest. Sarah uses the woods "as if the clearing were her drawing room" (146). One is at the pinnacle of society, the other is beyond the pale. The contrast between the two is so extreme that it makes them seem to be representations rather than people. They divide too cleanly down the middle.

It is Sarah who receives Charles's more curious projections. He foists upon her all the repressed contents of his psyche, making of her all the things he would like to be, the sum of his unrealized potential. But his transference causes her to become an abstraction. When she casts him that first piercing look she appears to be "a figure from myth." "That face" and "that look" take on tremendous proportions in this novel, as they always have the most devastating effect on Charles: "that face had an extraordinary effect on him . . . as if she was a figure in a dream, both standing still and yet always receding" (66). Sarah has many affinities with the anima figure that is so prevalent in Fowles's work. She also has many characteristics of the Conradian "other," the secret sharer. The situation itself also recalls Conrad: a respectable protagonist is attracted to a shady character, an outsider, who reflects the buried desires of the hero. Many emotional conflicts arise wherein the hero is nearly torn apart. Charles feels the gothic nature of the attraction instinctively: "That face . . . unsettled him and haunted him, by calling to some hidden self he hardly knew existed. He said it to himself: It is the stupidest thing, but that girl attracts me. It seemed clear to him that it was not Sarah in herself who attracted him . . . but some emotion, some possibility she symbolized. She made him aware of a deprivation" (130). His insight is acute but, like all other Fowlesian protagonists, he forgets his intuition almost immediately. Charles does not deal with Sarah qua *Sarah*, but with Sarah the fictional character of his imagination. Fowles reveals Charles's tendency to abstract her in the way Charles makes an art object of her every time he sees her. Whenever he comes upon her or she comes upon him suddenly, the narrator draws a frieze of Sarah through Charles's eyes. When he sees her sleeping on the cliff his aesthetic sense is moved, as it is when she intrudes on his test hunting: "An oblique shaft of wan sunlight . . . lit her face, her figure standing before the entombing greenery behind her; and her face was suddenly very beautiful" (139). The rather heavy and highly visual description recalls the affective intensity of the Rosetti paintings, in this case "Proserpina."

When Sarah finishes her first confession about Varguennes,

Charles tries to evade the distressing implications of her story by letting his mind wander. But (as Freud might predict) it stumbles onto a hidden truth. He looks out to the distant clouds and thinks about traveling again: "Even then a figure, a dark shadow, his dead sister, moved ahead of him, lightly, luringly, up the ashlar steps and into the broken columns' mystery" (177). The mention of Charles's dead sister is what Fowles might call an accidental: a note so jarring that it must assert itself. Charles links Sarah rhetorically to his sister, a "soul sister," a double, a sharer.

While it might appear that Charles distorts Sarah in a neurotic way, his case simply demonstrates how extremely difficult it is to know anything objective about another human being. If the narrator (whose brainchild she is) cannot grasp her truth, how could Charles? In fact, the narrator, by his own problematic and intrusive presence, forces us to examine the very word "I," to recognize what a shifty and complex thing it is.[10] Fowles poses the old problem of identity in a new way. The narrator brings up the problem himself as he has Charles on the train thinking about Sarah: "I say 'her,' but the pronoun is one of the most terrifying masks man has invented; what came to Charles was not a pronoun, but eyes, looks . . . a nimble step, a sleeping face" (332). Language contributes, then, to the difficulty of knowing the truth about one's neighbors; it allows one to limit, classify, and collect; it puts all things in parity. The narrator reproduces the entire text of "To Marguerite" to suggest these distances between enisled individuals.

The sustained theme of "hearsay" is an illustration of these same distances. Much of what the reader knows of the people in this book emerges from stories, usually several times removed. The first information of Sarah comes from a story the Vicar (who heard it from another vicar, who heard it from Mrs. Talbot) is telling to Mrs. Poulteney. She processes the information and categorizes Sarah based on criteria mentioned in the story (which, the narrator confides, the Vicar is amending slightly as he speaks). Sarah earned the appellation Tragedy through similar apocryphal stories that flew through Lyme. Through the novel many different versions of the Varguennes story are told (most notably the double version from Sarah herself), demonstrating the spurious or tentative nature of what the indi-

vidual tellers assume to be truth. In the opening scene the voyeuristic narrator establishes the specious nature of appearances by
giving first a long then a close shot of Charles and Ernestina: "The
local spy . . . might have deduced that these two were strangers. . . .
On the other hand he might, focusing his telescope more closely,
have suspected that a mutual solitude interested them" (4). The contradictory nature of the sightings (both of which are untrue) shows
the deceptiveness of visual information. Similarly, Sam first introduces Mary by a story in which she falsely appears to be a prostitute.
Mr. Freeman seeks to know Charles before he allows him into the
family. Charles gets top honors because the dossier of appearances
that he has constructed around himself defines him, ironically, as a
fine Victorian gentleman. When people see Sarah standing on the
Cobb and staring out to sea, "There it was supposed, she felt herself
nearest to France" (62). As we later learn, Sarah cares not a whit for
Varguennes, but the natives interpret her solitariness according to
the conventions of romance. In truth, any walk in Lyme commands
a view of the sea, and the Cobb and Cliffs are the only places to get
away from the local eavesdroppers.

The narrator enjoys playing a game of appearances. One of his favorite tricks is to set the reader up to feel one way about a thing;
then he makes a quick reversal and twits the reader for feeling as he
does. For example, he labors the fact of Charles's extreme and foolish
overdressing as he goes out to find fossils. He prompts a feeling of
superior judgment in the reader, then derides him for his condescension: "We laugh. . . . We make, I think, a grave—or rather frivolous
mistake about our ancestors. . . . Their folly in that direction was no
more than a symptom of their seriousness in a much more important one. They sensed that current accounts of the world were inadequate; that they had allowed their windows on reality to become
smeared by convention, religion, social stagnation" (47). If the laughter is unjust it is because all human beings are handicapped by having to see life through a haze of complex and virtually unavoidable
prejudices. The reader's laughter says much about the dirtiness of
his own windows, and points to his arrogance in thinking he has the
right angle on things, an attitude for which the narrator soundly
condemns Mrs. Poulteney. The reader may feel compassion for Sarah

that all condemn her on the strength of appearances; but the narrator often makes him feel guilty of the same crime.

Characters in the novel frequently sit in judgment on each other, and the bases for their decisions are always these deceptive appearances. The draconian Mrs. Poulteney presides, for example, over a great number of questions involving hirings, firings, matters of taste, and morality. She fires Millie for some minor domestic crime until Sarah, characteristically, uncovers the truth behind the crime and finds that the girl is ill. Sarah forces Charles to judge her by choosing him as her confessor. Grogan, at the end of the novel, finds himself having to pass judgment on Charles. The narrator spends much of his intellectual energy on judging an entire age. The narrator even judges himself at the end when he appears in fancy dress. All the judgmental situations meet in the breach-of-promise writ that Mr. Freeman hands down against Charles. The crude and only vaguely accurate language of that document conveys how ill founded most judgments are and how shortsighted we are when we seek to judge. The errors that mark and defile Sarah and Charles are the same errors that send LaRoncière to prison.

The story of LaRoncière, the other French lieutenant, is the most extreme case of maladroit judgment in the book. Like Sarah, he is a victim of the universal human penchant for collecting and categorizing. In the same way that the accumulation of apparent evidence sends LaRoncière to jail, various sorts of circumstantial evidence nearly send Sarah to the lunatic asylum. Grogan examines Sarah and accepts a good deal of slanted evidence about her behavior, and promptly diagnoses her as melancholic and hysterical (and he would have Charles do the same; Grogan is another who is convinced he has the right angle on things). Ironically, given all the extenuating and existing information, his diagnosis seems perfectly plausible. She does indeed suffer purposefully, as do all the other hysterics in Grogan's grisly catalogue. But to put Sarah in the same category as Charcot's famous patients is a gross parody of science similar to the diagnosis of Nygaard in *The Magus*. The only thing certain about Sarah is that she can be neither classified nor explained; she has motives that cannot be comprehended by Grogan's philosophy. It is not Sarah but Ernestina who commits hysterical acts in the novel, as when she "faints" as Charles leaves her. Charles smells that rat, as well as Grogan's.

Grogan himself best plays out the sense of crippling schizophrenia, the war between facile appearances and contradictory intuitions. When Charles refuses to admit that he loves Sarah, Grogan counters, "Do you think in my forty years as a doctor I have not learned to tell when a man is in distress? And because he is hiding the truth from himself? Know thyself, Smithson, know thyself" (225). Ironically, Grogan should be giving this advice to himself. He is a "dry little kestrel of a man" who has never known real commitment to another human being. He showed Charles the telescope with which he enjoys Lyme's bathing beauties, and as he did, "his tongue flickered wildly out and he winked" (150). In this rather disgusting image Grogan-the-voyeur reveals himself as one who looks but does not leap. In many ways Grogan is a retarded adolescent who plays with ideas rather than living them, as he demonstrates in his childish playing with Charles at a secret society of Darwinism, in his histrionic swearing on Darwin rather than the Bible. Both are embarrassingly juvenile acts committed by one who constantly conjures his forty years' wisdom. But there is much in Grogan that is likable, that is even wise; he speaks perhaps the most meaningful words in the book when he sends Charles off for the last time, warning him about the wages of freedom. The narrator also suggests that Grogan is a bit taken in by Sarah. But he is pathetically torn; as is Charles, who eventually goes way beyond his mentor in existential awareness.

Fowles creates in this novel an intricate web of errors in fact, judgment, awareness, intuition, and perception. Sarah elects Charles in order to save him. Her godgame involves training Charles away from contradictions, appearances, superficies, and conventions. Why Sarah chooses to work her game on Charles is a moot consideration. It seems easy enough to accept on simple faith her simple explanation: she loves him. With her uncanny perspicacity—"She saw through people in subtle ways. . . . She saw them as they were and not as they tried to seem" (52)—she sees the real Charles in hiding. She sees that he has the potential to become existentially aware (as she is). His trial is a test of his fitness, of his worthiness to be naturally selected. She does not see the same potential in Grogan, whom she knows to be firmly attached to the status quo, and she refuses to tell her story to him. She sees that Charles, caught in an evolutionary incident and metaphorically buried in a landslide, is becoming fossilized. She simply tries to show him the way out; or, as Ronald Binns suggests, her game is designed to make Charles aware that he has a destiny over which he has control.[11]

Her methods—like those of the god of the universe and the author-god—are strange. It is probable that she has her plan fairly well defined from the start. Before she and Charles have gotten very far he says to her, rather avuncularly, "If he does not return, he was not worthy of you. If he returns, I cannot believe that he will be easily put off, should he not find you in Lyme Regis, as not to discover where you are and follow you there" (142). What he says is an excellent description of his own future conduct toward Sarah. Her reply is, characteristically, a look: "Her expression was strange, almost calm, as if what he had said had confirmed some deep knowledge in her heart" (124). The test becomes a question: Will you follow me out of the landslide?

Sarah teaches, as Conchis teaches, by parable, by telling stories. Both involve their listeners in fictitious situations that seem to be real. Sarah's method is to tell a plausible story about herself and Varguennes and then to maneuver Charles into the plot in her former role, so that he always has a mysterious sense of deja vu. The Varguennes story is, for Sarah, a metaphor (like Conchis's masque) for how she achieved her own sense of freedom. She explains to Charles why she gave herself to Varguennes: "I did it so that I should never be the same again. I did it so that people *should* point at me, *should* say, there walks the French Lieutenant's Whore. . . . I threw myself off a precipice. . . . What has kept me alive is my shame, my knowing that I am truly not like other women" (174). What she means to do (to mirror what was ostensibly done to her) is involve Charles in a relationship far outside the bounds of propriety, to make it impossible for him to return to his former life. Then, like her, he will have to suffer the burden as well as the exhilaration of his freedom. In effect, she makes him walk in her shoes.

After Charles becomes enchanted by Sarah he walks as furtively on the Ware Cliffs as she does; he even learns all the paths only she knows, to keep away from the eyes, the spies. Sarah begins slowly to cut him away from Ernestina and respectability. When she relates how she and Varguennes deceived Mrs. Talbot, Charles becomes opprobrious until he realizes that he has been deceiving Ernestina about his meetings with Sarah. At the end of her confession Charles is extremely aroused by her, and he thinks, "He would be to blame, of course, if he did not now remove himself, and for good, from the fire" (189). Sarah offers him the same position she was in with Varguennes: the knowledge that he has a choice and that his choice entails responsibilities either way. He is at the point where, no matter what he chooses, he will never be the same again. Sarah takes him farther away from safety after she gets herself dismissed from her position. She sends him a note at his hotel (knowing that word will get around, which it does) where she again offers him the existential choice that, according to her story, Varguennes offered to her. She writes in French (allowing her to be more maudlin than she could be in English), reinforcing the equivalence that is being built up between her and Varguennes: "Une femme à genoux vous supplie de l'aider dans son désespoir. Je passerai la nuit en prières pour votre venue" (208). Even Charles gets the connection: "The French! Varguennes!"

Charles's demise becomes inevitable when he succumbs to her clever machinations. When he decides to go to Sarah on the Undercliff despite (and in opposition to) Grogan's diagnosis, he has already begun to walk in her shoes. After he spends a frantic night in self-questioning, he walks off into the dawn to this clandestine meeting. But instead of showing the meeting, the narrator interrupts with an entire chapter describing Charles's walk. The chapter is a lovely, lyrical pastoral, a hiatus in the despair and confusion. We see how gorgeous the morning is; we see Charles looking up rather than down, thinking of the living things rather than the dead. He stops to listen to the wren's song and feels that "the heart of all life pulsed there in the wren's triumphant throat" (240). He realizes that he now feels more outside the drawing-room world than inside: "Charles felt in all ways excommunicated. . . . He was like Sarah" (240).

Charles's undoing happens in many steps and runs parallel to other events in his life that prove helpful to Sarah's endeavors. He is, after all, stripped of his estate, title, and fortune. And then he is, to his horror, invited to go into trade. These circumstances help to create the air of fatedness that hangs over his relationship with Sarah. But his fulcrum moment arrives in Exeter. When he goes to Sarah's hotel he is literally in the same position she was in with Varguennes at Weymouth. The edict of both Sarah and her metaphorical French Lieutenant is: you must come to me of your own will; you must choose to cut yourself off with your own will. Sarah feigns a sprained ankle for this reason: so that Charles should have to come up to her room knowing fully what he is doing. As he climbed the stairs "he remembered Varguennes; sin was to meet in privacy" (344). She makes certain that she is helpless, that she can take no active part in the sexual encounter, because it must be all his doing. He must take command completely, become existential action personified. He appreciates the real spirit of the moment: "He felt borne on wings of fire, hurtling" (348). And he does indeed become action: he strides around the room, knocks over chairs, rips clothes, half kills Sarah with violent kisses, throws her across the bed. Sarah fulfills the requirements of the rest of her story by disappearing, as Varguennes did. Charles's education is not complete until he proves that he can bear the burden of freedom. In his exile he moves closer and closer to Sarah until the two virtually merge in an image: "One calm evening while still at Charleston, he chanced to find himself on a promontory facing towards Europe" (436). Immediately after that he is told, "She is found" (436).

There is another reason—and another facet of Charles's education—that sex must be the climax of this godgame, as it was in *The Magus*, and why both Sarah and Julie disappear postcoitus. Like Nicholas, Charles consistently confuses his lust with love, and ideas with people. His engagement, for example, comes about strangely. He had not been abroad for a long time and "was therefore in a state of extreme sexual frustration" (82). The combination of his lustfulness and the potency of Ernestina's bait con him into believing he loves the girl: "One morning he woke up. Everything had become simple. He loved Ernestina. He thought of the pleasure of waking up . . . and seeing that demure, sweetly dry little face asleep beside him." (82). The juxtaposition of the last two sentences is telling. Another time Ernestina forces Charles to kiss her, but Sarah's kiss is still on his lips. As he reluctantly performs his duty with Ernestina, "he felt there was a distinct stir in his loins. There had always been Ernestina's humor, the odd little piques and whims of emotion, a promise of certain buried wildnesses" (264). The lust whose cause he attributes to Ernestina is left over from his very passionate yet frustrated encounter with Sarah; he transfers his passion mindlessly from one woman to the other.

On the way to Ma Terpsichore's Charles hesitates about becoming involved in the Bacchanalian revels, but "there came out of nowhere Sarah's face . . . and the kiss. . . . He needed a woman" (301). When he leaves the narrator suggests that "as he was revolted, so was he sexually irritated" (305). And he goes out to pick up the first whore who looks like Sarah. Sarah has become for him, as far as sex is concerned, a goddess of passion, a sex symbol. When Charles first sees Sarah she is visually linked to sex, leaning, as she was, "against an old cannon barrel upended as a bollard" (5). As part of her game of encouraging Charles to participate in her fiction, she invites this fantasy relationship by making him a voyeur to her and Varguennes. She cleverly describes in much detail their tryst in Weymouth, and ends with "I gave myself to him" (174). The story has its desired effect. Charles has increasingly erotic feelings for this wanton, abandoned woman who gives herself illicitly. He is now convinced that she is a whore, but that is a large part of her fascination. He felt "beset by a maze of crosscurrents and swept hopelessly away from his safe anchorage of judicial, and judicious, sympathy. He saw the scene she had not detailed: her giving herself. . . . Deep in himself he forgave her her unchastity; and glimpsed the dark shadows where he might have enjoyed it himself" (176). This scene ends, properly, with another act of voyeurism. Charles and Sarah are forced to hide together and watch Sam and Mary making love. This titillation serves to inflame Charles further (his increasing excitement is one of the main narrative lines), and to infect and undermine the strait-laced side of him.

As Fowles demonstrated so graphically in *The Magus*, voyeurism is intimately related to pornography, which is essentially auto-eroticism. Pornography becomes a sexual encounter with images in one's own mind. Charles's climactic encounter with Sarah is the culmination of all his bunglings, confusions, and projections in the book. In their first embrace she is more like a phantom than an individual human being: "He strained that body into his, straining his mouth upon hers, with all the hunger of a long frustration—not merely sexual, for a whole ungovernable torrent of things banned, romance, adventure, sin, madness, animality, all these things coursed wildly through him" (349). Fowles undercuts this climax (toward which the novel has been speeding the way an arrow speeds to its target) pointedly: "Precisely ninety seconds had passed since he had left her to look into the bedroom" (350). To end the scene in this way, to stress its brevity, is to question its definition as two people making love. It has been an affair of one. To project one's own fantasies onto one's lover is a kind of irresponsibility, because the transference signifies a profound lack of commitment. Nicholas Urfe went on trial for this reason. And Charles has to suffer his own kind of trial.

When Charles discovers that all Sarah has told him is a lie, he realizes that he is at another beginning of the same game and he justifiably wonders why. Sarah's strategy is to unravel Charles, and this sexual act is a major step in his undoing. This inscrutable benefactress first tells him a story, then invites not only his participation in that story but the transference of his emotions onto the characters. In the next phase of her therapy she reveals the fictional nature of her metadrama and, by extension, urges him to progress beyond the illusion into true selfhood. She uses the same strategy Conchis uses with Nicholas (he is ostensibly speaking about Lily, but really about Nicholas): "I wish to bring the poor child to a realization of her own true problem by forcing her to recognize the true nature of the artificial situation we are creating here together. She will make her first valid step back towards reality when one day she stops and says, This is not the real world. These are not real relationships" (*The Magus*, 282). She takes the already divided Charles and makes of him a litter of parts; she dismantles him by systematically destroying the false assumptions, ideas, and codes of conduct that have kept him together. Her tools are frustration and tension because those two devices are effective in disturbing complacency. When she confesses that it has all been a lie, she effectively cuts Charles adrift from her, disintoxicates him. She is saying that she will no longer write his script. Ellen McDaniel sees exile as the most important part of the godgame: "[Godgames,] though instructive, cannot be substituted for life in the real world. . . . Conchis and Sarah have helped Nicholas and Charles see through their first mistaken identities, but the two men still must separate their real identities from their roles in the godgames."[12]

If Sarah's method seems a roundabout way to teach a lesson, it is, finally, the only way. The creation of and involvement in myth solve existential difficulties by mapping a real problem onto a story. In the beginning Charles's implicit question is, how can I be free of this conflict? Sarah's implicit answer is, let me tell you a story about a French Lieutenant. The difference between telling facts and telling stories is the difference between knowing and understanding. Charles has an insight into her method as he is railroading her out of Lyme: "She raised her face to his, with an imperceptible yet searching movement of her eyes; as if there were something he must see: a truth beyond his truths, an emotion beyond his emotions, a history beyond all his conceptions of history. As if she could say worlds; yet at the same time knew that if he could not apprehend those worlds without her saying them . . . (259).

The desired effect of this psychotherapeutic process is Charles's reconstruction of himself, which the reader never fully sees. Choosing Sarah over Ernestina is not enough; had it been enough, Sarah would have been waiting for him at Endicott's Family Hotel. In Fowles's definition of existentialism choosing is in itself a meaningless act; one must choose his destiny again and again, day after day, to meet the real test. Not only must Charles put himself back together, but the new Charles will have to stand up to considerable opposition from the conforming majority. In the church the meaning of Sarah's self-imposed exile comes rushing at him. Christ says to him, "Escape [from the prison of your future] is not one act, my friend. . . . Each day, Charles, each hour, it has to be taken again.

Each minute the nail waits to be hammered in" (361). Charles and Sarah meet in this Christ. As Charles speaks to the "spreadeagled figure" he sees Sarah's face hanging on the rood; and soon "he saw himself hanging there" (363). Both she and Charles are symbolically anointed with the blood from her spreadeagled figure, presaged by her pricking her finger during the telling of the Varguennes story.

Charles's crucifixion begins immediately as almost universal scorn comes down upon him. He considers escape, which he has prescribed for Sarah throughout. He imagines (again incorrectly) that when he finds Sarah life will be a lark, one long holiday of dressing her up and taking her abroad. In America he finds this futile and meaningless. Another of Sarah's lessons, and a reason for his exile, is that he must find the end to his dallying nonparticipation in life. If he is to be a true rebel he has to live his convictions in the real world and, furthermore, be an instrument of evolution. He saw this truth briefly in the church. Sarah "seemed there beside him, as it were awaiting the marriage service; yet with another end in view. . . . To uncrucify! . . . to bring about a world in which the hanging man could be descended, could be seen not with the rictus of agony on his face, but the smiling peace of a victory brought about by, and in, living men and women" (363). In Lily de Seitas's terms Charles is thinking about "charting the voyage," bringing about a social and moral evolution by setting a living example. Fowles, like Jung, believes that "the salvation of the world consists in the salvation of the individual soul."[13] Grogan defines for Charles the conditions for his election: "The elect, whatever the particular grounds they advance for their cause, have introduced a finer and fairer morality into this dark world. If they fail that test, then they become no more than despots. . . . If you become a better and more generous human being, you may be forgiven. But if you become more selfish . . . you are doubly damned" (397).

Charles's trial, then, will determine whether he can learn to be himself and accept the consequences of selfhood by living his convictions in the real world. But he must allow Sarah to be herself, not an abstraction or a projection. Even after he has taken his existential leap, the relationship he envisions with Sarah is still fantastic. During his travels an image that brings Sarah to his mind is an Egyptian statue "showing a pharoah standing beside his wife, who had her arm round his waist, with her other hand on his forearm" (399). Charles again tends to confuse life and art, and he clings to the outmoded concepts of man as king and woman as devoted underling. Implicit in the rules of Sarah's game is that Charles not approach her again until he can approach her as a human being, and that he allow her the same freedoms he has taken for himself. Clearly his education is incomplete by the "end" of this novel, for reasons that will be explored later.

Several critics dislike this novel because they feel it indicts the Victorian era. Ian Adam, for example, takes exception to Fowles's patronizing attitude toward the Victorians' faults.[14] Yet Fowles counterbalances the overpowering evil of a Mrs. Poulteney by an Aunt Tranter, who shows that you can be a good Victorian and a good person at the same time. To understand the considerable Victorian machinery Fowles has brought to this book, it is necessary to look at the theme of time itself. Underlying the seeming denunciation of Victorianism is Fowles's belief that many of its faults are shared by our age and, furthermore, by all ages. A series of constants runs throughout history making time, as it were, parallel. Fowles says in *The Aristos* that "All life lies parallel in each moment of time. . . . Evolution is horizontal, not vertical" (60); and "The whole is not a chain but a spinning top. The top spins on, but stays in one place" (176). The jarring time warp in this novel, the jostling back and forth between then and now, constitute a metaphor for the spinning-top model of history.

In examining how times are parallel, Fowles examines what things remain constant from age to age, what underlying structures endure as forms change. This theme has its first expression on the first page, when the Cobb is described as being "as full of subtle curves and volumes as a Henry Moore or a Michelangelo" (4). In a sense the constants that link Moore and Michelangelo are the constants that link us to the Victorians. These constants teach the differences between surfaces and depths, which is what Sarah is trying to teach Charles. Just as beauty is constant, so is love, despite all the peculiar encumbrances each age puts on that emotion. When Charles meets Sarah in Carslake's Barn he is prey to unlocalized feelings. All he can think of is Sappho: "Whenever I see you, sound fails, my tongue falters, thin fire steals through my limbs, an inner roar, and darkness shrouds my ears and eyes" (249). Charles thinks this feeling is lust but the narrator states that it is "the best clinical description of love in European medicine" (249). The feeling is constant, as shown by Charles's hurtling back through ages to be joined in emotion to Sappho, even though Charles's tortured behavior seems a parody of love. Ultimately they kiss and "the moment overcame the age" (230).

Fowles examines sex at length in this novel because it is on this subject that we are most likely to fault the Victorians' inhibitions and laud our own enlightenment. The narrator denies the existence of these facile categories. He devotes one of his discursive chapters to the subject of sex and, after a running comparison of how the Victorians felt and how we feel about sex, comes to the conclusion that the basic seriousness and importance of the act are constant, though attitudes certainly change. He says, for example, "I have seen the Naughty Nineties represented as a reaction of many decades of abstinence. I believe it was merely the publication of what had hitherto been private, and I suspect we are in reality dealing with a human constant: the difference is a vocabulary, a degree of metaphor" (268). The narrator dramatizes this idea with the scene at Ma Terpsichore's. He conspicuously fails to describe the whores' playlet himself, but transfers the responsibility for that task to *The History of the Human Heart* (1749), from which he quotes extensively. He points to the timelessness of the whores' dance (and of lust and longing) by adding further, "What was done before Charles that night was done in the same way before the Heliogabalus—and no doubt before Agamemnon as well" (303).

Time is played against timelessness all through the book. The point of Charles's education is that he learn that "all those painted screens erected by man to shut out reality—history, religion, duty, social position, all were illusions" (206). Evolution was in the Victorian air, and as Prescott Evarts says, "evolving is the chief energy of the plot."[15] Fowles uses the model of evolution to represent his ideas about time. He uses quote after quote from Darwin, examines the fossils that encrust the Cobb, shows the earth crumbling as characters walk on the cliff. But horizontal evolution must be understood not as a progress or an evolving toward, but as a metamorphosis. The specific *form* of Victorian gentleman is obsolete, but the narrator sees a constant of gentlemanliness that runs throughout history: "a kind of self-questioning ethical elite . . . to brace or act as a structure for the better effects of their function in history" (295). In trying to understand evolution one can easily be duped by the idea of natural selection. Charles thought he was naturally selected because he was above the rest of his fellows—richer, smarter, better educated, and all the rest. But real natural selection in human terms means that those who are committed to "uncrucify," to live in the world and work to build a community in which constants rather than superficies flourish, those are the natural elite.

To illustrate the idea of horizontality Fowles uses a web-like frame of parallelisms to structure the novel. Mary is like Sarah in her sensuality, and her perspicacity is described in language similar to that which describes Sarah's: "She knew, in people, what was what" (131). He draws numerous parallels between Sam and Mr. Freeman, most notably in their aping of gentlemen; they have both risen out of lower classes and eventually they become involved in each other's lives. Aunt Tranter is like Grogan in that they are both decent people, but unable to evolve. Both are liberal, unconventional, and unmarried. Ernestina is linked rhetorically with Mrs. Poulteney in matters of taste and judgment. And we have already seen how Sarah herself becomes Varguennes. These and other correspondences demonstrate that there are constants not only in abstract ideas, but in human behavior and character. The web of interrelatedness in this book shows that people *are* related on deep levels, and therefore the sentiment of "To Marguerite" (which informs the final ending) is belied.

Fowles constructs the novel itself as a parallelism in that he weaves two novels together. One is a parody of the Victorian novel, the other is a modern novel. The Victorian novel, for example, has a predictable structure; the chapters could almost be named by their function: "Ernestina," "Charles," "Ernestina and Charles Together," "Mrs. Poulteney," and so on. Fowles introduces story threads and interweaves them with Dickensian artfulness. The structure mirrors the attitude that life has a structure, or plot (which is what

Charles thought at the beginning). The modern novel is without structure. Its ending can come in the middle, at the end, or not at all. In the Victorian novel character is handled traditionally, as it is in Grogan's case, for example. The narrator introduces him in the space of three pages. He begins by defining him with broad strokes ("a man who had lived and learned"), and then narrows to fine strokes that pile atop one another ("a very good doctor," "liked good food and wine," "knew the world and its absurdities," "something faintly dark about him"). The narrator presents what is essentially a resumé of his characteristics, then shows him in action, bearing out the specifics. To present a character in this manner is to imply that a person is a dossier, easily understandable, that he is the sum of certain superficial traits. The modern novel (whose subject is Sarah) treats character differently. The narrator asks "Who is Sarah?" and answers, "I don't know." Other plot conventions in the Victorian novel suggest that there is a plan, or fatedness, to the actions of characters, and a god (or an author-god) who controls their destinies. The many parallel scenes, parallel events, and consecutivities create the impression of a consciously ordered world. While Charles is advancing with Sarah, for example, Sam is working, "at that very moment" to undermine his success. In the modern novel Sarah works of her own will, has an unconventional degree of autonomy, and surprises both the reader and the narrator with every move.

The narrator does not make a qualitative judgment on the relative merits of the Victorian and modern novels. Rather, he tries, as do Sterne, Robbe-Grillet, Nabokov, and other practitioners in "the genre of the book-being-written,"[16] to examine some of the specious assumptions novels and their readers make. Immediately and comprehensively he destroys the fanciful notion that what we are reading is really happening. One of his favorite games is to break into the middle of a scene (or in one case, in the middle of a sentence) and announce its artifice: "I have pretended to slip back into 1867," or these two characters are "two figments of my imagination." He also adopts an ironic, even flippant stance toward his involvement in the novel, as when he parodies his own omniscience by so grossly overstating it, such as seeing Marx working in the British Museum while Charles combs the cliffs, or arranging to have Ernestina die on the day Hitler invades Poland.[17] He has a facetious attitude toward his ability to arrange details that have audaciously symbolic overtones.

He undermines his own integrity by revealing himself to be a voyeur. He opens the book with a look through a zoom lens that can see both near and far, suggesting that the narrative stance *is* a voyeuristic stance. It follows that the reader, then, is a voyeur once removed. Peter J. Conradi notes that the reader's viewing of two Victorians making love is like the primal scene itself.[18] The narrator maintains the cinematic point of view throughout. In the chapter devoted to Sarah in Exeter the narrator uses a camera technique similar to the one Hitchcock uses to open *Psycho*. The camera circles high over Exeter, over to the shady district, down to the street where the hotel is, down to the hotel itself, up to the light in Sarah's window and comes to rest on Sarah's silhouetted figure in the doorway. It is an almost indecently intrusive camera, and this scene recalls a similar one where the narrator broke into Ernestina's bedroom, as well as Clegg's first view of Miranda in *The Collector*.

The narrator calls his authority into question by frequently losing control of his characters, such as when Charles disobeys his orders, or when Sarah disappears and even he does not know where she is. His credibility is questionable because he confesses to be a schizophrenic himself. On the train he is one person; at the end he is another—a sinister, rococo showman of dubious moral standing. One is a serious and stolid artist who is truly interested in his characters, the other a dandy who loves to go on show. He parades his flesh before us to show his humanness. He denies that he is the superhuman being Booth calls the "implied author." He is, in fact, not all wise (he cannot understand Sarah), nor is he without some of humanity's baser feelings (such as those Mrs. Poulteney brings out in him). He flaunts his imperfection, his humanness throughout: his ability to love (he *does* love Sarah) and hate, his quickness to feel lust (especially for Mary), his habit of committing some of the crimes for which he condemns his characters (such as atrocious punning and other ironic games of language), and his sanguine opinionatedness: "Amateurs . . . ought to dabble everywhere, and damn the scientific prigs who try to shut them up in some narrow *oubliette*" (49).

What the narrator does, finally, is to discredit himself as author cum authority. He tries to distinguish himself from those authors who pretend to be gods. He assesses his relationship to his story and his reader when he gets on the train with Charles:

> Fiction usually tends to conform to the reality: the writer puts the conflicting wants (of his characters) in the ring and then describes the fight—but in fact fixes the fight, letting that want he himself favors win. And we judge writers of fiction both by the skill they show in fixing fights (in other words, in persuading us that they were not fixed) and by the kind of fighter they fix in favor of. . . . But the chief argument for fight-fixing is to show one's readers what one thinks of the world around one. . . . I continue to stare at Charles and see no reason this time for fixing the fight upon which he is about to engage. (406)

He suggests that this kind of fictional contract is on the reader's part an evasion of responsibility and surrender of freedom, and on the writer's part an act of impudence and arrogance. The question he asks is: Who am I to tell you what to think? As he says in his first discursive chapter, "A genuinely created world must be independent of its creator" (97).

Then why should we read his story? An answer to that question forms slowly and involves a readjustment of the reader's assumptions and expectations, and a shift in emphasis from *what* is read to what the act of reading means to each *reader*. In the novel the reader can discern a close relationship between the narrator and Sarah. Most obviously they are both story-tellers, and both tell stories only to refute them. Their methods of instruction are virtually identical; in short, everything Sarah does to Charles, the narrator does to his reader, and for the same reason. The situation is similar to the one in *The Magus* where Conchis and Fowles played parallel godgames. Because Sarah is entirely inscrutable she is able to work a spell on the reader as easily as on Charles. Her lack of definition invites the reader's own transferences, as well as those of Charles. The narrator arranges the book as Sarah arranges her game, as a kind of tease, the structure roughly paralleling, in Scholes's terms, tumescence and detumescence.[19] One of the narrator's tricks is to build a dramatic line slowly, bring it to a near climax, and then change the subject for a chapter or two. He realizes what Sarah realizes, that tension energizes. His lengthy discussion of Hardy and Tryphena seeks to illustrate to what degree creativity is generated by tension and frustration. Tension, as Allen Tate has pointed out, undermines and then revitalizes perception.

Sarah tells Charles, "Do not ask me to explain what I have done. I cannot explain it. It is not to be explained" (355). This nonexplanation corresponds to the narrator's refusal to fix the fight. Both tellers give their listeners the freedom to make their own explanations. The appreciation of the novel is a joint venture of the reader and the writer, as Robert Scholes says: "Like the sexual act the act of fiction is a reciprocal relationship. It takes two . . . the meaning of the fictional act itself is something like love."[20] The ultimate example of Fowles's method is contained in the two much-debated endings.[21]

It is clear that neither ending is satisfying. The first is blatantly sentimental; the second ostentatiously bleak. Fowles impudently demonstrates that he has chosen only two out of the indeterminate number of endings to this novel, and in fact stresses their arbitrariness. Just as he refused to be a dictatorial author-god, so he refuses to end this story and take away its energy. As Sarah refused to finish Charles's script, the narrator refuses to end ours. He would hope that by his giving the gift of freedom, each reader would write his own ending. As Charles writes the first ending to the novel (in which he marries Ernestina) the narrator steps back to examine what is happening. He says, "I said earlier that we are all poets, though not many of us write poetry; and so are we all novelists, that is, we have a habit of writing fictional futures for ourselves. . . . We screen in our minds hypotheses about how we might behave, about what might happen to us; and these novelistic or cinematic hypotheses often have very much more effect on how we actually do behave, when the real future becomes the present, than we generally allow" (339). The ending Charles wrote was so ghastly that it did affect his behavior—he shrank away from an imagined end, in the same way that Dickens has Ebenezer Scrooge shrink away from his imagined ends. As Frank Kermode says, imagined endings give energy, while real endings take away energy.[22] Fowles leaves his book full of energy, then, because like Kermode he believes that "a finite creation is incomprehensible" (*The Aristos*, 20). The reader takes over the function of novelist and his imagined end becomes a disclosure of his identity. The epigraph to the novel, which virtually equates freedom and humanism, is a profoundly optimistic comment upon both life and art.

4 Daniel Martin

It is hard going to the door

Cut so small in the wall where

the vision which echoes loneliness

brings a scent of wildflowers in a wood . . .

I walked away from myself,

I left the room.

ROBERT CREELEY

"The Door"

D*aniel Martin*[1] is obviously very different from Fowles's other novels. It lacks the magic and sparkle of *The Magus* and *The Ebony Tower*, the strong plot appeal of *The Collector*, and the color and intensity of *The French Lieutenant's Woman*. This novel is for the most part a serious and sober piece of mature introspection, and its power lies in its richness of thought as well as its strong commitment to humanism. Fowles poses a popular modern situation: a middle-aged man looks back on his life and wonders where he went wrong. Yet there is something in Dan's dilemma that sets him apart from other protagonists in this category. Fowles arranges for the reader to see Dan living his life and writing it at the same time. "I'm going to try a novel," is what Dan tells everyone. The future and the present jar uncomfortably in statements like that. Dan's task is defined by Jenny, who says Dan must write "your story. The real history of you" (17). In seeking to do that, Dan creates a curious feeling of double entendre throughout the work, a strong sense of both the remembering and the shaping of the remembered at the same time, a novel union of character and author. It is this typical Fowlesian doubleness that is at the heart of this book and from which derives its peculiar complexity.

My discussion of this novel is divided into three parts. The first considers how Dan's cinematic writing style is symptomatic of the errors in perception that have brought him to his crisis. The second examines Dan's attempts to correct those errors by adopting a more novelistic stance toward his own life. I should point out that when I speak of cinematic and novelistic forms I am not referring to any absolute or ideal definition of either genre. In many ways the two forms are very similar.[2] But they appear as distinct categories in this novel by virtue of contrast. Cinema simply functions as a foil for the novel. The third part examines the dense texture and structure that results from the many angles of vision, and especially concerns itself with the swarm of parallels that are, ultimately, both the form and the substance of the novel.

Life as Cinema

The writing of Dan's real history involves a search for two things: himself and a medium. Throughout this book it is evident that Dan is a scriptwriter learning to write a novel. The extraordinary first chapter is an excellent case in point.[3] In trying to begin his real story, Dan chooses a "hinged moment" from his boyhood. The *way* in which he recalls the events of "The Harvest" is distinctly cinematic. The camera point of view, which tends to fall naturally into omniscient form, is immediately apparent as we get an extremely long pan of the field, an establishing shot: "The field sloped from the wall of trees . . . down to the open gate onto Fishacre Lane. The dark coats lay there in against the hedge, covering the cider-jar and the dinner-bundle. . . . Lewis sat perched behind the faded carmine reaper. . . . Captain hardly needed the reins; so many years of plodding, just so. . . . Sally, the younger horse . . . stood tethered beneath a thorn not far from the gate, cropping the hedge, her tail intermittently swishing" (3). The chapter continues in much the same way, with the camera maintaining a distant and sweeping perspective of the events. The entire chapter has this lavishness of visual detail, which betokens camera reality and its inability to exclude.[4] Thus, Dan gives a mountain of information (such as that the dishcloth that covered the lunch was "white with blue ends") which, while pleasing, is not necessarily what ordinarily comes from the novel's perspective. Novel writing implies an excruciating process of selection, a winnowing down to what is truly telling. In Dan's art, then, as well as in his life, he must learn to see what is really important.

Dan's lapses into present-tense narration mimic the present-tense tyranny of the camera: "Old Mr. Luscombe . . . smiles lopsidedly with his bad teeth, a wink, the cast in his eye, the sun in his glasses"

(4). As Dan later realizes, "Film excludes all but now: permits no glances away to past and future; is therefore the safest dream" (155). Thus, because by its nature film is a "constant flowing through now-ness," it (in Leon Edel's terms) "cripples the use of the mind's eye."[5] In using cinematic temporality, Dan thwarts the novel's boundless freedom to ruminate, to "see whole" all at once. In a sense he is going back into his past without coming to terms with the past; he is recapitulating rather than recuperating.

The camera point of view distances the reader from the pro-tagonist. The lens evades the boy, who is a vague shadow, seen in long shot, with no name: "A boy in his midteens, his clothes un-suited, a mere harvest helper" (4). The boy is at first no more signifi-cant than his fellows because the camera forces parity upon all things in its frame. He eventually achieves more notice as Dan makes brief and hesitant forays into his mind; but even these are distant because they are derivative in a literary sense, echoing ca-dences and styles of other writers. Of an apple: "Still Primavera's thinks the boy; and much better poems than bruised and woolly Pelham Widow. But who cares, teeth deep in white cartwheel, bread and sweet ham, all life to follow" (6). Or "Adieu, my boyhood and my dream" (4). In this poetic ostentation Dan communicates a strong sense that young Dan is a type rather than an individual, a Stephen Dedalus or a young Dylan Thomas, whom he echoes strongly else-where: "See him scythe, dwarf the distort handle and the blade, the swaling drive and unstopping rhythm, pure and princely force of craft" (4). The chapter ends with an appropriate action: Dan carves his initials in a tree. His signature is like our first perspective of him: vague, undistinguished, unfleshed. Thomas Docherty sees Dan's distance from his earlier self as a voyeuristic stance encour-aged by his cinematic training, a stance that "erodes one's ability to feel."[6]

Dan's evasion of that boy, like his evasion of selection, is symp-tomatic of his lifelong problem of self-evasion. Writing screenplays, as he tells Jenny, not only condones but demands self-effacement of its author: "It's such a soft option. You write, interior, medium shot, girl and man on couch, night. Then you walk out. Let someone else be Jenny and Dan. . . . You never really stake yourself. Let it be no one else. Just you" (15). In this fledgling attempt at a novel Dan is learning about the "just you," which is counterposed against the committee-like nature of cinema art.

The cinematic quality of the writing continues into chapter 2 ("Games"), with Dan and Jenny playing games, acting parts, compulsively and consciously engaging in histrionics. The two characters move as if by stage direction (again note the present tense rendition): "He turns and crosses the room to a fake Biedermeier table by the door"; or "She stands and wanders across to the window, stubs out her cigarette . . . in a pottery dish by the telephone" (13). Dan has even arranged his mise-en-scène very carefully, with the telephone always predominant in the setting. That telephone is about to ring and become the agent of Dan's adventure and, therefore, the rest of the book. The door, also of semantic and thematic importance, is also always visible. In creating these props for the mind's eye, Dan is making an uneasy graft of the conventions of theater and cinema onto the novel, which is singular in its ability to release the reader from the tyranny of the visual.

This staginess, or screenplay ambiance, permeates the novel, as in the excerpt below, which finds the young Dan and Jane at Oxford:

> The wind blows the indolent arms of the willows sideways and ruffles the water of the long reach. The distant wooded hills to the west and the intervening meadowlands are stained with summery cloud-shadow. On the far side of the Cherwell, a young man, an undergraduate, poles a punt upstream. In the bow seat, facing him, a girl wearing sunglasses reclines. She trails the fingers of her right hand through the water. He is twenty-three years old and reading English; she is two years younger, and reading French. He wears army-surplus denim trousers and a navy-blue polo-necked sweater; she is in a dirndl peasant skirt, a dark green busily embroidered white and red; a white blouse and red Paisley head scarf. By her bare feet lie a rush basket, sandals and a strew of books. (20)

In this passage Dan uses the same deadpan, uninvolved camera narration of the first chapter: the long establishing shot, the medium shot that alights on the subject, the closer shot that defines the subject, the glut of detail. The string of parallel independent clauses attempts to ape the visual in syntax, to mimic the action of eyes by the forward motion of words. The actions themselves are stagy and the details conventional, as they are in the following scene, which occurs after the precipitating phone call:

> He stares into the lit planes of the California night. . . . "Two fingers, Jenny. Straight, please." He stares at the glass when she silently brings it. . . . She holds his eyes, probing. "What's happened?" "My erstwhile brother-in-law wants to see me. . . ." He swallows half the whiskey. He stares down at the glass. He looks up at her, then down again. "We were very close once, Jenny. . . ." He turns away from her eyes, looks out again over the endless city. (47)

This passage has the studied emoting, the pose striking of soap opera. Dan is using conventional theatrics to recall his inauthentic, theatrical life; but in doing so he is merely rolling the camera in words, transferring his familiar medium into print.

The subject of the "Games" chapter is Dan's vague crisis, which he never clearly defines. He plays virtually the whole chapter in dialogue, the heart of which is as follows:

> *Dan.* I suppose it was about reality. Failures to capture it.
> *Jenny.* You don't even . . . *and* you know it.
> *He.* Only by local standards.
> *She.* Balls.
> *He.* Darling, when you're ———.
> *She.* Oh Gawd, here we go again.
> *He.* When I was your age I could only look forward. At mine you . . . .

The reproduction of this opaque gibberish is apparently the product of a suggestion by Jenny as to how Dan should write his book: "I don't know why people make such a fuss about it. You just write down what you remember" (228). And in this chapter there is a strong sense of Dan playing back a camera in his mind. So if he has captured reality in one sense, that is by communicating the tone and flavor of a vapid and artificial relationship, he has failed to use a distinctly novelistic mitigating intelligence to select, form, and reflect.

Perhaps the most noticeably cinematic aspect of the novel is its constant recourse to dialogue. Dan defines himself to Jenny as "a dialogue installer and repairman" (32). This volubility is evident everywhere, such as in the chapter "Solid Daughter," where virtually all that occurs is the marmalading of a piece of toast. Going up the Nile, Dan and Jane are often like talking heads as they discuss countless weighty subjects, or construct verbal responses to events.[7] "The Shadows of Women" is an excellent study of the possible abuses of dialogue. It is constructed of several parallel conversations between Dan and his many women, each of which shows him offering a different explanation for taking Jane to Egypt. Dialogue is the only tool of the scriptwriter, but it is only a part of the novelist's art, as Dan knows. When Jane tells him that he ought to have no trouble with dialogue in his novel, he replies, "It's the bits between I fear" (390). It is not surprising, then, that Dan uses the telephone conversation, which he calls "film without vision," as a predominant motif. The chapter called "Rain," for example, is a compendium of telephone conversations, again dealing with Dan taking Jane to Egypt. As in "The Shadows of Women," Dan prevaricates and constructs word barriers to keep truth away from others as well as himself.

A screenplay-like scenarism pervades the novel as Dan renders his life as a series of scenes or set pieces, making the chapters of the first two-thirds of the novel seem like short stories strung together rather wantonly. The chapter called "Interlude," for example, is a perfectly self-contained account of the Miriam-Marjory affair, as "Phillida" is of the Nancy Reed affair. The chapter called "Compton" is the most claustrophobic of the set pieces. Dan gathers all the characters together and shows them engaged in innocuous conversations. He moves them about, puts them into conversational pairs, shows how alliances shift, and reproduces conversations in which characters reveal themselves to be different from what they are in the group. Much of the talk is given to discussion of Caro's absurdly banal affair with Barney, talk that becomes a blind for more important things. The problems of evasion and identity that Dan brings up in this minidrama are relevant to the evasions and identity crises in the other stories of his past. But because he does not make these connections, because he tends to close off the significant details of his life from each other, these chapters remain a ragbag of oddities unsynthesized by their author.

Dan's familiarity with film editing techniques influences his novel writing. He self-consciously uses (and states that he is using) a continuity shot in picturing his flight from California to London—a gratuitous visual on which he superimposes much flashing back. He uses the match dissolve in the juxtaposition of remembering the young Barney Dillon in Oxford and seeing the present Barney upon opening his eyes on the plane. He also tends to use background music rather obviously, as when he ends his lovemaking with Jane at Oxford with a provocative but tasteful fade: "The student oboist began to play Delius, and she reached her free hand across the rug, almost formally, like a medieval bride" (59). There are jump cuts (as in the dissonant juxtaposition of chapters 1 and 2), voice-overs (Jenny's "contributions"), and montage editing (as in "Passage," which grafts together several layers of time). In fact, the first two-thirds of this book has more in common artistically with *Citizen Kane* (the most talked-about film in the book) than a novel. *Citizen Kane* is also a study in a single man's identity. Both *Kane* and *Daniel Martin* employ flamboyant stylistics, which in the case of the former established an exemplar of achievement in film art and revealed great expressionistic potential for the recalcitrant visual. In the novel, however, such stylistics are, while interesting, unnecessary, and ultimately detrimental to Dan's task. Dan's baroque techniques show a triumph of form over content, and because he adopts a cinematic stance toward his own life he places himself (as does the cinematographer) on the outside looking in.

Not all of Dan's writing, of course, maintains the safe distances of the cinema. Fowles brings out the differences between novel seeing and camera seeing in "Umbrella" (which Dan calls his "Rosebud"). This chapter has one of the three epigraphs from Seferis: "What can a flame remember? If it remembers a little less than is necessary, it goes out; if it remembers a little more than is necessary, it goes out. If it could only teach us, while it burns, to remember correctly" (75).

Dan then writes a chapter in which he tries to remember correctly his childhood, especially his relationship with his father. He tries two kinds of remembering. In the first he simply gives a bland, first-person, past-tense account of his dislike for his father. As Dan begins to become emotionally involved in his remembering the chapter breaks down and veers off into a diatribe against Englishness (a common type of evasion for Dan), and from there into an intellectual meditation on time and memory (another evasion of the subject). Toward the end he pulls himself back to the subject of his father and gives a present-tense (and highly visual, aural, and cinematic) rendition of a single important childhood event. This restless shifting shows Dan struggling to learn *how to remember,* indeed as if the process is more important than the content. The epigraph informs Dan's first attempt at remembering. In the lifeless discourse on his early life he remembers too little: "He wasn't a stern man at all, in spite of his lack of humor, which sprang much more from a diffuse absentmindedness, almost an unworldliness, than any intrinsic disapproval of laughter. There was nothing in his personal nature that overtly tyrannized the household" (78). And in the highly colored umbrella account, where once again Dan makes a screenplay of his life and a fictional character of himself, he remembers perhaps too much:

> I draggle kicking down the back lane. . . . Burning May, the hedges dense with cow parsley. . . . Late afternoon. . . . A wood lark sings . . . bell-fluting tri-syllable, core of green, core of spring-summer, already one of those sounds that creep into the unconscious and haunt one all one's life. My father appears, wheeling his bicycle up the hill. . . . On some days my stupid father will use his rotten old bicycle like this. His pale-beige summer visiting coat, his dark gray trousers in bicycle clips, the straw panama with the black band which can't blow off, there's an eyelet in the brim behind attached by a safety pin to a sort of black boot lace that ends in a watch chain bar pushed through his buttonhole. (87)

Both rememberings are inadequate for defining the real relationship between Dan and his father. The truth must lie somewhere in the central evasion where Dan seeks neutral ground. The problem of writing one's life, then, becomes one of remembering correctly, of getting as close as possible to the real, or as Dan poignantly puts it: "That other door [into his past], like reality itself, that ultimate ambiguous fiction of the enacted past, seems poised eternally in two minds; is always waiting . . . for someone at last to get the feeling right" (50). Part of the reason for the strange mix of techniques in Daniel Martin is that Dan is trying different ways of remembering.

Learning How to Remember

There is no one point at which Dan ceases to write a screenplay and begins to write a novel; indeed the two forms coexist throughout. What is evident is that a learning process is taking place during and as a result of his reconstruction. In all his novels Fowles shows that telling a story leads to understanding. Dan experiences the psychotherapeutic effects of remembering in peculiar ways, as when he recalls walking in his orchard: "He began to walk slowly among the old trees. From the bottom there was a familiar gurgle of water where the leat ran shallow over some stones. He did not hear it" (402). In effect, he experiences and understands more in his recollection than in "the implacable first person of the moment" (414). Telling is an important motif in this book, and many characters give accounts of their lives. Andrea tells the story of her depraved marriage; Miriam tells Dan the story of her unhappy childhood; Jenny tells many stories about both her life and her fantasies; the Herr Professor tells the story of his life with a detachment toward his younger self that recalls Dan's own narratorial stance. The first Seferis epigraph suggests the meaning of this telling. The first line poses the question of the book: "What's wrong with that man?" And the last line implies the source of the answer: "Then he told me the story of his life" (3).[8]

The novel illustrates the many ways in which individuals try to understand others. Dan allows the reader to hear the inquest that probes Anthony's suicide. The authorities presume to get at the truth of a man's life through a series of dry, clinical questions. They attempt to bring to quotidian terms an essentially metaphysical act. Jane tries to understand Gramsci by reading his Prison Notebooks;

Dan tries to understand Caroline by examining the contents of her bedroom. In this book Fowles poses what is his most thoroughgoing investigation yet into the nature of identity. Dan's writing of his own story is closely paralleled by his writing of the Kitchener script, in which he is trying to define the real essence of the man. In outlining his problems with that script, he might be talking about himself: "The mass of material that had to be included. . . . He had settled for one small formal trick. He wanted to catch Kitchener somewhere in mid-career and at some central focus geographically; and then sally from that point in flashback and flash-forward to the rest of his life" (279).

The problem of the *form* of one's recollections, then, is attended by the difficulty of knowing what one's identity is. Just as the problem of unconscious projection (which in this novel works in much the same way as it did in *The French Lieutenant's Woman*, especially in terms of Dan's perceptions of Jane) hampers our true knowledge of others, the strong unconscious motivations to which each of us is prey hamper our knowledge of ourselves. Dan is, for example, able to delude himself about his reason for taking Jane to Egypt, thinking of the act variously as a favor to Anthony or a nebulous humanitarian gesture. But his real feelings erupt in curious ways, as when he talks about how long they'll be gone:

> *Dan to Jane.* I have to go to Egypt for a few days.
> *Dan to Jane.* They run a jolly one-week cruise.
> *Jane.* It sounds heavenly. But I ———.
> *Dan.* Only ten days.
> *(Later) Dan to Roz.* Two weeks at the most.
> (397, 415)

Dan shows the same sort of protesting too much in the way he consistently and continually maintains that Jane is no longer attractive. He abuses Freud by using psychoanalytic jargon as a blind, as when he analyzes his attraction to Jane as Oedipal rather than admitting it is a case of simple love.

Most of the characters are uncertain about whether identity is constant or protean. In this compendium of reminiscences, a character commonly asks, what has *become* of so and so?—as if what a person once was is no longer what he is. Dan sees Nancy Reed again after twenty years and finds her to be not the lush beauty he knew, but a fat, coarse, middle-aged woman who reminds him of a barmaid. The chapter called "Jane" is a tissue of ambiguities, and Dan wonders who this middle-aged Jane is: "I knew I didn't yet know her well enough as she had become" (155). Jane complicates his problem by protesting, "I'm no longer the person you knew, Dan" (192). Identity must, it seems, be graphed against a temporal variable.

Dan divulges the difficulty of his search for himself in his nervous handling of point of view as he vacillates, sometimes in the same sentence, between "I" and "he." Of his affair with the "British Open" he says, "Dan left the flat feeling stunned with self-shock; and I remember he had a terrible afternoon" (138). He suffers much confusion over first and third persons, feeling on one hand that it is desirable "to see oneself as others see one—to escape the first person and become one's own third" (62). On the other hand, he feels the third person is a "flinching from the 'I' inherent in any honest recapitulation of his life" (63). After making love to Jane in Palmyra, Dan reveals that this same conflict affects his life: "The failure could have been put in terms of grammatical person. It had happened in the third, when he craved the first and second" (599). Similarly, Dan's use of shifting tenses shows, as Robert Alter says, "the subtle and shifting pressures of different pasts on present consciousness," and allows the reader to see "the precarious moral drift of 'a life awash in time.' "9 The problems of understanding identity are several and well-defined: What is one's nature? How does it change over time? At what angle can one view oneself clearly? And ultimately, how does one tell it?

In his other novels Fowles has shown characters coming to terms with themselves through the therapeutic effects of remembering.10 In showing Dan's growing ability to write a novel he suggests that the union of words and memory gives the closest approximation to "remembering correctly." The object of this, Fowles's most ambitious game, is not to arrive at an understanding of the quintessential Daniel Martin, but to examine by what process identity comes to be known to oneself and, further, how that knowledge can be communicated to others.

Remembering correctly, in Dan's case, is a matter of substituting novel vision for cinema vision. A good case in point is his meeting (in 1969) with Nancy Reed. He writes the scene for the most part in the cinematic mode with high color, luxurious detail, and copious dialogue. He even introduces the scene with "one last shot" (as a kind of coda to the "Phillida" chapter). Dan says of their awkwardness:

> I found it all vaguely amusing at the time; it hasn't really distressed me till now, when I set it down. . . . If only I had broken through the wretched plastic shell of that meeting, through her frightened gentility and my equally odious urbanity. We think we grow old, we grow wise and more tolerant; we just grow lazy. I could have asked what happened that terrible day: what did you feel, how long did you go on missing me? Even if I'd only evoked a remembered bitterness, recriminations, it would have been better than that total burial, that vile, stupid and inhuman pretense that our pasts are not also our presents. (381)

In this scene Dan freezes the frame and walks around it; he studies it before letting it fade. He is acknowledging that words aid remembering by contributing a dimension missing in the pictorial. Cinema vision closes doors, creates a sealed world that is forever done and past; the final cut allows no more than one angle. In writing the story of himself, Dan must learn to open doors, not only to himself, so that he can see himself more clearly, but to readers who are free to project themselves into the text and participate in the process. As Dan says, "Images are inherently fascistic because they overstamp the truth. . . . The word is the most imprecise of signs. Only a science-obsessed age could fail to comprehend that this is its great virtue, not its defect" (187). The same process takes place in his writing of the Tarquinia scene, where he, Jane, Nell, and Anthony form a circle in the night sea and dance naked in the water. Dan confesses, "I tried repeatedly in later years to put those few moments into my work—and always had to cut them out" (110). The problem is familiar: in either drama or film he had trouble making the scene seem anything more than "a faintly embarrassing midnight jape" (110). Now Dan has successfully put the scene in his work.

One of the most curious features of this novel is that it changes abruptly two-thirds of the way through. It changes, of course, at the section that deals with Dan and Jane going up the Nile. The crazy-quilt structure gives way to a very traditional, linear, sequential narration. The chapters flow together and are no longer set pieces. The section is ordered by a ruminative, reasoning faculty rather than by one that seems more subconscious and impetuous. In Palmyra Dan wakes in his room feeling disoriented, "in a familiar maze between sequence-despising dream and coherent reality" (602). That condition is a paradigm for this book, the first part being like a dream of his past from which he must awake, and the second being a coherence made possible by finding Jane. Remembering correctly is also contingent upon finding an order to experience that allows one to glance backward and forward while maintaining a steady course.

Dan also ceases to strain over his point of view in this section, as he uses a consistent third-person narration. Apparently Dan has his character in focus and has found that with the third person the author can be both inside and outside at the same time; he can hold himself out at arm's length to get the objective view and crawl back inside to get the emotional amenities of the first person. In this final portion of the novel Dan uses much less dialogue. He begins to let go of the safe habit of reproducing pages of dialogue and gives more freedom to the mitigating intelligence that is the province of the novel alone. His tone grows moody and sullen as he begins to understand what evasions dialogue can harbor: "He took the opportunity to be franker about Jenny McNeil and his own dilemma. That is, he started meaning to be franker; but it soon grew like an algebraic rendering-down, more a casual analysis of the general stresses of Jenny's kind of life. . . . The only real pleasure he took in that conversation was far less in its words than in its silences and pauses." (499).

Cinematic seeing is limited seeing, while novel seeing gives at least access to the ideal of "whole sight" that is expressed in the motto of this novel (which begins, cryptically, with the admonition "WHOLE SIGHT; OR ALL THE REST IS DESOLATION"). Anthony's deathbed wisdom is that whatever one makes of God, it is certain that the Devil is "not seeing whole" (181). The tragic "design failure" in Anthony's life is caused by his habit of looking at (roughly comparable to cinematic vision) rather than looking for. When he enjoins Dan to look for the real Jane (and by extension the real Dan), he is asking Dan to deal with the difficult problem of finding what does not change. His challenge again recalls the first Seferis epigraph: "I try to keep myself going with a flame / because it doesn't change" (3). Dan begins to feel an Eliot-like intersection of timelessness with time when he becomes reinvolved with Jane and Anthony: "It was . . . like going into a theatre and finding a production one had seen there half a lifetime before still on stage" (189). The city of Cairo becomes a metaphor for whole sight, for seeing all time at once ("Time—layers of time, so many stages of history still co-existing here" [461]) and all places at once ("All cities grew one. Cairo was simply denser, older, more human. The medieval injustices and inequalities still existed, and everywhere; in the West they had simply been pushed out of sight" [461]). Fowles constructs complex layers of time both in the minds of the characters and in the outside world, and he mirrors the complexity in such tortured chapter titles as "Forward Backward" and "Future Past."

The Nile voyage is by its nature a journey back in time, and along the way Dan begins to see a pattern of continuity, as when Jane buys him a third-century Coptic head that is the "spitting image" of Jimmy Assad; or when Dan sees the Egyptian wild geese "whose remote ancestors he also saw much closer at hand, painted on temple walls" (508). Dan perceives intellectual constants as he compares two seemingly disparate historical figures in the same breath: "The wretched Rameses II, Il Duce of the dynasties" (476). Dan often feels that there is a metaphysical survival of spirit after death. He feels the presence of the ancient Etruscans at Tarquinia, and of the Pueblos at Tsankawi, and of the humble Reeds in his own home: "I could live a thousand years in this house where I write now, and never own it as they did, beyond all artifice of legal possession" (379). Dan sees reflected in the Nile itself the "Heraclitean same and not the same" (493); and he recalls the Bible: *"The earth abideth forever; and there is no new thing under the sun"* (493). The Professor illustrates this doctrine called Qadim (i.e., that the past is also the present) with his story of the ghost in the empty tomb. The experience was "like a broken link in time. . . . One exists, but it is somehow not in time.

In a greater reality, behind the illusion we call time. One was always there" (525). Fowles shows, as he did in *The French Lieutenant's Woman*, that beneath history's chronic bouts of chaos and change there exists a substructure of constants. In this novel he explores how constants relate to the subject of identity as well, and he examines the difference between being and becoming. When Anthony asks Dan to resurrect the old Jane, it is because he has realized the truth Seferis expresses in the final epigraph:

> At the hour when one day ends and the next one has not begun
> at the hour when time is suspended
> you must find the man who then and now, from the very beginning, ruled your body
> you must look for him so that someone else at least
> will find him, after you are dead.
>
> (615)

One's nature, though it can be compromised almost beyond recognition, does not change; and it is only by seeing whole, by seeing one's past, present, and future together, that one can detect the degree to which he has become inauthentic. Dan's attempt to see whole is mirrored in the technique of the last section, with the unions of "I" and "he," of showing and telling, of silence and speech, of past and present.

Dan begins at last to get the feeling right when he finds Jane again. She had always been almost metaphysically disturbing to him, strangely bound up in his fate and his identity. He realizes as they travel together that he is seeing through her eyes. Dan, like Charles Smithson, consistently projects his insecurities onto the woman he loves. The imagined rebukes he fears from Jane become almost a paranoia. He says, "I had also, behind the apparent deference, felt obscurely condescended to the way intellectuals will condescend to peasants" (155). All the ways in which Dan has sullied his true nature and talents stand out accusingly when he is with Jane. She is the standard against which he measures himself: "Making him think was essentially a making him look at himself through her eyes" (414). In Jane's presence Dan is able to step outside of himself and examine himself objectively, as when she first comes to Thorncombe. He thought he had decorated the place shrewdly, in stark Scandinavian white and wood, with a sprinkling of family pictures for atmosphere, until he sees it as he imagines Jane must see it—as a sterile home, a mockery of the home made by its former inhabitants. Like Sarah Woodruff, Jane is a shadowy figure about whom Fowles gives very little objective information. The reader perceives dimly that she is haggard and defeated. Virtually all her feelings and thoughts are imputations that come from Dan's transferences. So when Dan says, "She appeared to be implying that I couldn't accuse Barney of my own nature and crimes" (187); or "I know I was being tolerated for Anthony's sake" (188), these insecurities tell more about Dan's sore points than Jane's true feelings. She is his true mirror.

This strange relationship of mirror and object constitutes a definition of love that is only hinted at in Fowles's other books and that boldly speculates on the interrelationship of identities. When Dan finds Jane again he has the strong feeling that they have consummated fate. Dan feels a sense of almost biological bonding in their union, as if once mated they belonged to each other forever: "There are some people one can't dismiss. . . . Who set riddles one ignores at one's cost; who like nature itself, are . . . dissolvent of all time" (413). Dan sees a reflection of their relationship in the ankh at Karnak: holding the "ancient keys of life" are "Iris and Osiris, brother and sister, husband and wife" (477). Dan understands the exclusive and reflexive aspects of love when he says to Jane: "What I need from you is that something inside you, between us, that makes half-living, half-loving like this impossible. . . . I meet you again, I suddenly see all this, what went wrong from the beginning, why you were the one woman who might have led me out of it" (567). Like Yin and Yang, true lovers are a completion of each other.

Love, the human bond, counteracts fear of the "frozen distances" that are symbolized by the landscape of Palmyra. Dan finds that he wants "to know one could always reach out a hand and . . . that shadow of the other shared voyage, into the night" (561, Fowles's ellipsis). Just as the lovers are the complements of each other, the love relationship itself is the complement of death. The many deaths in the book give rise to love and life, from the beginning, when the young Dan's having seen "the agony in the mower's blades" makes him feel, on reflection, "pregnant with being" (11). Dan and Jane are first brought together by death, by the woman in the reeds. Many years later Anthony's death brings them together again. Love and commitment become appropriate and necessary responses to what is otherwise an empty and unintelligible existence.[11]

It is Jane who is responsible for Dan's ability to see whole, and that ability in turn makes it possible for him to write his novel. With Jane as his mirror he is able to see the travesties he had made of his life, and he also begins to understand what he calls "reality." Dan uses that word glibly throughout as though its meaning were a given and not a matter of contention. His artistic credo is based upon that polysemous word: "To hell with cultural fashion; to hell with elitist guilt; to hell with existential nausea; and above all, to hell with the imagined that does not say, not only in, but behind the images, the real" (405). Or, in Oxford, Dan says, "It's been the most marvelous three years of my life"; and Jane counters with, "But has it been real?" (27). Dan never defines reality. Instead, Fowles shows how its meaning accrues for Dan until it has a shape and tone, rather than a definition. Dan discovers what is real by writing his novel, by rediscovering himself with new eyes.

Certainly, strong agrarian values make up a large part of what Dan means by reality. Dan becomes conspicuously lyrical when he writes about Ben and Phoebe and their "elementary decencies of existence—method, habit, routine, . . . continuity" (343), or about the Reeds and Thorncombe. The "Phillida" chapter is an intense, sustained pastoral, defining much of what Dan feels he has lost: home, stability, earth, love, constancy, and simplicity, all the true desires of his life that he has flouted, only to pursue their opposites with demented fury. Of Thorncombe he says, "It has some mysterious warmth, some inner life, some grace that we lacked at the Vicarage" (347). Dan conceals his profound love of nature as though it were a disease, and that concealment is a large part of his self-betrayal and perversion of reality.

Dan comes to believe that what is real may be perceived only by the faculty he calls "right feeling," a close cousin to D. H. Lawrence's notion of intuition. Dan suggests the meaning of right feeling in his explanation of why modern men are so evasive of their real natures: "We've let daylight usurp everything . . . all our instincts, all we don't know in ourselves. When we're still just as much animals as that poor creature over there" (610). Intuitive feelings dominate the Tsankawi episode. Dan thinks about how isolated he is, how Jenny can never understand what is happening in his mind, and that he must therefore leave her. He feels, however, that he is hiding his feelings well and says nothing to spoil the day. The point of view switches abruptly to Jenny, who reveals that she understood everything silently: "It was so sad, these sudden bad vibes between us, and not being able to say anything. . . . Knowing I'd lost Dan but not why" (333). Intuition, silent understanding, "tensions, poles, the mysterious architecture of secret reality" (391) are given, in this novel as well as in the others, a legitimacy that a rational approach to reality cannot claim. Relationships with ourselves, others, and the outside world are thoroughly contingent upon biases, circumstances, points of views, and rationalizations, and the ultimate recourse to truth lies in silence. Dan considers this idea as he and Jane listen to Bach. The music spoke "of other languages, meaning-systems, besides that of words; and fused his belief that it was words, linguistic modes, that mainly stood between Jane and himself. Behind what they said lay on both sides an identity, a syncretism, a same key, a thousand things beyond verbalization" (561). The Professor also understands that there is a numinous substructure to human relations: "Learn never, but never, to believe your eyes" (483).

This novel is epistemological in that it inquires how one comes to know oneself and one's relations to others, and it proposes the epiphany as the model of real knowledge: the sudden flash of insight, the momentary recognition of right feeling, what Dan calls "fulcrum moments." Obviously one does not go through life seeing whole and feeling right all the time. For example, roughly halfway through the novel Dan has a devastating insight wherein he realizes that his life has been dominated by a love of loss: "Then he did something absurd. He got out of bed and found his notebook. . . . He jotted down not something profound . . . but the words: Remind Ben—*mangetout peas*. He had remembered they were one of Jenny's greeds" (456). This major change in key reverses the profundities of the previous paragraphs. Dan goes from contemplating a lonely, searching vigil at Thorncombe while he works on his novel to imagining the continuation of game playing (and seeing Jenny at Thorncombe). The brilliant realization that the protagonist soon forgets or contradicts is a typical Fowlesian inversion; the trivial business of living so soon overwhelms the profound. In most novels a character proceeds toward some climax of understanding that thereafter reverses either his actions or his attitudes. Fowles's novels always leave the major characters in a quandary, and this one is no exception, ending as it does in a conundrum: "Dan told her . . . that at least he had found a last sentence for the novel he was never going to write. . . . And in the knowledge that Dan's novel can never be read, lies eternally in the future, his ill-concealed ghost has made that impossible last his own impossible first" (629). Knowledge of self is never so thoroughgoing as most novels suggest, and such knowledge is, anyway, not to be had by following traditional novelistic models. It is neither decisive, quick, nor finite, and is a process rather than an event. Thus at the end Dan has a hazy notion that he is doing the right thing, even though a life with Jane is a tissue of hazards. His self-knowledge is not complete, even though he shows himself to be learning by means of his changing writing style. He shows us, rather, that all knowledge (and communication of knowledge) is at best an approximation, gained by occasional "moments of intense vision" (547).

Approaching Whole Sight

In endeavoring to "say the real," Dan has used the "oomph of mimesis" (21) to construct an analogue of reality. His complex novel has dozens of characters, locations, and time levels, mirroring the large, complex business of life, which stands as the greatest impediment to understanding. Yet there is an extraordinary number of parallels in this book, a substructure of coincidence, correspondence, recurring events, motifs, even leitmotifs, that serve to tame the chaos by the logic of, say, an Escher drawing;

that is, if one reads life (and this book) properly, one can begin to see the connections.[12]

The chapter titles themselves suggest parallel layers of meaning. "Breaking Silence," for example, refers to Dan's speaking in an otherwise silent train compartment; to his coming meeting with Jane and Anthony after sixteen years; and to his marital problem with Nell, which is the major subject of the chapter. The chapter entitled "Behind the Door" sees Jane revealing much about her relationship to Anthony. Physical doors figure largely in the chapter, as characters go in and out of rooms, opening and closing doors in what seems an orchestrated game of hide and seek. Jane takes the terrible phone call announcing Anthony's suicide behind a closed door. Doors are symbolic throughout this novel as they are in *The Magus*. Dan and Jane have connecting doors on the Nile trip; after Jane seduces Dan at the beginning she slips out the door, having heard a distant door close, whereupon Dan goes upstairs and knocks on Barney's door. As he is talking to Anthony in his hospital room, Dan looks out the glass door—the same door Anthony leaps through to end his life, a literalization of Dan's comment that Anthony is at "death's door." Dan uses the door as Lewis Carroll uses the looking glass, as a portal through which one makes quantum leaps.

Semantic correspondences abound in the novel, and certain words act like descants over a musical composition. When Dan becomes angry at Jane in Palmyra for all her evasions, he calls her "bitch"; and the next chapter is called "The Bitch," to ally Jane with the animal who exhibits "distraction behavior" in order to survive. Dan talks about "ghosts" many times in differing contexts, and ghosts come to signify a sense of the past that coexists with the present.[13] Dan feels the ghosts of the Reeds at Thorncombe; he feels Anthony's ghost on the Nile journey; he feels the ghosts of the Pueblos at Tsankawi; the Professor tells him "a ghost story without a ghost," about his union in a rock tomb with the "greater reality." Dan himself later experiences, in that same tomb, a sense of "being outside his own body" (534). In the end Dan feels Jane's ghost, who "watched him watching himself" (624), inside his own body.

Archaeology is perhaps the most persistent idea in the book. In the second chapter we find Dan "in ruins somewhere," and the rest of the book is an archaeological investigation into his life that is paralleled by his many visits to historical ruins: at Tarquinia the foursome explores Etruscan tombs; in Tsankawi Dan and Jenny pore over the Pueblo ruins; and in Egypt the ruins provide the backdrop and frame for Dan's and Jane's mutual explorations. In fact, Dan and Jane go as far back into history as they can, ending in Mesopotamia (Palmyra is in the valley of the Tigris and Euphrates), where civilization began. In the first chapter Dan escapes to his high hill and sees "the parallel waves where an ox-plough once went many centuries before" (11). He sees the same waves when he and Nancy Reed escape to their hill; and many years later Dan brings Jane's son (who has inherited his father's penchant for looking at) to see the same lines. The ruins of many civilizations lie at his feet, ready to teach him that forms die and constants—like the fellaheen, poverty itself, megalomania, or love—remain. The Professor, who like Conchis is an arrived individual, offers a connection between identity and archaeology. "He began to talk in more detail of his past—quite objectively, as if he were a site . . . not unlike the way in which he had outlined Queen Hatshepsut's life to them at Thebes" (520).

The many extraordinary coincidences in this book create the feeling that reality does fall into discernible patterns. Just after Jenny tells Dan that a door will open onto his past, he receives the call from Jane. It is Andrew who finds the woman in the reeds with Dan and Jane, the same Andrew who comes back as Nell's second husband. On that same day Dan and Jane speak of death, and Dan tells Jane of his experience with the rabbits. As he speaks "a huge American bomber, a Flying Fortress" roars overhead, just as the German bomber had appeared on that other long-ago day of death. Later, when Dan and Andrew stroll at Compton and lament the dying of the aristocracy, their idyll is shattered by the thundering of a Concorde. The most blatant coincidence is Dan running into Barney Dillon on the flight to London.

Fowles uses repetitive situations as part of his strategy of patterning. The party—at Assad's, at Compton, on the Nile steamer, in Jenny's "Third Contribution"—is one such situation and shows how identity falters in a crowd. Dan demonstrates his restlessness in the many long and important conversations he holds in cars: Dan and Jane renew their acquaintance in the drive to the hospital; Dan and Caro dissect their relationship on the drive home from Heathrow; Dan and Jane discuss the problems of a mutual future in the long taxi ride to Palmyra; Dan comes to know Paul in the long drive to Thorncombe, and so on. Other important conversations occur on planes (Dan and Barney on the way to London, Dan and Jane going to Cairo). The boat trip is also a part of the motif of moving vehicles. Dan and Jane first appear together poling on the Cherwell. Later, they boat together up the Nile and recapitulate an identical voyage Dan had taken with Andrea years before. When they step off the steamer they board a felucca. Dan is always moving, leading Jenny to compare him to a battered suitcase. This obsessive peregrination—flying, driving, taking day trips and walking tours (such as at Compton and Kitchener's Island), sailing, steaming, taking the train, vacationing (such as with Nell in France), moving from one home to another (Dan going from the mews to the Hampstead flat to Thorncombe)—is the shifting background against which we see Dan, who compares himself to "a bird that has forgotten how to stop migrating" (276). He presents himself in his most characteristic mode: on the run. Significantly, the novel ends with the static image of Dan in Oxford "leaning beside Jane in her kitchen while she cooked supper for them" (629). The image answers the question Dan posed earlier for his novel: "What makes him stop?" (276).

An examination of two of Dan's trips, Palmyra and Tsankawi, divulges an even greater depth to the paralleling going on in this novel. Both trips are stolen (Tsankawi from a busy shooting schedule, Palmyra as an unscheduled, last-minute divagation), rushed, and almost illicit. The couples explore ruins of different natures. Tsankawi demonstrates the positive endurance of a creative and noble culture; Palmyra is utter negation, the remains of a decadent empire, a reminder of the constant presence of a destruction principle. In both a question of marriage hangs in the air; and in both Dan is silently angry at the woman. Both are attended by flocks of ravens— Dan's "totem bird." The similarities in the situations reflect other similarities between Jane and Jenny, the first of which is the close-ness of their names. They are also both intelligent and beautiful actresses. In fact, Dan often draws the two together in his mind. When Jane sets Dan an enigma, which she often does, Dan charac-teristically retreats into thoughts of Jenny: "I felt baffled. . . . Once again I had a sharp and sudden longing for the girl who was phys-ically far away in Los Angeles . . . for her . . . simplicities" (155). Jenny is, perhaps, enough like Jane to fill a temporary subconscious need, to be a surrogate, but she could never be Dan's mirror.

The guided tour is a more specific version of the journey motif. During virtually all of Dan's trips he is led by a guide who tries to teach him the significance of what he sees. Even the Professor is a guide, and, to Dan, a mentor. Andrew takes Dan around Compton, Assad shows him around Cairo. Dan usually tries to pull away from the guide but is never very successful. Sometimes it is he who is the guide, the urbane interpreter, as he takes Jenny around the sights of Los Angeles and Jane around Thorncombe. Yet one of the last images of the novel is Dan standing alone in a museum before a late Rem-brandt self-portrait. A group of school children being led by a guide passes through the room. Aloneness is part of what the painting teaches him, "the distances he had to return" (628). The guided tour, then, is a metaphor for yet another misleading way of seeing.

A characteristic variation of the journey is the exile. Dan is first exiled from his fellows as a child because he is different. Later he is exiled from Nancy in one stroke, and she is exiled from her own home. With an equally swift cut Dan is exiled from Jane and An-thony. And the Professor is in political exile from Germany. Exile is paralleled by retreat, especially retreat to a Sacred Combe, *la bonne vaux* of Restif de la Bretonne. Tsankawi, Tarquinia, Kitchener's Is-land, and Thorncombe are all idealized domains, niches apart from the real world that have the same attraction for Dan that the de-Galais domain has for Le Grand Meaulnes (another wanderer). The reverse side of exile and escape is the return, and Dan goes back to Oxford, back to Thorncombe, back to Compton, even back to Egypt. Coming full circle suggests again the wisdom of "Little Gidding," which played such a large part in *The Magus*:

The end of all our exploring
will be to arrive where we started
and know the place for the first time.

Relationships between people fall into complex correspondences. The ménage à trois, the love triangle, as well as incest, are curious examples. In the first category, the consenting threesome, we find Dan-Miriam-Marjory and Jenny-Steve-Kate. The classic triangle has many manifestations: Dan-Jane-Nell (as students); Dan-Jenny-Jane (of the fictional present); Jane-Anthony-David (Jane's Harvard "friend"); Caro-Barney–Barney's wife; Dan-Nell-Andrea (as well as his other adulteries). Incest is merely a suggestion in the novel, though it is a strong undercurrent. When Dan and Jane and Nell and Anthony were involved together at Oxford, Dan "felt an inherent poison in the situation . . . an almost Jacobean claustrophobia, incest" (106), as if by marrying one sister he can, according to Freud's theory, have the other. There is a strong tint of incest in Dan's relationship with Caro. They toy with the idea, banter with innuendo, and at one point Dan says, "I half sensed what could drive fathers and daughters to incest . . . that need to purge the spoken of the unspoken, to institute a simplicity in place of an obscuring complexity" (123). There is a strong suggestion of sexual transference in all the May-December relationships in the novel—in Caro's adultery with Barney, in Dan's affair with Jenny, and in Jane's relationship with her lover, which she realizes is not healthy: "He was Anthony's student originally . . . there's always been that Oedipal undertone. The Jocasta thing" (204).

Sex is on everyone's mind a great deal in the novel, and Dan describes many sex acts outright. Sex becomes another way in which people try to get the feeling right. The threesomes, adulteries, and implied incests are all situations of disequilibrium and are frequently generated by unhealthy motivations. Dan's affair with Jenny is time defying. It is an evasion of his past, which in the context of their relationship is "like an infidelity, something one has no right to remember or refer to . . . like a past mistress" (387). This tangle of parallel affairs and transferences is the physical analogue of the other difficulties with identity, projection, and interrelationship. The difficulty in one's sexual affairs, as in all other relationships, lies in purging the encounters of the always-absent other. The symbol of hand holding (which is obsessive throughout the novel) acts as the corrective to these sexual excesses and depradations (in much the same way that intuition is the corrective for overintellectualization). In Syria the desolation of the landscape has a disorienting effect. Jane says, "I feel as if I'm on another planet. Nothing seems real any more" (583). Dan tries to fill the void with true human warmth: "He reached in the darkness and took her hand. . . . The two hands lay joined on the fabric of the seat between them; the last contact with lost reality" (583).

There are countless other parallels and motifs in this novel. As John Gardner points out in his famous panegyric on *Daniel Martin*, "Incredibly, every vivid detail works symbolically, as does nearly every other detail in Fowles's huge novel."[14] Some of the motifs are major considerations and some are curious oddities: birds, sisters, rain, the epiphany in the dark, the giving of jewelry, and even the act of reading itself. These recurrences and correspondences are analogous to a *symboliste* perception of reality (in the same way that the ideal of whole sight suggests the *cubiste*). The vastness of life and overwhelmingness of experience[15] tend to obscure the patterns and parallels, to dull one's perception of what is constant, enduring and therefore real. The symbolist brings order to life by, in Eliot's terms, unifying disparate elements. Dan attempts this kind of synthesis in his novel. As he begins to see patterns emerging from his life, especially the self-avowed "repetition compulsion" he has regarding his intentional loss of everything he loves, his first response is anger and a sense of fatalism: "[Life] just exhibits a repeated pattern, and all one can predict is the recurrence of the pattern" (267). The black mood of that pronouncement is reversed when he thinks about how satisfied he feels in Jane's company again: "The ghost of that one carnal knowledge of her . . . did still faintly haunt the air. . . . But I knew something in Jane's presence satisfied some deep need in me of recurrent structure" (396). One type of recurrence is bad, the other good; one attests to Dan's destruction compulsion, the other to his recognition of right feeling. What Dan is to learn as he steps back from his text is that the recurrences in our lives are of our own making (recalling the Marxist epigraph to *The French Lieutenant's Woman* —that history is the chronicle of men pursuing their ends), and that one must perceive them and act on them according to how one judges them. This is yet another facet of whole sight.

In the novel Fowles considers only a few ideas, albeit very large ideas—identity, reality, memory, perception—but in such varied ways that the novel becomes very dense. He uses Dan's style and technique to reflect the differences between novelistic and cinematic modes of perception. He often brings up themes by having the characters engage in lengthy, open-ended discussions. And he injects meaning into even the humblest details, charging them with a dialectic life of their own.

Coda

Even though he is distant from his novel, Fowles is, of course, the agent of Dan's revelations. He asserts his presence in this, his most autobiographical book, in strange ways. That is, Fowles seems to be, either consciously or unconsciously, paralleling his other novels. He plays several extratextual games in the novel, such as when Dan says to Jenny, "One day I shall make you up" (17); or when Jenny makes Dan swear he'll never show her writings to anyone. In the chapter called "Games" Dan chooses his pseudonym: S. Wolfe, which is an anagram of "Fowles." "Jane," who is the protagonist's mirror, is the feminine form of the name "John." Fowles himself becomes one of the ghosts who haunts these pages.

Fowles creates resonances, moods, and situations that sharply recall his other novels. Jane first seduced Dan so that nothing could ever be the same between them again, which is what Sarah does to Charles. Then both women "disappear" and enforce a lengthy period of exile (the comparison also extends, here, to *The Magus*). Then Jane is rediscovered after a trial. In each novel sex immediately precedes the loss of the woman. This story of the lost true love harks back to the Tryphena story in *The French Lieutenant's Woman*, and Dan and Jane even make a point of driving past Hardy's statue.

The conflict between sisters (or two women) seems to be one of

Fowles's favorite situations. There are many sisters in this book, as well as June and Julie in *The Magus*, Sarah and Ernestina in *The French Lieutenant's Woman*, the Freak and the Mouse in *The Ebony Tower*, Miranda and her sister in *The Collector*, and Erato and Nurse Cory in *Mantissa*. With each mention of sisters Fowles makes an oblique suggestion of those other sisters, the Muses.

Music, even specific music for specific situations (leitmotifs) resonates through Fowles's work. In Egypt the love Dan has kept hidden from Jane (and largely from himself) comes tumbling out in a confession while a Russian lady plays Chopin in the distance. In *The French Lieutenant's Woman* Charles pours out his love to Sarah while a lady plays Chopin in the distance. In *Daniel Martin* the pianist goes on to play a Goldberg Variation while Dan and Jane sit quietly in mutual reflection. In *The Collector* Miranda and GP also listen silently to the Goldberg Variations as they consider the difficulties of their relationship.

Even the cadences of characters' speech and writing styles are sometimes strikingly similar. Jenny's writing about Dan, for example, is much like Miranda's writing about GP: "He wasn't a playwright, a dramatist turned scriptwriter. All he did is write dialogue. Once he put it: I'm a dialogue installer and repairman. Another time: at least most screen-actors never learn to act" (32). This excerpt has the same studied slapdash of the intelligent nonnovelist that we see all through Miranda's diary: "GP as artist. Caroline's 'second-rate Paul Nash'—horrid, but there is something in it. Nothing like what he would call 'photography.' But not absolutely individual. I think it's just that he arrived at the same conclusions" (*The Collector*, 183). The situations behind these two extracts are closely related as well: a beautiful and talented young woman endeavors to write an objective account of an older man (an artist) with whom she is infatuated, and who has rejected her.

There are semantic correspondences between similar situations in the different novels. Both Miriam and Jojo are women of distinctly lower class whom the respective protagonists pick up and take home as temporary expedients. Of Miriam Dan says, "I rather treated her as a pet animal—someone I was prepared to feed and dress and make love to" (244). The language clearly recalls Nicholas's definition of

Jojo as his "poor mongrel." Both women slip away from their bene-
factors unannounced, leaving a scrawled message of farewell.

Anthony's godgame, whose main victim is Dan, has certain similarities to Conchis's. When Dan finds that Anthony has killed
himself, he thinks, "It was like being the victim of a bad practical
joke" (197), echoing almost exactly the reaction of Nicholas Urfe to
Conchis's machinations. And as Dan leaves Anthony's hospital
room, Anthony "raised his hand: and still that smile. It had the faint
air of a benediction" (183). The gesture recalls the "hieratic gesture"
Conchis characteristically gave to Nicholas, and the smile recalls
the talismanic smile of Conchis's elect. Yet if Conchis has a true
avatar in this novel it is certainly the Herr Professor. The Professor
has the power of the magus; he is capable of drawing Dan and Jane
under his spell. Like Conchis, he is a manifestation of the archetype
of the Wise Old Man. As Dan remarks: "Behind his self-irony, his
authority, there lay a stillness, almost that of an Indian sage" (511).
(Breasley of *The Ebony Tower* is another of Fowles's wise old men.)
Like Conchis, this hierophant or mentor tries to teach Dan and Jane
lessons by telling them stories, especially about his life. Even the
lessons are the same: that peace lies only in "the river between."
Both Conchis and the Professor have transcendental experiences
that their pupils in turn undergo. The two even compare on lesser
points: both love a woman who has died, both are scholars, both
were German prisoners of war, and both face imminent death from
heart disease.

There are at least two instances in *Daniel Martin* where it seems
that Fowles is writing a scene that he has written before. The first is
the scene with the rather dyspeptic man on the train. Dan shares a
train compartment on his way to the reunion in Oxford and is re-
buffed when he breaks silence by asking if he ought to shut the window: "I stood and shut it; and received a frozen grimace, meant to
represent gratitude. . . . I had committed the cardinal sin not of
shutting the window, but of opening my mouth. . . . I noted it, like
an anthropologist, and understood it, as an Englishman. Being forced
to share a confined space with people to whom you have not been
introduced was an activity dense with risk; one might be held to
ransom and forced to give some item of information about oneself"

(132). Virtually the same scene takes place in *The French Lieutenant's Woman* when the bearded man enters Charles's compartment on his anthropological task.

The closest parallel of all, however, is when Nancy Reed and Sarah Woodruff take their respective males into their woodland hiding places. Fowles writes the scene in *The French Lieutenant's Woman* as follows:

> [Sarah] stood obliquely in the shadows at the tunnel of ivy's other end . . . again he had that unaccountable sensation of being lanced, of falling short, of failing her. . . . "I know a secluded place nearby. May we go there?" He indicated willingness, and she moved out into the sun and across the stony clearing. . . . She walked lightly and surely, her skirt gathered up a few inches by one hand. . . . Following her, far less nimbly, Charles noted the darns in the heels of her black stockings, the worndown backs of her shoes. . . . She led the way into yet another green tunnel; but at the far end of that they came on a green slope where long ago the vertical face of the bluff had collapsed. Tussocks of grass provided foothold; and she picked her way very carefully. . . . Sarah waited above for Charles to catch up. He walked after her then along the top of the bluff. The ground sloped sharply up to yet another bluff some hundred yards above them. . . . On the far side of this shoulder the land flattened for a few yards, and there was her "secluded place." It was a little south-facing dell, surrounded by dense thickets of brambles and dogwood; a kind of minute green amphitheater. . . . Someone—clearly not Sarah—had once heaved a great flat-topped block of flint against the tree's stem, making a rustic throne that commanded a magnificent view of the treetops below. . . . The banks of the dell were carpeted with primroses and violets, and the white stars of wild strawberry. . . . Charles sat silent, a little regal with this strange supplicant at his feet; and not overmuch inclined to help her. But she would not speak. . . . Plucking a little spray of milkwort from the bank beside her . . . she went on. (163–65, *passim*)

Dan's meeting with Nancy is like an echo of that scene:

> I was pushing up the steepest part, thinking of nothing, counting steps. Then something moved, where the old lime kilns were hidden behind the August leaves. Nancy stood out in the little path. . . . Now she looked at me, then down at the sycamore leaf she was shredding. . . . "Where are you going?" "Old quarry. Mabe. . . . There's a path. . . . It's a secret." She turned before I reached her and led the way up through the trees to where the rocks rose vertically, for twenty feet from the earth. . . . She stopped where the cliff gave way and there was a steep scramble going up. . . . It was difficult at the top, one had to yank oneself up the last yard or two by holding a tree-root. . . . She wore old black shoes, school shoes, no socks. . . . She walked quickly. . . . At last she turned up toward the common and soon we were pushing through the green bracken. Still she led the way. Then suddenly we were on the brink of the old quarry, looking out across the valley. . . . He felt out of his depth. . . . She seemed waiting. . . . She led him on to her "real secret place," which was out of the wood and through a patch of high bracken and gorse. . . . A large, flat-topped limestone rock stood there, the "Pulpit." (354–57, *passim*)

The similarities are remarkable: an illicit woodland meeting (which is a seduction on the part of the woman); the woman, mistress of the forest and keeper of secret lairs, leads the man up a hill; she is sure-footed and nimble, while he is clumsy; he notes, with pleasure, her ankles; the arrival at the hilltop clearing, the flowers, the brambles, the view, the rock; the woman who is silent, waiting; the man who feels insufficient, abashed.

Of course, all writers tend to repeat themselves in some ways. But in *Daniel Martin* Fowles appears to be recycling the actual materials of his other books: motifs, characters, words, and scenes. Because he has intimated that the novel is autobiographical, and because the shadowy S. Wolfe haunts these pages, it is tempting for the reader to posit the existence of an older man, a mentor, in Fowles's past, or of extraordinary sisters, or of an important woman who once led him

up a high hill. It is not even certain that these repetitions are conscious or unconscious; it is only certain that they are there.

Speculations about autobiographical specifics are, while good
sport, frustrating and ultimately not very important. What Fowles
does call upon the reader to do, by virtue of his games, is to specu-
late on the relationship of an author to his work, how the work and
the life relate. As we have seen in his treatment of Alain-Fournier, he
is fascinated by that subject himself. Writing is, for Fowles's characters, always a heuristic activity. It does not require much of a leap to
see that, as Sue Park says, *Daniel Martin* "provides [Fowles] an opportunity for self-exploration, for examination of personal motives
and needs and quirks—but at one remove from the unmitigated vul-
nerability of total exposure."[16] The standout parallels I have pointed
out, as well as others, exist in two modes: the mythic and the real-
istic. In *The French Lieutenant's Woman*, for example, Sarah exists
as anima personified, a shadowy goddess. In *Daniel Martin* her
counterpart is a homespun Devon farmgirl. To borrow Northrop
Frye's shorthand, Fowles has created a myth displacement. Whether
there is a real Sarah or Nancy is in this context irrelevant. What is
important is that something or someone in Fowles's life was important, and that he has surrounded it with this form, or metaphor. In
writing his own story in this veiled way, he has taken the event out
of the mythic mode and translated it to the real. Perhaps Fowles's
endeavor parallels Dan's in that he, too, is trying to remember correctly. In all the speculation the reader is asked to do about Dan's
stance toward his personal history, one must include the superimposed image of Fowles. Dan becomes, then, not his persona but his
comrade.

5 Mantissa

His stories are not the worst, though, I'll say

that, said Lamont.

O he can talk, he can talk, I agree with you

there, said Shanahan, credit where credit is due.

But you'd want what you'd call a grain of *salo*

with more than one of them if I know anything.

FLANN O'BRIEN

At Swim-Two-Birds

M*antissa*[1] fully reveals a side of Fowles that we only glimpse in his earlier novels: a spirit of exuberant playfulness and a well-developed sense of comedy. The novel was perhaps too playful for its first reviewers, who did not receive it well. Certainly the meaning of the novel sometimes seems as obscure as the fog from which Miles awakes. The plot is constantly being rewritten before our eyes by the characters themselves, who change both shape and identity with the snap of a finger. The only thing that is sure is that the action (if indeed action can be said to take place inside a brain) represents the monumental struggle between the author and his protean Muse, whose actual existence is highly suspect. But at the heart of that struggle is a wry treatment of one of Fowles's favorite subjects, one he treats elsewhere with great seriousness, the matter of author-ity.

If one begins with the reasonable premises that a novel creates its own logic and that all the materials necessary for its comprehension are imprinted upon it, *Mantissa* reveals itself as being dominated by a strategy of irony and metaphor (in the loose sense of including all other tropes), by great distances between what is said and what is meant. The reader is immediately immersed in irony when, after a weighty epigraph from Descartes that posits the existence of pure reason, he sees the protagonist living, homunculus-like, in his own brain. The distinction between physical and mental states is hazy at best in this novel. Fowles generates other ironies by revealing inconsistencies in the role a character is playing at any given moment and his or her true feelings. Miles professes great moral indignation at being raped by his medical attendants, while he is obviously enjoying himself very much. Later, he appears to defend his manhood staunchly against Erato's belittling, even though in the role of shrew she seems to be the wish fulfillment of his female domination fantasy of part I. Fowles creates a strong tension between Miles's wish to be "bereft of pronoun," to be, like Leopold Bloom in "Circe," in the charge of female authority figures, and his wish to protect himself from "castration." His chagrin at being unmanned is counterpointed by his flight from manhood in the amnesia fantasy.

Erato is equally ambivalent about her femaleness. On one hand, she wants to be the virginal and gossamer fantasy pictured by Lemprière; but her actions seem to distinguish her more, as Miles points out, as "a by-blow of the randiest old goat in all theology" (114). Her relationship with Miles is also dominated by ambivalence. She professes to want fair play, affection, gentleness, and open honesty; yet she brutalizes him in both word and deed, and her "honest" comments—"You're such a bloody pedant"; "You're a typical capitalist sexist parasite"; "You're just a degenerate tenth-rate hack"; "You have always had such a rare talent for not being able to express yourself"—are perhaps less than constructive.

The mighty battles that take place between the two result mostly from their failure to interpret correctly each other's irony. They become lost in a miasma of words as they play off each other's supposed moods and masks. Each picks up and drops roles as easily as he or she takes on and off clothes, and they play an eternal, unresolvable game of catch-up. It is understandable, if not entirely laudable, that Miles's ultimate fantasy is of the Geisha, with whom "any dialogue but that of the flesh is magnificently impossible" (189).

The characters' relationship is deformed by uncontrolled irony, and the context and language in and by which Fowles writes of their affair are dominated by the distancing devices of metaphor and symbol, most of which are so ludicrous as to be self-parodies: quilted grey walls stand for brain tissue, the rose carpet for meninges; Staff Sister (who represents Clio) advocates "surgical intervention" in Miles's case, "after the manner of Dr. Bowdler"; hospital corresponds to the literary world and medicine to literary art. The cuckoo clock, an oddly anomolous feature of the scenery, represents the obsessively repetitive activity of writing, as well as the cuckolding of man by his

Muse. Even the name "Miles Green" is a long and somewhat face-tious stretch to Flann O'Brien's *At Swim-Two-Birds*, which is, as we shall see, the guiding spirit of *Mantissa*.[2] The epitome of shameless metaphorrhea is Erato's story (told while she is wearing "Jane Austen glasses") of the literary lady and the banana importer. Erato illustrates the lack of mimetic dimension in this novel, even in such rudimen-tary considerations as character and place, when she warns Miles that he cannot walk out of his own brain; he retorts, "It's only my meta-phorical brain" (125).

The issue of metaphoricality extends to the dubious existence of the Muse herself. One moment she is the raging feminist, demand-ing that she be considered as an individual rather than an archetype. She also seems, ironically, to be autonomous, if only by virtue of her being able to complain that she has no reality at all, but is a projec-tion of Miles's fantasies. When Miles asks, appropriately, "Who the devil do you think you are?" she answers with an extravagant conun-drum: "I'm just one more miserable fantasy figure your diseased mind is trying to conjure up out of nothing. . . . I only seem real because it is your nauseating notion that the actually totally unreal character I'm supposed to be impersonating should do so. In fact a real me in this situation would avoid all reference to the matter, especially as she would never have got herself into the situation in the first place. If she had any choice. Which she doesn't. As she isn't real" (85).

If she is merely a metaphorical Muse, she joins the ranks with Fowles's other heroines who are more projections of anima than in-dividuals. Miles says, "You've always been my perfect woman. . . . Even though I've never understood you" (61). Erato agrees: "All you ever see in me is what you choose to see" (149). As she tells the erotic story of her satyr lover, Miles describes her much as Nicholas describes Alison or Charles describes Sarah—as a "human oxy-moron," all women: "[Erato] contrives all at the same time, to be both demure and provocative, classical and modern, individual and Eve-like, tender and unforgiving, real and dreamed, soft and . . ." (71). She is, in effect, the "other" we have seen so often before in Fowles, the woman through whose eyes the man sees both the world and himself. In the case of the satyr story the reflection is not partic-

ularly flattering to Miles. If it is indeed just his own libidinous fantasy channeled through her, it shows him to be lecherous (the girl's
age shrinks to eleven before the tale is done) and satyric. His later
physical metamorphosis into a satyr is the logical extension of this
tale. Erato says smugly of his transfiguration, "But darling, this is
what they called the anagnorisis" (190), which in classical literature
is the recovery of identity.

The incident of the implied satyr later becoming the actual satyr
is one of many such common structural tricks in this book, a structure that suggests the odd, rather Kafkaesque (recalling Joseph K. and
his shadow) relationship between Miles and Erato. Because the
novel is full of music (and there is a compelling case for seeing a pun
in muse-ic), the structure might logically be called fugal, especially
as Erato suggests the metaphor herself during one of their arguments: "I may not be the musical one in my family, but I can recognize a fugal inversion when I see it" (68).[3] By the terms of this musical metaphor it appears that the two characters are carrying the
same melody, which has been fragmented into two voices that alternately harmonize, battle in counterpoint, repeat, circle, and recapitulate. The same themes, for example, are taken up by the two
voices at different times, as when each feigns indignation over an
alleged rape: Miles's rape by Dr. Delfie and Erato's rape by the satyr
are the same story. Both share an ambivalence toward their sexual
identities: she wants and does not want to be a sex object; he wants
but does not want to be the man in charge. These inconsistencies
lead to much comic bickering, as when the two accuse each other of
being pornographers. After Miles's story of Dr. Delfie, Erato says,
"I've had my clothes taken off by sensitive geniuses. I'm not going to
be impressed by a composer of erotica" (69). After her tale of the
banana importer, Miles charges, "I know your game. You are simply
trying to spin out an erotic situation beyond all the bounds of artistic decency" (115). Physical parallels match the many rhetorical parallels as well. After their one truly successful sexual encounter, "the
oblivious pair lie slumped, in an unconscious reprise of their position after the first and clinical coupling" (155).

Fowles interweaves the characters' identities in this fugal manner.
Each voice, for example, is allowed one long solo. Miles accom-

plishes a literary tour de force when he extemporizes a three-page sentence while Erato is silent. Later, Erato strikes Miles mute in a kind of angry counterpoint and spins her yarn. Each delivers at one point a catalogue of complaints against the other that are, in spirit and detail, identical in their imputations. The ability of each to perform magic sets up an equivalence between them: he snaps his fingers to make things disappear, she twangs her lyre; he makes clothes appear, she turns him into a satyr. Many times they seem like duelling magicians, Merlin and Morgan Le Fay vying to see who has the stronger magic. The circularity of the narrative, which ends more or less where it began, is symbolized by the monotonous repetition of the Greek alphabet, which to Erato means sexual variations and to Miles, "the alphabetical conjunctions which make words" (192). The two voices go around and around in a closed pattern of stylish echoing and, as in a fugue, reveal themselves to be one voice shattered into variations.

The same sort of inconclusive power struggle goes on over who is in charge of the narrative. There are countless confusions about who is doing the writing and who is putting words in whose mouth. For example, Erato, cum punk rocker, flies into a towering rage because Miles parodied her as Dr. Delfie. Miles confesses sheepishly, "It was just an idea. . . . A little tryout. A first sketch" (51). His authorship is plausible until Erato later admits to collusion on that very sketch. Miles would also seem to have the upper hand, judging from Erato's many complaints that she is merely his slave. She protests, "All I ever do is parrot whatever lines you give me. They're yours, not mine." Miles counters with a typical confusion: "I'm not putting a word of this into your mouth" (86). The battle goes on in many small ways also, as when Miles makes Staff Sister appear when Erato (cum Dr. Delfie) had rung for Nurse Cory ("He clears his throat, and gives a winning little smile of confession. 'Just an impromptu notion.'" 137); or when she makes the Geisha appear as a teasing gesture. Miles (again in the spirit of the fugal structure) also complains bitterly that he has no say in the narrative: "You've ruined my work from the start, with your utterly banal, pifflingly novelettish ideas. I hadn't the least desire to be what I am when I began. I was going to follow in Joyce and Beckett's footsteps. But oh no, in you trot. . . . I have about as much say as an automatic typewriter. God, when I think of the endless pages the French have spent on trying to decide whether the writer himself is written or not. Ten seconds with you would have proved that one forever" (127).

The thick texture of irony, metaphor, ambivalence, ambiguity, and schizophrenia, the insistent doubleness that runs through this work, is largely the product of Fowles's virtuoso games playing. He strongly suggests that a Muse is a vivid projection rather like an author's alter ego. Yet, like Henry James, who refuses to answer conclusively whether the ghosts are real or imagined in *The Turn of the Screw*, Fowles impishly leaves open, by virtue of his own inconclusiveness, the possibility that Muses really do exist. On a more serious level the reality or unreality of the Muse becomes almost irrelevant, subordinate to the process by which Miles Green's writings come about. In this dialectic between man and Muse (be she autonomous or projection), Fowles allows the reader to witness the murk that lies behind the text. *Mantissa* is a kind of alter novel, the dark underside of an ordinary novel. It contains all the deliberating, the haggling, the incessant rethinking and revision that go on during the process of writing; and its main subject is its own coming into being.

The work's theatricality, its prodigious amount of dialogue, its boastful adherence to the unities of time and place, and its stage conventions indicate that once again Fowles is undermining generic conventions. Fowles uses props (the rubber sheet, the chair, the bed, the cuckoo clock, the call button) as self-consciously and obsessively as Beckett in his plays. The long drone of dialogue performs the same function as the dialogue in *Daniel Martin:* characters use words to play games, to avoid having to step back and consider, to avoid having to exert a controlling intelligence. Dr. Delfie's diagnosis of Miles is perhaps correct: "You are overattached to the verbalization of feeling, instead of to the direct act of feeling itself" (38). Fowles further suggests the alter reality of this novel when both the text and the protagonists disappear during their one perfect sexual congress. Good lovemaking is a metaphor for good writing, a symbolic harmony of writer and Muse. In this scene Fowles suspends theatrical time and allows novel time, fluid and nebulous, to take over in the silence. He breaks the unity of place as well, as the walls disappear and the scene becomes a placeless fog or mist. The reader is excluded because Fowles's fanciful metaphor demands that Miles's flawless text (symbolized by his and Erato's harmony), be published to a hypothetical outside world, while the readers of *Mantissa* get what would presumably find its way into Miles's wastebasket.

The exertions of Miles and Erato, then, illustrate and define the process of authorship, a process that, Fowles suggests, raises many ethical questions. One large moral concern is that in playing with language the author is perpetrating deception upon the reader. As we have already seen, metaphor has the power to distort reality. What one usually understands to be the positive aspects of metaphor—its ability to expand knowledge by suggesting subtle correspondences, its ability to revitalize perception—Fowles shows here in a more negative light. Metaphor, taken to extremes as it is in this book, can be abused to the point where it loses its referential function and becomes simple deceit. Miles at one point becomes so confounded by the shifting metaphors he and Erato construct that when she says, "You know I love the real you," he counters with, "I wish you wouldn't use the word 'real.' You've totally undermined my confidence in it" (182).

All the other tropes and literary flourishes that make up the substance of this work serve also to show that wordplay, or manipulation of language, has its dark side. The sentences that go on for pages, the foul language, the bad puns and jokes, and outrageous metaphors show language play as a kind of treachery by virtue of which the characters use words as weapons rather than as tools of communication. The novel starts with very simple language, with Miles remembering only "disconnected morphs and phonemes," with language broken down into its purest form of "images and labels" (3). As the novel progresses and the games intensify, the purity of language breaks down. The visuals, the evocations of the seen spectacle, become sparser and sparser as the talk takes over. Ironically, at one point Erato has to remind Miles that he had better look to his narrative and release them from the "quite ludicrously inappropriate sexual congress" (82) he has maintained during a particularly heated argument. As each tries for victory in this game of one-upping the other's irony and outmaneuvering the other's metaphors, Fowles illustrates the power of language both to confound and control.

By extension, part of an author's intention in using what Robert Scholes calls "deceptive communication"[4] is, in its most extreme implications, to overpower his reader's sense of reality and identity. That is, what is usually lauded in the literary product—its brilliant use of rhetoric—may be seen in a different light. Fowles examined this tyrannical activity, the use of verbal trickery to bring a reader around to the author's thinking or state of emotion, in *The French Lieutenant's Woman*, and he labeled it "fight-fixing."

Mantissa is a graphic illustration of the clinical relationship of writing to the writer's libido. The blatant sexual element serves to define the origin of the literary work. The most obsessive repetitive action in this novel is the creation of fiction during some kind of sexual engagement. For example, as Dr. Delfie and Nurse Cory become successful in their ministrations Miles does not, as they promised, remember his identity, but creates several rousing personae for himself, fictional representations of Miles Green, all based on "something to do with rows of watching attentive faces" (32). He casts himself variously as lawyer, headmaster, navy captain. His ultimate vision is appropriate: "Was it not most likely, he thought, as the black girl, having seized his hands, now led them up, like lifeless flannels or sponges, over her smooth stomach to ablute the cones of dark-tipped flesh above, that he was a Member of Parliament? A determined opponent of the forces of evil and permissive morality in society?" (33). The Jamesian sentence structure, with its main clause interrupted by a string of telling phrases, mirrors perfectly this union of word and flesh that is elsewhere illustrated by the Greek alphabet's curious relation to sexual positions (Erato is raped by twenty-four black Marxist guerrillas, which is the number of letters in the Greek alphabet). Even the rhythms of the sex he is experiencing are reflected in the jounciness of the sentence, with its many commas.

Similarly, Erato tells her fiction of the satyr while Miles makes love to her. "Inspiration," then, takes on quite a new light. If the origin of the story-telling impulse is with the Muse, then she is, to use Miles's phrase, an "old whore." Telling stories, by the logic of this novel, is intimately and mysteriously bound up with the writer's libido, and writing is an autoerotic activity. Fowles suggests in a rather lighthearted way that literature, which is popularly conceived as a respectable and dignified act of the intellect, really has its origins in shadier places. Literature becomes more the expression of an author's sexual fantasies than the revelation of noble thoughts. This is the major alter suggestion of this alter novel.

Fowles questions the value of fiction as he brings clearly into focus the relationship between language and deception, inspiration and titillation. He also shows that fiction is not very far removed from lying; and, as fiction allows one to lie, so it allows one to evade responsibility. As Dr. Delfie points out to Miles, writers have an extremely long and well-recorded "general incapacity to face up to the realities of life" (27). Miles's amnesia, as well as Erato's extremely poor memory, are expressions of this desire to be severed "from all one was or might be: to be not expected to do anything, to be free of a burden" (12). Erato finally compares Miles to Old Doodah (Plato) who can only deal with shadow figures on the wall. She says, "You are always trying to turn me into something I'm not. As if you'd like me better if I was perfect. Or Nurse Cory" (180). The writer evades reality by dwelling in the world of make believe, and as an idealist he shuns both personal and social responsibility. The specter of Lukács and his admonition to writers against the heresy of idealism loom here as they did in *Daniel Martin*.

Thus Fowles lays bare the seamy underside of fiction. For every virtue with which we usually credit fiction, he offers a different perspective. But it is the nature of the author himself that is brought under the most serious fire. The fantasies of part I reveal much about the hidden motives of authorship. Throughout the book an unflattering picture of the writer as neurotic emerges, highlighted by the suggestion that the hospital ward Miles finds himself in is the psychiatric ward (the cuckoo clock, which is the central symbol, fittingly has the last word of the novel). Erato diagnoses him acidly during her disappearance: "I was trained as a clinical psychologist. Who simply happens to have specialized in the mental illness that you, in your ignorance call literature. . . .[You have a] marked tendency to voyeurism and exhibitionism. I've seen it ten thousand times. You also obey the usual pathology in attempting to master the unresolved trauma by repetitive indulgence in the quasi-regressive activities of writing and being published" (143). Fowles demonstrates the writer's exhibitionist tendencies in the scene where rows of faces watch Miles and Erato's perfect coupling. Erato brings out his voyeurism in virtually every encounter. Fowles always suggests that the writer is basically a voyeur, especially in his depiction of the bearded man on the train in *The French Lieutenant's Woman*. He has stated that while working on a novel he sometimes feels that he is in the grip of an unhealthy obsession.[5] Thus the person from whom conventional expectation demands wisdom and sensitivity—the author-god whom Fowles consistently parodies— may also be characterized by such passions as satyriasis, regression, infantilism, voyeurism and exhibitionism.

It is, however, the author's despotism that is his worst obsession. He lusts after power and the text is power made manifest. The ability to play with language is one kind of power, but the ability to dabble with the identity of one's characters is fascistic. With just the drop of a few words the author can metamorphose a character. It is in this respect that *Mantissa* takes its inspiration from *At Swim-Two-Birds (ASTB)*,[6] and a brief comparison of the two works might be fruitful here.

The narrator of O'Brien's novel (who remains nameless) is writing a novel about Dermot Trellis, who is also writing a novel. Trellis exercises maniacal control over his characters, forcing them to live with him at the Red Swan Hotel, forbidding them to marry when they are in love, forcing them into various undignified situations. "Trellis has absolute control over his minions but this control is abandoned when he falls asleep" (*ASTB*, 47). While he sleeps the characters conduct their own lives, which consist mainly in scheming how best to effect the demise of Trellis. As they form a posse and come to deliver Trellis "the razor behind the knee," a cleaning lady inadvertently throws Trellis's manuscript into the fire, and the characters disappear like smoke. The narrator says he hopes to show that

> the novel is an inferior art form inasmuch as it causes the reader
> to be outwitted in a shabby fashion and caused to experience

a real concern for the fortunes of illusory characters. . . . The novel, in the hands of an unscrupulous writer, could be despotic. . . . A satisfactory novel should be a self-evident sham to which the reader could regulate at will the degree of his credulity. It was undemocratic to compel characters to be uniformly bad or good or poor or rich. Each should be allowed a private life, self-determination. (*ASTB,* 32)

The case that O'Brien comically overstates echoes Fowles's own feelings. In *Mantissa* not only does the author have the ability to manipulate the reader by regulating the fortunes of his characters, but the relation he has to those characters is unhealthy and predatory. Erato, who like Trellis's characters has come to life to claim autonomy, levels this accusation at Miles: "You just collect and mummify [your characters]. Lock them up in a cellar and gloat over them like Bluebeard. . . . [It is] a plurally offensive habit. Otherwise known as necrophilia" (95). This sidelong reference to *The Collector* places Miles-as-author in the same category with Clegg. This comparison brings up the complex subject of an author's relationship to his characters. The problem becomes this: how can a humanistic existentialist (which both Miles and Fowles claim to be) square his penchant for tyrannizing people (that is, characters) with his philosophy, which states that, as Erato and Miles both say, one must have elementary freedoms to exist. In short, it is unseemly for the author to play god, even with imaginary people. The author-to-character relationship is an extremely poor paradigm for decent human conduct.

All these considerable, though humorously hyperbolic jabs at both the writer and the work do not, however, add up to a condemnation of fiction. Fowles's treatment of fiction is in itself ironic. By his own admission he loves to play games with his readers, and in this work his own playful games are superimposed upon the characters' games with each other. For example, when Miles asks Dr. Delfie how long he has been in the hospital, she answers, "Just a few pages"; or when he makes blatant reference to having been around for about 183 pages, on page 183. Rather, *Mantissa* is a corrective to the way in which literature is sometimes both conceived and received today. Fowles's disgust with the modern novel that takes itself too seriously breaks through all the metaphor and irony with a Swiftian vigor. Miles says of the novel:

> Even the dumbest students know it's a *reflexive* medium now, not a reflective one. . . . Serious modern fiction has only one subject: the difficulty of writing serious modern fiction. . . . Writing *about* fiction has become a far more important matter than writing fiction itself. . . . There is in any case no connection whatever between author and text. . . . The author's role is purely fortuitous and agential. . . . Our one priority now is mode of discourse, function of discourse, status of discourse. Its metaphoricality, its disconnectedness, its totally ateleological self-containedness. (118–20, *passim*)

Fowles directs his satire against the novel that is a hostage of cant or is overbearingly self-important. He condemns even more strongly the kind of literary criticism that both expects and nurtures the kind of novel he satirizes. Again Miles speaks of Erato:

> What I was wondering was this: whether there aren't really . . . areas that merit further investigation by both the written and the writer, or, if you prefer, between the personified as *histoire* and the personifier as *discours*, or in simpler words still, by you and me; and I feel sure that we have at least one thing in common: a mutual incomprehension of how your supremely real presence in the world of letters has failed to receive the attention (though you may regard that as a blessing in disguise) of the campus faculty-factories, the structuralists and deconstructivists, the semiologists, the Marxists, academic Uncle Tom Cobbleigh and all, that it deserves. (62)

Fowles objects mainly to the drab and unimaginative seriousness that surrounds much of modern fiction and criticism. *Mantissa* is a strategy to undermine the hyperintellectualization of literature by exposing its underside and reminding readers that it is a sometimes shady business surrounded by complex ethical problems. What is truly positive in fiction may be deduced from what Fowles reveals on the dark side. As we have seen throughout Fowles's work, the exposition and demise of the author-god should be an exhilarating liberation. When the reader realizes that the god is only human, reading becomes an existential act. Literature becomes (as Miles finds when he opens the door only to find his own face mirrored back to him) both a door and a mirror—a world we walk into and a reflection of ourselves. Thus, even though Fowles makes the reader see vividly the author's despotic tendencies, the value of reading fiction should not be diminished by that vision. Instead one learns that the reader is free to create his own text.

The same may be said of all the deceptions and literary strategies that Fowles has parodied in the novel. Obviously, though irony and metaphor are tricks, they also have a great value. They always cause thought and in using them the author assumes that one can deduce what is visible from what is not. Reading is the act of making conceptual replacements for disorienting details. Fowles makes heavy use of similes in this novel and they are, unlike the other florid figures, uniformly superb. They underscore the positive aspects of metaphorical expression: when Miles's wife lists the names and places he should know, it sounds to him "like evidence of crimes he had committed"; or when she lists their children they sound "more like overdue bills, past follies of spending, than children" (9); or, of Staff Sister: "She stands surveying the unconscious patient, as she might an unwashed bedpan" (134); or the expression on her face is like "some psychological corollary of the starch in her uniform" (155). This kind of metaphoricality broadens the scope of mere words and preserves the polysemy of language. In the beginning of the novel, during his brief period of analphabetic purity, Miles feels this power behind language, the way in which complex feeling clusters surround labels: "Images and labels began to swim, here momentarily to coalesce, here to divide, like so many pond amoebae; obviously busy but purposeless. These collocations of shapes and feelings, of associated morphs and phonemes, returned like the algebraic formulae of schooldays" (3).

Mantissa is, finally, like all Fowles's other novels, about seeing correctly and seeing whole. By the logic of this book the novel should be taken very seriously, as it has the infinitely humanistic potential for allowing each reader to discover himself. But it should not be taken so seriously that it becomes narcissistic, drowned in a bog of cant and theory. The parody of artifice and authority are meant to put the novel in proper perspective.

6 A Maggot

His opinions, who does not see spiritual agency,

is not worth any man's reading; he who rejects a

fact because it is improbable, must reject all

History.

WILLIAM BLAKE

"A Descriptive Catalogue of Pictures"

In *A Maggot*[1] we find familiar Fowlesian themes: the elusive nature of truth, the limits of perception and language, the metatheatrical godgame as a vehicle for self-understanding, and the endorsement of freedom as the highest human good. Yet in this novel Fowles pushes the conventions of his genre to their limits and all but totally abandons the reader. The novel has no controlling plot; several plots alternately vie for attention. The question-and-answer depositions are devoid of point of view. Excerpts from the *Gentleman's Magazine* and other topical sources make their way into the text without comment. Fowles gives us a part-time narrator who has neither authority nor irony, whose discoveries are simultaneous with the reader's. The novel has no consistent protagonist, but a shifting one, as the focus changes from Dick to Bartholomew to Rebecca to Ayscough and, finally, to Ann Lee. In this chapter I will try to see this difficult maggot whole; that is, to see how the unusual technical strategies reflect Fowles's characteristic concerns.

From the beginning Fowles defines the limits and weaknesses of ordinary perception. The first teller is a present-tense narrator (who occasionally lapses into a past-tense mode that is merely a disguised present) who reports events as they unfold before him. Like the camera narrator of *Daniel Martin*, he is the hostage of a devouring present that requires persistence of attention and prohibits him from stopping and ruminating. Like a movie camera he cannot exclude information and therefore places all he sees in parity. One instant he watches as Rebecca "tucks her violets inside the rim of white cloth"—a momentous gesture in terms of the whole novel—and the next he sees that Jones has "stopped to piss beside [his horse]" (8). This narrator illustrates the difficulty of seeing present-tense information selectively and meaningfully because the evidence of the senses is anarchic.

The narrator's knowledge of the characters advances (as does the reader's) by the slow accretion of tentative and superficial information. In Rebecca's case he begins in complete darkness; he sees, "a young woman . . . enveloped in a brown hooded cloak, and muffled so that only her eyes and nose are visible" (6). Next, she lowers her hood and he adds another stroke to her portrait. She is "hardly more than a girl, pale-faced, with dark hair bound severely back" (6). Yet disturbing new information consistently surfaces to negate his conclusions. Even her name keeps changing. The narrator conducts the same trial-and-error examination of Lacy (whom he thinks is Brown) and Bartholomew. At first he sees that "the uncle and nephew have just finished supper"; but his intuitive suspicion mounts: "The two men bear little physical resemblance"; and, furthermore, "They do not speak like uncle and nephew" (16–17).

His narratorial task is complicated by physical limitations. He is at some remove from the action and often cannot hear or see what happens. He reports, as the naked Rebecca embraces Bartholomew on that last night, "She murmurs something in a low voice, inaudible across the room" (44). His testimony is as qualified as that of Dorcas, who admits to Ayscough, "The door is thick and they spake low" (80); and as that of Jones, who says of the company in Cleave Wood, "They spake briefly, but I could not hear" (215). This narrator becomes another deponent and his only means of understanding is to allow his experience to play subjectively over the unknown. As a result, he is an obsessive simile maker. His perception is like Dorcas's when she projects her domestic experience into the curious figures on Bartholomew's papers: they look to her "like a cheese-rind, sir" (78). Projection, then, is another impediment to perception.

After the first fifty-two pages of unruly narration, Fowles examines another traditional approach to truth: the sworn testimony of witnesses in the context of awesome judicial power. Yet the tellings of the deponents are slanted by the same subjective biases as the narrator's account. Sampson Beckford's response to all experience is homiletic and he reduces the vast mystery of Bartholomew's disappearance to "divine retribution . . . acted upon gross deceit" (95). The superstitious Jones reports that Dick makes the sign of "Devil's horns" in Cleave Wood: "They say 'tis how witches greet" (215). John Tudor, Ayscough's clerk, describes to Rebecca the distance between truth and projection: "There are two truths, mistress. One that a person believes is truth; and one that is truth incontestable. We will credit you the first, but the second is what we seek" (344).

Ayscough never does reach truth incontestable, nor does the reader. Rebecca's long-awaited testimony, the account that will ostensibly answer the urgent question of the novel—what happened?—is as inconclusive as the rest of the testimony. She witnesses and participates in actions that are beyond her ken and that she organizes by metaphor. While Jones again sees "Devil's horns" in the silver woman's gesture, Rebecca sees hands that are "folded as 'twere in prayer" (361). She has a religious experience because she needed to be saved, and she superimposes over the bizarre maggot episode bits of Bible lore that shape the experience to her need. Her June Eternal becomes alternately "Heaven itself" (371) and a New Jerusalem. The highways appear to her to be "paved of gold" (368), a projection of John's vision of New Jerusalem: "The street of the city was pure gold" (Revelation 21:21). Inside the maggot she perceives "a wall of precious stones, whose colours shone, of topaz and emerald, ruby and sapphyr, coral and peridot, I know not what" (360). Again she weaves strands of New Jerusalem into her seeing. John says, "The foundations of the wall of the city were adorned with every jewel" (Revelation 21:19). The typical plot question of "what happened?" does not proceed in an orderly manner to an answer in this novel. Rather the question, the absolute mystery, continues to expand.

The prominent drug and toxin motif casts a different shadow on the reliability of telling. Rebecca rubs toxic ceruse into her skin and drops belladonna into her eyes. At the climax of Jones's testimony Ayscough recesses the hearing and drinks a glass of ale laced with wormwood—a powerful toxin and the chief ingredient of absinthe. Fowles begs the question of Ayscough's sobriety during the remainder of Jones's testimony. Rebecca's account of all she saw on the maggot is compromised by the glass of strange amber liquid she drank. She admits of her experience, "It seemed no ordinary passing of time; of one far more slow, like to the motions of a dream" (374). Jones testifies that after she came from the cave, "All her movings were most slow, I might believe she had drunk some potion" (225). Sleep is a drug that negates perception. Jones's insistence that Bartholomew never left the cave is overturned by his admission that he had dozed on and off that afternoon. Likewise, Rebecca falls asleep in the maggot and misses the conclusion of the episode. The physical foundations of perception are as fragile as the psychological.

While some tellers relate, however imperfectly, what they see and experience, others relate what they have trustingly learned from others. But in this novel people lie and propagate only falsehood. Telling is vulnerable to deliberate tampering as well as to inadvertent errors. Puddicombe had all his information from Jones, who "lied in all" (62). What he does not hear from Jones he fills in with superstition and gossip, as he admits to Ayscough: "I say no more than what is said" (69). Lacy is in all respects a perfect witness. He is honest, forthright, and his memory is preternaturally sharp—a result of his actor's training. He remembers dialogue verbatim, recounting discussions as though he were playing them back in his mind: "He asked me what I should say . . . to playing a part for him alone. I requested to know what kind of part. He replied, One I should give you. . . . So said I was sure I should be pleased to serve him in such a thing. Very well, he says, but say it should not be here and now, Mr. Lacy" (122). But despite his keen recall, his testimony is but a recapitulation of Bartholomew's riddles and lies. He warns Ayscough at the beginning, "All that followed was proven false" (122). Rebecca, of course, lies to Jones about what happened in the cave, thereby setting off Jones's false deposition. Ayscough at one point throws up his hands at this hall-of-mirrors lying: "One witness is known liar and transparent rogue, and here does inform of another we may fear to be a greater liar still" (269).

Telling is contingent upon the caprices of memory and the teller's habits of selection. Rebecca forgets to mention the huge circular burn outside the cave (a feature that greatly impressed others), and we must therefore wonder what else she forgets. She also censors her testimony, tailors the story to fit Ayscough's alphabet. She divulges that she is doling out her story, alternately withholding and advancing tentatively. She withholds Bartholomew's riddle of the stars, one of the most important scenes in the book:

> *Ayscough.* Nothing else was said to you by his Lordship?
> *Rebecca.* No.
> *He.* You hesitate.
> *She.* I sought my memory.
> *He.* Mistress, there is that in your answering I like not.
>
> (332)

She advances boldly in her fervor: "And 'tis time I tell thee this more. His Lordship was not lord of this world alone" (417). Other information she withholds altogether: "Other names beside I have not told thee nor shall not" (423). Rebecca's testimony resonates as much with what she omits as with what she tells.

The very medium of expression—language—tends to obscure meaning and inhibit understanding. Ayscough consistently demands that Rebecca use words in her telling that will fit his alphabet, but she is equally adamant that words cannot describe her experience. He insists that she describe the smell of June Eternal:

> *She.* I could not say in words.
> *He.* I command you to describe this smell.
> *She.* Of life eternal.
>
> (358)

Ayscough's legal talk is foreign to her. She is habitually slow to answer, "as if she must have Ayscough's words first translated from a foreign language before she can frame a reply" (410). Her response to his constant bullying is, "Thee has thy alphabet, and I mine, that is all. And I must speak mine" (313). People have different uses for and expectations of language, and the depositions often become a Babel of cross-purposes.

Beckford's characteristically bloated language and baroque syntax illustrate the power of language to drown meaning: "I thought to assure them that they had not arrived in wildest Muscovy, as I doubt

not they might well have supposed at the appearance of the place—
to show that we are not quite without *politesse*, for all our exile
from speakable society" (89). The same game exists in the master-
fully verbose and obsequious letters Pygge and Ayscough write. It is
the same language game Charles Smithson plays with Sarah and for
which he receives stinging silence and a turned back. In this novel a
problematic verbal communication is played against the perfect, silent telepathy between Dick and Bartholomew.

Telling is compromised in all these ways; but telling only represents the "answer" part of the depositions. Questioning is subject to
unique stresses as well. Questioning is the honored cornerstone of
the scientific method, but in this novel each question takes us farther away from "the" answer. The back-and-forth dynamics of question and answer are like an eternal deuce game in tennis. Ayscough
plays a power game with his forensics, and his self-righteous, vi-
tuperative attitude colors both the nature and tone of his questions,
as Wardley says: "Inquisition sits well in thy mouth, master lawyer"
(403). He views his deponents as quarry to be tripped up, caught, and,
as he says of Jones, "well hung for the roasting" (186). His questions
are based on his expectations of answers that he will understand.
His narrow insistence on literal truth leads Rebecca to say, "Thee's
cloud, thee's night, thee's Lucifer with thy questions, thee'd blind
me with thy lawyer's chains, that blind thee worse theeself" (426).
He leads witnesses into this hermeneutic circle, assuming their answers in his questions. He limits truth with his questions by probing
arbitrary and disconnected parts of a whole picture that is too large
for him to see all at once. Question-and-answer truth is a hybrid
truth, an imaginative construct fashioned of projection, prejudice,
and innuendo.

His scientific approach to the truth also fails. The sample of baked
earth resists Stephen Hales's exhaustive scientific attacks. Hales, a
distinguished member of the Royal Society, must confess, "I may
come to no certain conclusions to its nature" (282). Richard Pygge
assaults the cave with instruments and measuring devices, but only
succeeds in proving that what clearly was in the cave could not have
been in the cave. Fowles looks askance at the age of Enlightenment,
which does not allow science to mingle with other systems of know-

ing. He conjures the names of Newton, himself a closet hermeticist, and Whiston, the brilliant but disgraced predecessor of Saunderson, as examples. He plays the fishbowl struggles of the scientists of the Enlightenment against Rebecca's finding of pure light. In *The Enigma of Stonehenge* Fowles warns about the limitations of science: "More and more Western society threatens to forget that other systems of perceiving, understanding, and deriving benefit from reality exist. . . . Science is the most formidable of the idols that man has ever realized" (124).

The characters in the novel are limited by their time-bound notions of existence; they are comfortable seeing life as a progress, mapped out against their seeping mortality. The narrator conspires in creating this sense by plotting the travelers' last day against the setting of the sun: another day, another town closer to the end. In their depositions the witnesses use place names—Basingstoke, Wincanton, Amesbury, and so on—in an attempt to order events. At first the journey is literal, geographical, pleasant to plot on the map. But Fowles withholds the name of the last stop, C——, after which the place names may be found more easily in myth than Michelin. While the characters cling to their linear reconstructions, the macrostructure of the novel belies such complacency by splintering and reorganizing the journey; in the different tellings the journey keeps folding back over itself, and it is more like a Möbius strip than a straight line. The great cyclonic sweep of the novel overwhelms all the attempted chronologies.

The *Gentleman's Magazine* is a linear history of its time, ordered by successive months rather than towns. In it we follow several ongoing stories: the arrival of the Princess Saxe-Gotha; the debacle of Captain Porteous; the crimes of the turnpike levelers; the indicting and sentencing of thieves and murderers; and the rise to fame of Crazy Sally, the bonesetter. The last entry creates the illusion that these stories are coming to an end, that loose ends are being tied up, whereas the seven extracts represent only a slice of history, excised at random from the larger picture. The author and the reader create arbitrary endings in their desire to order experience. In this way history courts fiction. Fowles draws equivalences between the contents of *his* plot and history's plot to suggest this kinship. The travelers

fear turnpike levelers; the gathering of dissenters outside Ayscough's office recalls the mob who lynched Porteous; the arrival of
the princess mirrors the arrival of Bartholomew's great lady: the former wears a "habit of silver" (54), as does the latter; her marriage to
the Prince of Wales parallels the marriage in Cleave Wood; the princess is "not so well versed in the English language" (17), and Bartholomew's lady does not "speak our tongue" (48). Fact and fiction
mesh hypnotically throughout the narrative. Nearly all the characters are actual historical personages, and Fowles uses them to demonstrate that human lives do not necessarily have definite beginnings and ends. In this novel, as in *The Magus*, "the dead live," and
the eighteenth century becomes now.

Fowles defies the notion of forward progress with his characteristic use of interruption. He stops Rebecca just as she is about to
tell what happened in the cave. The narrator interposes with a short
history of women's underwear and then plays out a bit of low
comedy with John Tudor. Ayscough (and the reader) search for answers with a passion that has almost physical energy. The story is a
game of titillation, a sensual interplay of cause and effect, stimulus
and response; and Ayscough is dragged on by desire toward a hoped-
for consummation. While Fowles frustrates beginnings and endings
with his method of interruption, he often illustrates an escape from
the "Debtor's prison of History" stylistically, as in the first sentence
of the novel: "In the late and last afternoon of an April long ago, a
forlorn little group of travellers cross a remote . . ." (3). The startling
juxtaposition of "long ago" with the present tense suggests a Jungian
conception of time: "Space and time have a very precarious existence. They become 'fixed' concepts only in the course of [man's]
mental development, thanks largely to the introduction of measure-
ment. In themselves space and time consist of *nothing*. They are
hypostatized concepts born of the discriminating activity of the conscious mind."[2]

Fowles repudiates the classic approaches to knowing: questioning,
telling, scientific investigation, and historical mapping. He also examines the consequences of these various forms of tunnel vision.
Partial sight leads to collector-consciousness, the insidious mentality that limits existential freedom. The narrator immediately and

instinctively categorizes the travelers' characters by their clothes, but he is, of course, deceived in each case. Rebecca defies easy definition because she changes her costume throughout as she moves through her diverse roles. Appelations similarly dehumanize characters by abstracting them. Dick slips from being into legend when by consensus he becomes "the violet man," just as Rebecca's identity is effaced by her title, "the Quaker Maid." Ayscough reduces Jones to his Welshness: "You [Welsh] are . . . a nauseous boil upon this kingdom's posterior" (265).

Collector-consciousness is a general affliction. Because characters see themselves in terms of classes and categories, they become commodities. The narrator tells us that the predominant sentiment of the time was the "worship, if not idolatry, of property" (227). The characters in the novel are part of the property mentality, as all—even Ayscough—are servants, owned and controlled by someone slightly higher on the scale. Rebecca is the ultimate servant, and before she meets Bartholomew she feels she is a victim of fixed destiny. Her servitude encompasses both body and soul, since she profanes the Bible for her clients' pleasure. The buying and selling of human beings form a significant part of the texture of this novel. Bartholomew first baits Lacy with five guineas and eventually buys his services for one hundred. In turn, Lacy buys Jones's complicity, and Jones later begins a scheme to blackmail the duke. He tries to buy Dorcas, but fails. Ayscough later gives her that shilling in the spirit of Virtue Rewarded. Bartholomew rents Rebecca, who is actually owned by Claiborne. Rebecca is the most owned of creatures. Even Ayscough scuffles with Claiborne over who owns her, as he says, "Now I warn thee solemnly, Claiborne. That wench is mine now" (158). But the duke is the most unabashed in his proprietary behavior. With her he acts like "a person sizing an animal, a mare or cow, as if he might at any moment curtly state a price that he considered her worth" (314). In this world human contact is reduced to business negotiation, behavior that is supported by a society that does not see limitless human possibilities everywhere but confines individuals to categories.

Thus Fowles anatomizes the subject of misperception. If the characters move about in a shadowy world, the reader meanwhile has problems of his own trying to unify the eclectic material of the text. Tudor casts a last, mischievous slur onto the veracity of his "official" depositions, as he says to Rebecca, "Where I cannot read when I copy in the longhand, why I make it up" (343). Fowles involves the reader in one more difficulty to which the characters are not a party. He exercises his artistic control by imprinting on the novel a dense web of myth, symbol, and archetype, and he invites the reader to test the acuity of his vision against this calculated polysemy. We see a touch of his invisible hand early on in his description of the shepherds outside C——: they are "monolithic figures in cloaks of brown frieze, like primitive bishops with their crooks" (9). The shepherds suggest Christ but they also recall the diabolical duke, who snares Rebecca with his crook. "Monolithic" anticipates Stonehenge, a temple variously associated with the holy, the pagan, and the profane, as well as the monolith (the Devil's Stone) in front of the cave. The brown frieze cloaks mirror Rebecca's own, and become an image of collective pupation. "Bishop" suggests orthodox religion, a sentiment that is at odds with some of the affects of the other words. Thus Fowles works out of many traditions and contexts, and they are often contradictory.

Dick Thurlow is similarly ambiguous. He is alternately "a dog in human form" (438) to Ayscough, Rebecca's "pet dog" (25) and, in relation to the silver woman, "a faithful dog long kept from its mistress" (438). Superadded to the common and archetypal significances of the dog is his association with Attis, the great Phrygian vegetation god. Cybele, his mother and the mother of all gods, loved Attis excessively and in her jealousy compelled him to kill himself—which he gladly did—in a forest, alone, under a tree. Violets sprang from his blood, as violets spring from Dick's dead mouth. This typical aspect of vegetation mythology—life springing from death—is comprehended in Rebecca's words for her heaven, June Eternal. Holy *Mother* Wisdom is perhaps an incarnation of Cybele, whom Dick approaches humbly.

Attis was revered by a succession of emasculated priests (Bartholomew is sexless) who served Cybele through sacred prostitution, as Bartholomew offers the Quaker Maid–prostitute to the silver woman. But Bartholomew also has affinities with other mytholo-

gies. In his manic seeking after forbidden knowledge he is like
Faustus, and Ayscough solemnly believes he has made a pact with
Satan. Yet Fowles allies him just as closely with Biblical figures.
Like Christ, he speaks in riddles and parables, and his disappearance
from the cave mirrors Christ's disappearance from the tomb. Certainly Rebecca ultimately sees him as a Christ figure, a kind of pure
light, which is the metaphor with which Christ describes himself:
"I am the light of the world; he who follows me will not walk in
darkness, but will have the light of life" (John 8:12). Christ's admonition to his followers is the same as Bartholomew's: "You will seek
me and you will not find me" (John 7:23). "Bartholomew," of course,
was one of Christ's Apostles, but the only distinction achieved by
Bartholomew the Apostle is that absolutely nothing is known about
him.[3] Our Bartholomew's mission is clearly apostolic, especially in
regard to Rebecca. The Apostle is associated with the sword in pictorial art, and one of Bartholomew's most conspicuous props is his
sword. Bartholomew also acts as Father confessor, who shrives Rebecca on that last evening, and John the Baptist, who makes her
wash her body before she enters the cave.

Together, Dick and Bartholomew suggest the twin archetype in
both its pagan and Christian manifestations. In most mythologies
twins represent opposite halves of a divided and tormented being.
Dick is the carnal half, Bartholomew the spiritual half. In pagan mythology, such as the Winnebago myth of Flesh and Stump, one twin
must be sacrificed to unite the split soul. Rebecca's vision on the
maggot is consistent with this myth and prefigures Dick's suicide:
"He with the scythe pointed to the uncut grass beside him, where I
must look, and there hidden was laid his twin, seemed asleep upon
his back, with his scythe beside him, tho' strewn with flowers as one
dead" (374). She puts the same phenomenon in Christian terms: "As
Jesus Christ's body must die upon the Cross, so must this latter-day
earthly self, poor unregenerate Dick, die so the other half be saved"
(417).

Rebecca is a Pandora figure as she looses onto the world the secrets of Bartholomew's mysterious chest. But Pandora's Christian
counterpart is Eve and, as Jones says of Rebecca, "Know Eve, know
all" (200). Cleave Wood evokes Eden, and it is the location of a fall

into knowledge. The garden even has its serpent: Jones says, "I crouched and crawled upon my belly, sir, and found a good place among the whortles" (218); and its fruit, as Holy Mother Wisdom offers Rebecca a strange fruit from the orchard. Fowles suggests the Edenic imagery as he has Lacy, in our first glimpse of him, reading Milton. Rebecca is also associated with Mary Magdalene, who wept outside Christ's tomb for His disappearance. Christ visits her in a vision (as Bartholomew visits Rebecca) and tells her to teach the others why he has disappeared. This is Bartholomew's implicit edict to Rebecca. Mary Magdalene, then, becomes the first Apostle, just as Rebecca becomes the first teacher of her new creed. Fowles draws parallels between Rebecca and Mary, mother of Christ, as well. She received her annunciation at Stonehenge: "a light upon us from above, a light more large than any human making" (321); and she later gives birth to Ann Lee, who believed herself to be, and was, worshipped as Christ of the Second Coming. Fowles further draws together Rebecca and Christ Himself. Jones watches her make her May chaplet, which is also a crown of thorns: she "made a chaplet of May-flower on her lap, paring the thorns with a pocket-knife. . . . As I watched she pricked her fingers more than once, and sucked upon them" (214). The allusion prefigures her later "crucifixion" in the real world.

The journey is an archetype of multifarious meaning. It has an insistent westward course, betokening death, and is attended by ravens (also the death bird of *Daniel Martin*). The question of T. S. Eliot's magi applies as well to this journey: "were we led all that way for Birth or Death?" It ends with Dick's death and Rebecca's rebirth, and the consequent literal birth of a savior in humble surroundings. Thus this journey reflects both the light and dark elements of the archetype. It begins with foreboding, progresses through the waste land (here reflected in the "bleak landscape, . . . the peaty track, . . . the waste of dead heather") and ends in grace at a holy place. It is the same archetype that guides such works as *Canterbury Tales*, Eliot's *Waste Land*, "Journey of the Magi," *Pilgrim's Progress*, and "Childe Roland to the Dark Tower Came." The culmination of the journey takes place on May Day, a celebration of rebirth and fecundity, and a day of savage cocksquailing and "blood on the setts," recalling pagan sacrifice. May Day Eve is Walpurgisnacht, the night the witches fly. The journey ends at the cave, which is both womb and tomb.

The novel affirms a vast creative energy through the numerous births it contains: Puddicombe's daughter gives birth on the night the travelers arrive in C——; the *Gentleman's Magazine* notes that shortly thereafter Anne Boynton is delivered of quadruplets; and the novel ends with a monumental birth. But as the journey archetype encompasses light and dark, so does the mother archetype. Jung tells us that mother symbols represent "the goal of our longing for redemption, such as Paradise, the kingdom of God, the Heavenly Jerusalem. . . . The archetype is often associated with things and places standing for fertility and fruitfulness: the cornucopia, a plowed field, a garden. It can be attached to a rock, a cave, a tree. . . . The magic circle of mandala can be a form of mother archetype." He goes on to say that the dark, devouring aspect of the mother is expressed through witches and dragons.[4] Rebecca sees both faces of the mother as she is first attached to the devouring Mother Claiborne, but in her "longing for redemption" finds Holy Mother Wisdom. Rebecca herself becomes a mother (when before she had been barren) and gives birth to the child who would become Mother Ann Lee.

Fowles employs a narrative mode, then, which challenges the reader to participate in the same epistemological difficulties that his characters experience. The life of this novel operates on a maelstrom model, in which everyone, including the reader-participant, gets caught up in a swirl of ambiguities, uncertainties, untruths, and misperceptions, and in which their knowing is limited by the very tools with which they seek to know. We must wonder how Rebecca assimilates and comprehends her ordeal and emerges as an arrived individual, having rejected her servant self. The answer is that she learns by godgame, the same kind of game Fowles plays in each of his novels. Bartholomew goes on a personal quest for freedom as he tells Lacy: "I am born with a fixed destiny. . . . I have no liberty, Lacy, unless I steal it first" (37); but he turns his journey into a public lesson on the power of individuation and nonconformity. Bartholomew's godgame begins with his gathering of a conspicuous, excessive train. Ayscough shakes his head at this contradiction between secrecy and ostentation as he writes to the duke: "It is to be presumed that to travel alone with his man had best suited the secrecy of his intent" (101). In fact, Bartholomew leaves a blazing trail behind him that he may be discovered and followed. The way in which he disposes of his brassbound chest is symbolic of the way in which he disposes of himself: " 'Twas thrown in a goyal of thick bushes, four hundred paces from the road. But he who found it saw a glint of the brass, amid the leaves" (68). He chooses as his companion a famous actor who had just acted in a popular play ("all London saw it"), and London's busiest whore. He chooses as his confidant a notorious gossip, Lord B——, who "has the most evil tongue in London" (350). Even Dick is like a radioactive isotope tagged onto the group. Because they form such a fascinating train they draw a crowd wherever they go. In C—— "some seventy or eighty faces were waiting, when they approached the inn" (15). Virtually all the disguises are penetrated immediately (though all the players carry on in their roles), and Dick and Bartholomew are recognized at once by an acquaintance of the duke. It is obvious that Bartholomew is determined to be investigated, as he prophecies to Lacy: "No one shall ever find in you any but an innocent instrument. Should it come to that" (21).

After many tests Bartholomew elects Rebecca as the centerpiece of his godgame. He says to her after Stonehenge, "You are she I have sought" (324). To be elect in Fowles's terms is to be existentially prepared to change one's wayward, inauthentic, and self-debasing course. When Bartholomew found her, Rebecca was on a path toward total depravity, determined to test the limits of sinning, as she explains to Ayscough: "I sinned the more brazenly because at heart I would sin no more" (305). She seals her election when she tells Bartholomew, "I would not be what I am" (47). Because she had hit moral bottom she was the more open to a regeneration. The logic of her election is quite simple, as she explains to Ayscough: "There was that in me matched what he willed. . . . That I had sinned and would sin no more" (325).

Bartholomew begins by disorienting Rebecca and ends by deconstructing her. This is the typical strategy of all Fowlesian godgames. He upsets her equilibrium by estranging her from familiar surroundings and keeps her off balance with his conflicting postures of cruelty and kindness. One moment he says, "Modesty sits on thee like silk on dung. . . . Even the pox is afraid to touch thy morphewed carcase" (42); the next moment he smiles, kneels before her and kisses her hand. By acting in this bizarre manner he denies her easy understanding by collector-consciousness. He demands that she begin to look into herself to understand his anomolous behavior.

Fowles habitually uses twin sisters (or two women)—June-Julie, Rat-Freak, Sarah-Ernestina, Erato–Nurse Cory—to play out meta-theatrically the warring desires of the godgame's victim. In this novel Fowles employs the twin brothers, Dick and Bartholomew, to that end. Bartholomew is chaste, "insusceptible to the temptations of the flesh" (182), and Dick is lust incarnate. They engage in an unusual sexual threesome (another familiar aspect of the Fowlesian godgame), founded on voyeurism, as Rebecca says: "There was such closeness between them they needed no words, they were as one person, tho' two in body. I might almost believe his Lordship did enjoy me, despite he would not bear my touch, yet through Dick's enjoyment" (311). When Ayscough points out this seeming contradiction to Bartholomew's noble mission—"Did he not keep you in sin and lechery?"—she replies, "That I should see it better" (325). Bartholomew forces her to the limits of depravity by making her couple with the "dog" when she clearly desires the master, who only watches and viciously berates her performance. He assures that her fall will be total and obvious. He performs the final humiliation when he makes her stand naked before him and denounce herself.

Bartholomew places Rebecca in the center of a morass of conflicting stories. He prepares individual scripts tailored to the character and interests of each player. All the versions he creates are differently clad metaphors for the essential story, that of his journeying toward a meeting with an important woman. He tells Jones a story that would fit his alphabet: that he was going to curry favor with a rich aunt. He creates for Lacy a romantic plot, which is doomed to discovery by its very complexity. It is a Romeo-and-Juliet story, one Lacy would be accustomed to playing and that would appeal to his tender heart. It has the stock characters and situations of typical melodrama: star-crossed lovers, angry parents, surreptitious communication, the go-between maid, intercepted letters, and missed meetings. He flatters Claiborne's vanity by saying he will make her famous for her part in a wild orgy. These players have only to be concerned with their own roles, but Rebecca must fit herself into the others' plots by pretending to be either a maid for Bartholomew's intended, with whom he is eloping, or a maid for the Bideford aunt. In addition, she must uphold the terms of her own plot, which Bartholomew matched with her alphabet. She believes she is to cure him of impotence (bait for a brilliant whore) through voyeurism with his servant and, to assure the outcome, they would travel to curative waters with a famous doctor (Lacy)!

The masque relies for its effectiveness on the logic of metaphor. Rebecca reports that Bartholomew "said none of us were what we seemed" (311); his words recall Conchis's confession of artifice: "We are all actors here, my friend. None of us is what we really are" (*The Magus*, 404). In her bagnio life Rebecca assumes poses and masks that hide her real identity, but because she believes her destiny is fixed, she acquiesces to her inauthenticity. The masque works to disturb her habitual mock self by forcing her into provisional identities. The masque is an existential adventure whose aim is to deconstruct its subject and force her to disassemble the elaborate gearwork of lies and appearances. Yet Fowles has demonstrated how ineffectual are traditional methods of knowing. Rebecca must come to see the meaning of the masque as readers come to understand the meaning of fiction, by the process of self-discovery through metaphor.

Fowles illustrates the process in the numerous dumb shows of the novel. When Rebecca undresses before Dick, she communicates through sign and gesture ("she shakes her head . . . she points to the floor") and through silence creates a potent situation. The only words she speaks—"Oh my poor Dick. Poor Dick"—are ludicrously parodic, and they deflate the latency of the scene. Jones sees a dumb show in Cleave Wood, as he admits: "I could not hear, sir, or only their voices, not what was said, they spake low" (219). He construes deviltry from what he sees, and thereby reveals his nature in the way he decodes the metaphor. The most fully extended experience of this kind is Rebecca's vision in the cave, during which not a word is spoken. She receives wordlessly the attentions of the silver woman and is made to view silent moving pictures in the maggot-theater. She witnesses a glut of bizarre images and is abandoned to discover her own meaning. In this, as in all godgames, the gods abscond.

This silent seeing relates to Dick, who sees all life as a dumb show and therefore "more wholly than normal" (28). Rebecca feels power and integrity in his nonspeaking: "He loved me the more, with all his strange heart, and despite he could not say it in any words. . . . In his no-words lay more speaking than in any spoken. . . . I heard what he would say better than if he had spoke it out loud" (329). Bartholomew echoes these feelings in his admiration for Dick's ability to "brush aside the specious veils of speech, of manners and dress, and the like, to the reality of man" (166). Thus, experience, to be truly understood needs to be divested of telling, questioning, and rationalizing. The "wordless interview" between Rebecca and the duke is highly charged precisely because it is silent, because it is not limited by words. They estimate each other "like two eternally alien species" (342). Tudor gives her "two swift movements of a bent finger" whereupon the duke stops her, then pulls her forward with his crook. The masque is, like a Bergman film, woven of studied silences, but the novel seems noisy, as witnesses put endless, futile words to experiences that transcend verbal expression. The depositions are like voice-overs in a silent film and are clearly inadequate to communicate. The language of truth is, as Wardley says, "the glorious tongue of light" (400).

The maggot experience, then, is a metaphor of unassigned meaning. The modern reader will generally see in it spaceships and beings from other planets, for such is the alphabet of contemporary life. We seek new and better worlds in physical space. But Rebecca saw, finally, what was inside herself—the desire for a better, fairer, more civilized society than the one she lived in. In effect, she discovered her real destiny in her interpretation of June Eternal. She also rediscovers her humanity, her real kinship (not the mock kinship of prostitution) with others, and she finds it in the vision of the burning child, the climax of the godgame. Our alphabet says the child is an all-too-familiar victim of napalm warfare, and that the battle has marked affinities with Vietnam. But Rebecca sees something far more profound in her, something that makes the child more than a statistic or a certain category of battle casualty. She says, "I should have died a hundred times to reach her, for I saw myself in her, as I was before I sinned" (377). She is able to project herself into the suffering of another and thereby share that suffering in a moment of pure empathy. This joining of spirits is the way to break through the walls of categories, words, lies, and games that people build to keep each other out. Rebecca finds her identity as a person who wants no more pain for herself or others, who wants only "more love."

We can see the distance Rebecca has come by comparing her profound emotion for the child with the sangfroid with which she repulsed another girl with arms upraised, the shepherd's daughter who begs from the travelers: "The young woman raised her left hand and took a pinch of her spray of violets and threw them at the small girl. They fell across the child's arm, over her bent crown of no-doubt lice-ridden hair, then to the ground: where the child stared at them, nonplussed by this useless, incomprehensible gift" (10). Of the burning child she says, "I did spring from where I sat and ran to the window to succour, for she came toward me. . . . Yet stayed the glass stronger than a stone wall between us, dear God I could not break it, tho' the poor child was burning there not three feet from me and cried and wept most piteously. I see her still, I would e'en weep now for how she reached her hands for help" (377).

The movement represented in these sentiments constitutes metamorphosis, a major theme in the novel, one suggested by the title and by Bartholomew's joke that he is out to "make a man of a toad, and a fool into a philosopher" (441). Rebecca goes through several stages in her personal evolution. We first see her wrapped, cocoonlike, in her cape (as we see Sarah Woodruff, who undergoes a similar metamorphosis). She changes from simple maid to whore as she piles on layers of cosmetics and fine clothes. The narrator says of her change, "Only those tawny irises . . . remain of the simple young woman who dozed on the bed" (27). In Cleave Wood she becomes the May Queen. In her final stage she comes out of the cave-cocoon-womb naked, a new kind of being—an Ur-Shaker—and thoroughly individuated. She transcends the limits of the earthbound larva and becomes a winged creature that soars above the formerly incompre-

hensible glut of detail (as does the maggot-machine). This final metamorphosis is realized in clothing as well: "In her coarse grey dress
and pure white cap [she was] . . . a new self, defiant, determined by
new circumstance and new conviction" (287).

Rebecca evolves, as does the winged creature, toward freedom. Bartholomew teaches her that her chains are self-made, as he tells her:
"The stocks you sit in [are] not of iron and wood, but of your blind-
ness" (51). While she acquiesces to her perceived fixed destiny and
feels herself to be without choice, Bartholomew counters with,
"Shall I tell thee why [the stars] scorn? . . . Because thou dost not
scorn them back" (50). Before she goes into the cave he forces her to
make her own May chaplet, saying, "Thou shalt be queen, Fanny,
but thou must crown thyself" (336). She must learn to direct her own
destiny in spite of pressures to make her conform to narrow categories. Claiborne wants her back, and Ayscough strives to keep her in
her category, as when he says, "What right has a brazen strumpet to
know God's will?" (266). But she kicks herself free from any authority that seeks to compromise her ideals, as she shows in her defiance
of Ayscough. Her conviction is tested daily, as we see in the living
conditions she must endure—the public outhouse that serves five
hundred, the filth of Toad Lane, the open pile of community offal on
which grows the plant fat hen, the meal of "thin gruel, watery oat-
meal mixed with one or two specks of salt bacon and a few dark
green leaves of fat-hen" (288). Her will to be true to her vision must
be hard and muscular. The test of her conviction to be free lies in her
willingness to be crucified anew each day. But she accepts the per-
petual testing as the condition for her freedom: "I am repentence
with each breath I breathe, until my last, or still I sin" (297).

Bartholomew constructs a proliferating godgame. He leaves Rebecca behind to tell the story, which then becomes a godgame for
Ayscough, the duke, and the reader. The meaning of the masque is
equally unassigned for all who hear the story. Therefore, Bartholomew offers the opportunity for all to undergo personal growth. In
this light Ayscough fails to metamorphose. He clings to the fold
while Rebecca advances beyond the pale. He fears Rebecca's vision
because it represents Dissent, which in turn conjures in his mind
the "rabid political" mob. He needs reality to conform to his expec-

tations, as his wall of "cased tomes of precedent" (107) indicates. He is a slave to his collector impulses, and in his desire to retain the status quo he often appears foolish. He says of the silver woman, "It is not heard of, that any woman whatsoever, far less a lady, and one of foreign birth, should be alone in such a place" (354). He is limited in his ability to imagine, as we see in his question about the houses in June Eternal: "Of stone or brick? Had they thatched roofs or tiled with slate?" (368). He is equally deaf to anything but Book truth, and he responds to Rebecca's notion of a female component in the trinity by saying, " 'Tis writ clear in the Book of Genesis that Eve came of Adam's seventh rib" (375). He is horrified most of all by Bartholomew's trespass: "He sets his face against all that Providence most clearly designs for him" (179). Ayscough clings to the peace of perfect stasis, and his failure to grow must be seen as a failure of both nerve and imagination.

Ayscough's final letter to the duke is much like a final deposition in that he adds his version of what happened. But Ayscough projects an ending to the story, an ending (like Clegg's) where everything stops, everything ends in the acceptance of human limitations. He has Bartholomew commit suicide because "he did seek wickedly to pierce some dark secret of existence, and moreover grew besotted by it" (440). Ayscough halts the energy of the godgame by affirming the existence of human boundaries: "Man would of his nature know all; but it is God who decrees what shall or shall not be known" (443–44). He is like Plato's cave dweller: "Suppose he were compelled to look toward the real light, it would hurt his eyes, and he would escape by turning them away to the things which he was able to look at."[5]

Bartholomew clearly desires the masque to go on, and to this end he carefully secures its inconclusiveness. Ayscough's frenzied quest for sensible answers confirms the power of indeterminacy: "I shall find the bottom of this. . . . I work slow but I sift small. . . . I'll not rest till all's laid bare" (97). The many stories within the novel stop but they do not have closure. Lacy's story stops at the gibbet as he confesses to Ayscough: "I have told you all that I know. I am sorry to disappoint where you would most have me say more" (177). Richard Pygge comes to a similar halt at the cave: "I fear I must leave you thus with a great enigma, sir" (277). Even Rebecca's story has a false ending, since it raises far more questions than it answers. When Lacy complains that he does not understand the "final design," Bartholomew counters with, "We might all say that, might we not? *In comoedia vitae*" (18). His strategy suggests that knowing is a process of ongoing self-examination rather than a fait accompli, and that mystery provides the energy for the quest. Bartholomew affirms, with Lily de Seitas, that "an answer is always a form of death" (*The Magus*, 626).

When we examine the terms on which the novel operates, they lead to an apparent quandary. Fowles illustrates that the evidence of the senses and of reason is specious; that language obscures rather than clarifies truth; that ordinary conceptions of time, history, and science are inaccurate; and that the godgame, and by extension the novel, is predicated on indeterminacy and inconclusiveness. Yet *A Maggot* is not an antinovel. Both Fowles and Bartholomew suggest the way to unify the contentious material of the masque. We see Fowles's hand in the way he exploits the numinousness of the number three. The number runs deeply and obsessively through the text. We first glimpse Bartholomew in his "tricorn hat" with the silver braid. The silver and the three points anticipate rhetorically the silver woman in her three incarnations. Dorcas's casual remark points to the same trinity: " 'Twas May Day, and much to do, work for three" (82). Fowles tends to set his scenes with groups of three characters: Ayscough, Tudor, and a deponent form the most common trinity, but Dick, Rebecca, and Bartholomew form a sexual threesome; Jones has three witches in his story; three people gather in the meadow of June Eternal; and three men wait in the street below Ayscough's office. Rebecca is Claiborne's whore for three years, and Bartholomew must visit her three times before she consents to leave. When she comes out of the cave she repeats three times, "They are gone."

But correspondences in the first section of the novel cause the Dick-Bartholomew-Rebecca trinity to become unity, just as the three phases of the silver woman merge into one. Three scenes in this section—Dick's longing for Rebecca, Bartholomew's shriving of Rebecca, and Bartholomew's praying when the others leave—are variously equivalent. In the first, Rebecca is superior and she treats Dick like a dog: "She points to the floor beside where she stands, as one might to a pet dog" (25). In the next scene she assumes Dick's position before the superior Bartholomew. "He examines her as he would an animal" (41). In the first scene Dick is on his knees, begging from Rebecca. In the next scene Rebecca is suppliant before Bartholomew. Dick bares his private parts to Rebecca while she is in complete undress before Bartholomew. Bartholomew himself recapitulates both these scenes when the others leave him. With his "bald head" unwigged he "sinks to his knees on the broad planks" and becomes suppliant to some higher power as though "seeking undeserved forgiveness" (52). The narrator suggests the merging of identities as he notes that on Bartholomew's face there appears "a translation, in terms of his own sex and features, of the meekness the girl's face has shown him" (51). The persecutor of one scene becomes submissive in the next as they move in and out of each others' roles. The merging of these three vastly different persons suggests a constant at the base of humanity. The three are joined in their longing for peace and forgiveness, and in their desire to live better, freer lives.

Bartholomew expresses his notion of unity in his theory of the "divine cipher." With his astonishing memory Lacy gives us enough information to discern that the divine cipher is the same as what Kepler called the "divine proportion" and the Greeks called the "divine section." It is the number "phi," the ratio between any two numbers in the Fibonacci series (a series in which each element is the sum of the previous two elements; viz. 0, 1, 1, 2, 3, 5, 8 . . .).[6] Bartholomew believed that phi was the common denominator of creation "that all living things must copy" (140). He found the number everywhere, "in the motions of the planets and the arrangement of the stars in the heavens, . . . in all plants, . . . in the history of the world, both past and to come" (188). Indeed, the curious significance of the number phi has always been a theme in mathematics.[7] In Bartholomew's view all parts of the creation share the same existence, a notion for which Dick's violets are an apt metaphor: "the plant took sustenance from the flesh, finding it soil at heart, as us must all come to" (67). Dick also uses the flowers as a final message

The American Shakers

A Celibate, Religious Community

Coeval with the American Republic; First Shaker Family formed at Watervliet, N. Y., 1776; First organized Shaker Community established at New Lebanon, N. Y., 1788; Fifteen Shaker Societies in seven States of the United States of America.

Beginnings.

Founder, ANN LEE, of Manchester, England, (1736-1784). In religious revival of 17th Century, arose the "Shaking Quakers," or "Shakers," 1754. Nine persons from Manchester and Bolton, emigrated, May 1774, for the purpose of founding a Shaker Church in America. Eight remained faithful. They were ANN LEE, William Lee, James Whittaker, John Hocknell, James Shepherd, James Partington, Mary Partington, Nancy Lee.

FROM ANN LEE'S TEACHINGS.

Basic Principles of the Shaker Order,

VIRGIN PURITY, PEACE, JUSTICE, LOVE,

expressed in CELIBATE LIFE, NON RESISTANCE, COMMUNITY OF GOODS, UNIVERSAL BROTHERHOOD-- held to be the Divine Order of Society.

Resultant Beliefs and Practices Held as Ideals

TO BE ATTAINED IN THE INDIVIDUAL AND SOCIETY.

Equality of the Sexes, in all departments of life,
Equality in Labor, all working for each, and each for all,
Equality in Property,--No rich, no poor, Industrial Freedom,
Consecrated Labor, Dedicated Wealth, A United Inheritance,
Each using according to need,
Each enjoying according to capacity.
Freedom of Speech, Toleration in Thought and Religion. Often persecuted,
Shakers have never been known to persecute.
Abolition of all Slavery,--Chattel, Wage, Habit, Passion, Poverty, Disease.
Temperance in all things.
Justice and Kindness to all living beings.
Practical Benevolence. Thou shalt love thy neighbor as thyself.
True Democracy, Real Fraternity, Practical Living of the Golden Rule.

Religious Ideals and Worship.

All life and activity animated by Christian Love is Worship. Shakers adore God as the Almighty Creator, Fountain of all Good, Life, Light, Truth and Love,--the One Eternal Father-Mother.

They recognize the Christ Spirit, the expression of Deity, manifested in fulness in Jesus of Nazareth, also in feminine manifestation through the personality of Ann Lee. Both, they regard as Divine Saviors, anointed Leaders in the New Creation. All in whom the Christ consciousness awakens are Sons and Daughters of God. Spiritual man has, as his divine prerogative and highest destiny, to live in clear conception of and in active harmony with the Highest Good. The Life of the Spirit not the form of expression is essential.

Practical Issues.

Beautiful, comfortable Community Homes, in each a Christ Family.
Daily manual labor for all, according to strength and ability. "Hands to work and hearts to God." *(Ann Lee)*
Opportunity for intellectual and artistic development, within the necessary limits prescribed by the common good.
Sanitation, Health, Longevity.
Simplicity in dress, speech and manner.
Purity in thought, speech and personal habits.
Freedom from debt, worry and competition.

Government.

No Government, No Body without a Head.
The Head of the Shaker Order is Christ. The Visible Human Representative is vested in a

DUAL ORDER OF LEADERS.

Spiritual Leaders, of both sexes, a Ministry over Societies, Elders over Families.
Temporal Leaders, of both sexes, Trustees, Deacons and Care-takers, in charge of Business and Industrial Interests.

The Inner Life,

according to the Shaker Faith, is twofold, embracing
Repentance--confessing and forsaking all sin;
Regeneration--the growth and unfoldment in the individual of the Christ Spirit, through living according to the teachings and practice of Jesus Christ. As opposed to the common life of human generation and selfish gratification, this is held to be the Resurrection Life.

Physical development, mental growth and spiritual unfoldment form the only rational basis for a harmonious and happy existence; self-denial the corner-stone of the structure. The truths inherent in Shakerism are the underlying truths of God-life in all ages and the mission of the Shaker is to unfold and demonstrate these truths.

A broadside outlining the tenets of Shaker belief.

to Rebecca in this silent language, just as Bartholomew takes his leave with the name of a flower on his lips: "Forget me not, Rebecca" (378).

The divine cipher is a metaphor for the equality and orderliness of all natural things. Any number is, as Jung says, "an archetype of order which has become conscious."[8] To Bartholomew the builders of Stonehenge had discovered the divine cipher: "We mortals are locked as at Newgate . . . within the chains and bars of our senses and our brief allotted span, and as such are blind . . . for God all time is as one, eternally now, whereas we must see it as past, present, or future, as in a history" (143). He laments, "These ancients knew a secret I should give all I possess to secure. . . . These rude savages may have entered a place where we still fear to tread" (142).

The Shakers rediscovered the divine cipher. June Eternal is Rebecca's vision of what the world could become, the vision that became Shakerism. In Shaker communities Fowles finds the expression of freedom, whole sight, and true civilization. The movement grew out of a repressive, propertied class culture and became a model of true communism. Rebecca foreshadows Shaker social ideals when she gives Jones half the money she has sewn in her hem and shares with him half her meager crust of bread. In June Eternal, as in Shaker villages, all goods are shared equally among the inhabitants and all work for the common good. No servitude exists because "all worked because they would, not that they must" (371). Individuals of all races gather in the community without fear of persecution. While clothes set off and define "the world's people" (as Shakers call those outside their communities), the Shakers use clothing to define the equality of all their members. In June Eternal all wear the silver habit, as in Toad Lane, and eventually in the American communities, all wear simple gray-and-white garments. The world's people close themselves off in arbitrary biological family units that often direct the destiny of their members. We see this especially in Bartholomew's case. In Rebecca's vision all members of the community, living and dead, are "one family," bound by common humanity rather than blood. Marguerite Fellows Melcher speaks of the profound bond between all Shakers: "Contradictory as it may seem, family life was emphasized and cherished by the Shakers. The word family had, of course, a larger meaning for them than the usually accepted term. . . . To be brothers and sisters in a consecrated communion of the spirit was to be joined not only in human companionship with one another, but also in a spiritual relationship with Mother Ann and all Believers living and dead—a mystical relationship that reached back to the beginning of man's yearning toward God and forward into eternity."[9]

In all their institutions and beliefs the Shakers seek to level hierarchies and destroy artificial codes and categories. Shakerism represents a commitment to pure socialism. In June Eternal there is no persecution, no envy, and no rivalry. Rebecca says: " 'Twas plain all were content to be of a sameness in their circumstance, that none might be without. . . . Not as it is with us, each man and woman's heart cased in iron by their greed and their vanity, and forced thereby to act and live for themselves alone" (370). This sameness leads to solidarity and a unity of purpose that the "mob" outside Ayscough's rooms illustrates: "All thirteen pairs of eyes seemed fixed on one point only: the window where Ayscough had appeared. . . . He was made out; and in a ragged but rapid sequence, thirteen pairs of hands rose in prayer to their breasts" (383). The gesture is the same as the silver woman's sign. Those who do not understand Shaker ideology often point to this show of sameness as evidence of mindless conformity to dogma, but as Virginia Weis points out, and Fowles understands, this sameness is the highest expression of individual freedom:

> Both simplicity and unity, in the Shaker experience, are very affirmative. It is others who have made them negative. To see Shaker furniture—and life—just as "stripped of ornament" and somehow barren of all human pleasure, is to fail to see the whole point of Shaker simplicity. To be truly simple is to know one's self honestly, yielding neither to pride nor to false humility. Similarly, to equate unity with uniformity . . . is to mock it. For Shaker union is profoundly internal, not a superficial adherence to an external code. It is a coming together, and being one, in Christ. It is not primarily an act of obedience, but an experience of loving and being loved. Neither simplicity nor

unity, rightly understood, was ever meant to be a negation or denial of human nature. Rather, these were the qualities in which and by which one's human faculties to know and love might be most truly realized.[10]

Shaker unity is a literalization of Bartholomew's divine cipher. The orderliness, the clean and simple regularity of their way of life, are reflections of the habits of nature. The Shaker community accepts its parity with nature; it is not governed by artificial, unruly, and unnatural forces, as is Ayscough's world.

In June Eternal Rebecca found the place that could be defined by its freedom from the bonds by which the world's people imprison themselves. The Shakers express an extraordinary indifference to received ideas. They are freethinkers in all matters, "unsullied by stock belief, learned tradition, and the influence of the other kind of enlightenment" (452) and, like Amos Hocknell and Joseph Wardley, express a fierce determination to be neither owned nor led. What mattered to Hocknell "was that a thing, an opinion, an idea, a man's way of life, should be plain, exact to its purpose; well built, well pinned and morticed, well fitted to its function; and above all not hidden by vain ornament from what it truly was" (451). This "marvellously inventive practical life" (451) led to Mother Ann's famous edict, "Every force evolves a form." Thus, the slate-cleaning attitude of the Shakers spawned many inventions for which we are in their debt. One of those is the broom Rebecca sees in June Eternal. The legendary cleanliness of Shaker communities is a "physical emblem of a psychological cleanliness" (287), in keeping with Mother Ann's admonition, that "there is no dirt in heaven."[11]

Fowles notes in his epilogue that the Shakers have been much despised for their fresh, unfettered thinking: "Orthodox theologians have always despised the sect's doctrinal naivety; orthodox priests its fanaticism; orthodox capitalists, its communism; orthodox communists, its superstition; orthodox sensualists, its abhorrence of the carnal; and orthodox males, its striking feminism" (450). Much of *A Maggot* deals with this last point. The Shakers called for a "new archetype of the Father-Mother God. Man's exploitation of women for thousands of years had been, according to the Shakers, one of the principal causes of failure in human history."[12] They insisted, in the face of much ridicule, that the creation is not possible without a female principal, and that the trinity is not credible without a female component. Rebecca suggests that Christ is inherently androgynous as she insists, "Christ is my master and mistress" (297). The followers of Ann Lee found it perfectly fitting that Christ's second incarnation would be a woman. The oneness of male and female is an extension of the Shakers' profound sense of the unity of all things.

Fowles illustrates the many ways in which we are bound by the chains of language. He sees liberation from language in silent, intuitive communication, and in metaphor, which opens rather than restricts possibilities. Rebecca comes to mistrust words and she tells Ayscough, "Truth may not be said of seen things" (423). The Shakers revere silence and when they worship they speak in tongues, a "richly metaphorical language" (450). In our last glimpse of Rebecca, she is singing in tongues to her new daughter: "Vive vi, vive vum . . ." over and over again. The phrase reaches outward in both sound and sense toward countless meanings, yet it cannot be understood definitively. The vibrato alliteration suggests the palsy that is the worship gesture of the Shakers, and the circularity of the lullaby mirrors much that is circular in Shaker thought—the coming again of Christ, the whirling Shaker dance, and the circle symbol in their art. "Vive" suggests life, while "vi" approaches many Latin words that are relevant to Shaker theology—"vis" as force or energy; "vis" as sight and vision; "vibr" as shake; "vicis" as whirl; "vincere" as overcome. The "vum" brings us to America (the destination of the Shakers) and is a colloquial term for "vow" or "swear." Shaker language is limitless rather than limiting.

Like the primitive builders of Stonehenge, who lived before the book of history was written, the Shakers move about freely in time; they are not caught in the treadmill momentum of the present. Spirits from the past routinely visit and communicate with the Shakers. Rebecca sees a vision of Bartholomew during her inquisition and is astonished that the others are blind to him. "The dead live" quite literally in their philosophy and they often leave "gift songs" and "gift drawings." Shakers can see equally well into the future, and

One of two staircases that rise in a three-story spiral in the Trustees' Office at the Shaker community in Pleasant Hill, Kentucky. All Shaker art forms mirror the regularity—with mathematical precision—of nature. These twin staircases reflect the tendency of natural objects to spiral in a regular way. In Bartholomew's terms, Shaker art is a manifestation of the divine cipher. (Courtesy of Shakertown at Pleasant Hill, Kentucky)

prophecy is a major activity of their faith. Rebecca receives her first vision—the sex of her child—in Ayscough's rooms. It is important to note that these prophecies and visitations are not imposed by an outward force, but are skills learned through the exercise of keen perception.

While Fowles repudiates traditional ways of knowing, he sees in the Shakers' notion of revelation a worthy epistemology. In their search for truth they are not circumscribed by the Bible, as Ayscough is. Wardley explains their position: "The Book is good witness, and

"A Present from Mother Ann to Mary H.," a spirit drawing dated November 29, 1848. While in a trance state, living brothers and sisters often received graphic messages from the spirits of departed faithfuls. This automatic drawing is a brilliant example of how the Shakers move about freely in time and also shows how rich in metaphor Shaker thinking is. Many images in this vision are characteristic of all such drawings and are parallel to images in A Maggot. The winged prince in a flying vehicle trailing the banner "FREEDOM" recalls Bartholomew. The birds, moon, and circle appear as glyphs on the outside of the maggot. The sectioned circle appears in Bartholomew's astronomical drawings. (Abby Aldrich Rockefeller Folk Art Center, Williamsburg, Virginia)

much wisdom; yet it is not all. . . . We say 'twas writ by good and holy men, they lied not by their lights. Such were their understanding then; in some things not certain truth. 'Tis but words that are fallible in their season. The Lord was never beholden to letters, nor the Book His last testament. . . . He is not dead. He lives" (396). Wardley sees that the Bible is testimony, precisely akin to the voluminous testimony in this novel, which is metaphorical in nature. The Shaker faith is organic. It lives, grows, and changes, and is therefore the antithesis of the stasis Ayscough champions. Prophecy and communication with departed spirits, the collective whispers of past and future voices, are an integral part of the faith because Shakers believe in the ongoingness of revelation rather than in a finite, attainable truth. Truth emerges from the process of revelation and reconstruction. Rebecca says that her vision was a series of swift glimpses, "So swift I saw not all; for all was no sooner glimpsed than gone" (369); and she assigned meaning to the vision during a period of reconstruction and self-discovery. She explains the process to Ayscough: " 'Tis not as people say, truth may come in one second; it may come more slow, and so 'twas for me. . . . I speak of it to thee more plain now than it was to me at this first, when it was but a trembling, a suspicion, a whisper" (374). The Shaker model of knowing excludes the existence of a truth accompli and affirms a truth that is consonant with human growth. Finally, Fowles sees in Shaker thought an eloquent expression of humanism, the antithesis of the spirit of materialism that he illustrates in the novel. Shakers worship the "eternal spirit" or "first principle" of life in human form rather than in a distant, disembodied god. The Shakers return Christ to earth in the form of Ann Lee and uncrucify him/her. Theodore E. Johnson expresses the Shakers' gentle and innovative way of looking at the world:

> Christ as spirit had come to establish the millennium, not on clouds of righteousness, not in glory on the Mount of Olives, but unobtrusively, quietly, as the scriptures had foretold, "like a thief in the night." . . . It is this concept of the indwelling presence of Christ in an active, ongoing way that lies at the heart of all Shaker teaching. Yet it is not the teaching in itself that has constituted the uniqueness and the greatness of Shakerism, but

the way in which that teaching has through the daily activity of men and women expressed itself as a way of life, a way of life that shaped a community and was consonant with community by its very nature.[13]

Fowles uses Shakerism itself as a broad analogy to his fictional strategy. Because his fiction aspires to a truth that lies behind metaphor—to the light beyond the impediments that cast shadows—it places faith in the ability of human minds to meet in the place beyond words. This novel, like his others, is an affirmation of the humanizing influence of fiction. As Johnson points out, Shakers live their faith, and their daily life is a continually rich and metaphorical expression of their faith. One need only casually study Shaker drawing, dance, and singing to see how much their lives seek to express "the relation of fiction to reality" (451). Fiction itself anticipates a kind of faith and, Fowles says, "We novelists also demand a farfetched faith, quite often seemingly absurd in relation to normal reality; we too need a bewildering degree of metaphorical understanding from our readers before the truths behind our tropes can be conveyed" (451).

In the "divine maggot" of Rebecca and Ann Lee, Fowles recognizes a moment of human evolution toward light. Though the vision bred in some a "narrow-minded bigotry," he admires "that first fuse, that spirit that was in them at the beginning" (452). They created a decent and humanistic world in which the brothers and sisters could be harmonious individuals. Rebecca states her mission to Ayscough: "Most in this world is unjust by act of man. . . . Change, that is my purpose" (424). Her purpose reflects Bartholomew's purpose, as he suggests when she begs him to say what he wants of her: "What I want of far more than thee, Fanny" (51). Fowles calls Ann Lee's word the "Logos"; and indeed the historical Ann Lee said, upon receiving her calling, "I am Ann the Word."[14] John the Apostle equates Logos with creation: "In the beginning was the Word, and the Word was with God, and the Word was God" (John 1:1). God's word is effectual, then, as He said, "Let there be light; and there was light." Ann's word created a new world as well. But the novelist is a creator, too, and he also creates worlds with words. His words flow on, even as he protests the limitations of his medium, creating a world where before there had been nothing. His creation, like God's or Ann Lee's, would be sterile and static, all frozen, outward form without the animating intelligence of the human observer, who is free to make what he will of the creation. Without choice creation is static, like the uncorrupted Eden with its unfallen couple. In this novel, as in all his others, Fowles and his reader are cocreators; he sketches the maggot and the reader turns it into a winged creature.

Such is his design, but he is uncharacteristically pessimistic at the end of the novel. He acknowledges that dissent, " a refusal to believe what those in power would have us believe" (453), is the catalyst of evolution, and that dissent leads to personal and collective freedom. But he is disheartened about the lack of dissent, the mindless conformity, in our own time: "We grow too clever now to change; too selfish and too multiple, too dominated by the Devil's great I, in Shaker terminology; too self-tyrannized, too pledged to our own convenience, too tired, too indifferent to others, too frightened" (454). In his lament he mourns the "lost spirit, courage, and imagination of Mother Ann Lee's word" (455). But even as he laments he is asking us to create new worlds in which we can be true to ourselves and each other. In his hope he is the compleat humanist.

Appendix.
Interview
With
John Fowles

I conducted the following interview with Mr.

Fowles at his home in Lyme Regis, England. The

text has been transcribed from tapes and edited

by both Fowles and me. Fowles authorized the

final draft, and I have tried to preserve his style

of speech as nearly as possible, while still

maintaining clarity.

You said in *The Aristos* that you would never want to be called a novelist. Are you happy with the name novelist now?

Fowles. I don't think of myself as only a novelist. I suppose I could say the novel is something I happen to enjoy, and I suppose I'm fairly good at it. But I do write novels mainly to discover myself and life. Really, I'm much more just an experiencer of life. I don't honestly mind being called a novelist. In my own private mythology it's rather too limiting.

Q. Are your novels more dear to you than, say, your nonfiction works, or do you care equally for both?

Fowles. Inasmuch as an author can rank his work, I did enjoy *The Tree* very much. It was a great pleasure to write that; that's the one I prefer of the nonfiction. I enjoyed bits of *Islands,* too. Certainly I wouldn't distinguish between writing them and writing novels. But there's always a certain surreptitious excitement when you're writing a novel, because you never know what's going to happen, whereas in nonfiction books you do start with much more of an idea of what you're going to say; and I hate the planned in everything. In fiction there is a certain first-draft mood which comes upon you, which is marvelous and is the nicest of all literary experiences. When you're into a narrative and it seems so full of forks and possibilities, and you're full of ideas, that is marvelous. That's the best of all literary experiences.

Q. What are you working on now?

Fowles. At the moment I have three or four possibilities. I suppose I'm lazy now. I don't feel any pressure to publish, and I also have a

Side view of Fowles's house in Lyme Regis.

strong belief that the longer you keep books to yourself, the better they finally go. So, you know, they're just kicking about, and perhaps one day the mood takes you and you finish them.

Q. It's all up to chance?

Fowles. No, well . . . no. I think probably deep down it's not up to chance, because the unconscious is such a large part of every artist. There are probably unconscious things that make you slow about finishing a text or make you feel you must absolutely finish it, as I did with *The Collector*, for instance. I wrote *The Collector* in one month—the first draft. But I don't think I could ever do that now, because the whole business gets more difficult as you grow older. It was just that the idea hit me, and once it started it demanded to be sort of raced through. When I say I wrote the first draft in a month, it went through lots of revisions afterwards, but the basic story did come quite exceptionally fast for me.

Q. Do you feel that writing is a calling? Are you driven to write, as the cliché suggests?

Fowles. Yes, absolutely. In old-fashioned terms it is a vocation. With a lot of writers, of course, I don't think it is a vocation, but I would say for every writer I admire it is truly a vocation. Of course lots of writers write to make lots of money, and it clearly isn't a vocation for them. It's just a trick they've picked up and a straight profession like any other.

Q. What's the most difficult part of writing for you?

Fowles. I should think the revising part. I write lots of drafts, but so does almost every writer I've ever heard of. I don't know anyone who can sit down and write a perfect text. I've quoted quite often the hypnotism chapter in *The Magus*, which I left out because I couldn't cope with it. All it was in the typescript was just a page with a note "Conchis hypnotizes Nicholas," or something like that. I couldn't actually see how to do it. I did it right at the very end; I wrote it in one morning, in fact. The accursed Erato was on my side on that occasion. This does happen in narrative: you'll get a chapter down very fast and then the most ridiculous little thing in some other one causes you hours and hours of problems. On the whole, dialogue is the most difficult thing, without any doubt. It's very difficult, unfortunately. You have to detach yourself from the notion of a lifelike quality. You see, actually lifelike, tape-recorded dialogue like this has very little to do with good novel dialogue. It's a matter of getting that awful tyranny of mimesis out of your mind, which is difficult. Evelyn Waugh is the man I admire. I don't like him on social or philosophical grounds, but I think he was an admirable handler of dialogue.

Q. All through your books there is a great deal of emphasis on music and painting. Do you paint or play?

Fowles. No. Well, when I say I don't play, I can just about get my fingers around a recorder; and, oh, I've tried to draw, but I have no skill.

Q. How do you feel about the fame you have achieved? Have there been adverse effects?

Fowles. Yes, many. I don't like it. I don't suffer it here because I have a sort of understanding with the town. They know I don't like being treated as famous. Yes, it has all sorts of problems, especially with old friends. I used to resent it because I used to think relationships had changed with old friends; but I realize that it is a traumatic experience for them, in a strange sort of way. And I think it's disagreeable because you can be taken too seriously, and you can get the feeling that you're being treated as if you were already dead—which I hate. I also get a very large correspondence, you see, especially from America. It takes—if I answer it all—too much time. Lots of well-meaning people write really rather lovely letters to me, and I can't answer them as humanly as one should. And the nicest letters are often the most difficult to deal with. You get a lot of other minor things like autograph hunters. Or "Will you please trace your hand?" and "Can I have a signed photograph?" That last is the one I particularly loathe—as if you're a pop star. I have a basic sympathy with writers like Salinger or Pynchon, who have a kind of shyness, or a neurotic complex, about all this. I fully understand it; I feel it myself once in a while. It's because you've had so many bad experiences, unfortunately.

Q. Do you still have a great interest in films?

Fowles. I see a few when I go to London, usually Continental films, because we never see them here. Yes, I enjoy films very much.

Q. Are you aware of all the cinematic qualities in your work?

Fowles. Yes. Films must have altered literary imagination greatly, I think. I did have periods in my life when I was seeing an enormous quantity of films, several a week. You can't pick up a modern novel without seeing techniques of editing—cutting, and all the rest of it. Flashbacks. The funny thing is, of course, that the cinema in fact got them from literature in the first place, so I don't feel bad about this at all. I just think it's a curious feedback, in effect, from how the cinema directors first used literature to develop their own art, and now we've got this sort of repayment from them.

Q. You've put yourself in exile down here in Lyme?

Fowles. In exile from literary England.

Q. Well, you've spoken several times about a feeling of alienation, a feeling that you've come from another planet, and that sometimes you don't understand the beings around you.

Fowles. Yes, I do feel that way. That's really not so much why I live in Lyme, but has to do with my whole feeling about nature. In many ways I have closer feelings to nature than I do to other human beings. I suppose living in a comparatively remote place like this is a kind of exile. But I think most novelists are implicitly in exile from most of society around them because of the elements in the novel which require you to look at your society objectively and criticize it. That immediately makes you different from most other members of that society. Therefore, that is a kind of inner exile which I should have thought every ordinary novelist would have felt. I mean, we do see life differently from most other people—and not only in a political way or a social way. We're so . . . what's very important for us is this whole business of writing. You've read up deconstruction, no doubt? The distinctions between *lecture* and *scripture* also put you in exile. We're all suspicious, you see, and we're always thinking in printed text terms, whereas most people, I suspect, think much more in terms of spoken, oral speech. I suppose I've always enjoyed being something of a solitary, anyway. There is certainly something in my private character, but it seems to me inherent in the fact that one is a writer.

Q. How different do you feel to be Fowles-the-man from Fowles-the-writer? Is the implied author of your novels significantly different from yourself?

Fowles. I hope not too different. I mean, it's part of the con man side of writing that of course you try to present yourself to the reader as enormously sensitive, intelligent, and perspicacious. But I suppose I would have to say that I really feel I *can* see through things sometimes better than most people around me. So in a sense I share the notion of—Thackeray was the one, wasn't he—of being the urbane compeer of human life. I suppose part of that is part of my private self inasmuch as that's an image I like to present to the world. I would say that on the whole a strong "voice" is usually very closely linked to a highly personal style, which I don't have and don't want. I hope my public "voice" is fairly close to my own; but of course you know you're being read, and I think you are probably slightly tainted by the fact of the whole business of the reading of a text, and that it goes on out of your sight. It's very difficult to impress what you really mean on somebody you can't even see and you won't know. Anyway, we don't know what goes on when people read. That's the great mystery. You can't do it yourself, you see. You can't say, well,

I'll read a passage and analyze what I think. It's like the same situation in physics—as soon as you start observing and thinking consciously, how do I read myself as I read, it's all distorted. It's a very strange blank. It's a dead end; you can't get past it.

Q. There's no right reading of a text?

Fowles. There's no right reading of a text, certainly not. And there's no way, I think, of knowing what actually happens mentally as the process is going on. We don't know to what degree people visualize, for instance.

Q. The act of reading, you think, is as creative as the act of writing?

Fowles. I'm all with deconstruction on that side. What I don't like is the corollary they've made. You know, the author is a mere irrelevant detail, who sells half a pound of text like half a pound of sugar. I rather object to that. I still haven't got over J. Hillis Miller's book on Hardy—when he said that all the biographical data are irrelevant to the true understanding of Hardy.

Q. Do you think you can be more honest in your writing than in ordinary social life? Are you ever inhibited in your writing by outside circumstances: social relationships, personal circumstances, and so forth?

Fowles. In writing? In what I say? No, no, I don't feel that. This is a problem for many young writers. I mean I did feel that at the time of *The Collector.* You have your close friends and your parents, your teachers—your dreaded ex-teachers—and I think that is a difficult period for many writers, younger writers. All art *must* be a kind of striptease. I don't, thank God, get sent many novels to read, but I would say it's the commonest fault: inhibition caused by private circumstances. It's very difficult to get over. The wife is a very special category, I think. One is still frightened and apprehensive about how the person who knows you best is going to react, and that is a problem. It's far worse for young writers who haven't really got out of what is the natural human position, which is to fear your neighbors and elders. It's another reason we're in exile. We've said forbidden things. I think a bad category here, especially, are one's ex-teachers, because they have generally taught you some traditional standards, certain rules which must be obeyed in art. And it's very difficult to shake off that whole credo they've fed you. To break rules, especially aesthetic rules. They're very difficult to crack. That's another sort of incubus you've got to shake off before you can write.

Q. You are conscious, I assume, of an audience when you are writing. Who is your audience?

Fowles. Well, I try not to be too conscious because the audience I usually try to keep in mind is one other person. This is because the reading experience is always, however many million times it takes place, one to one. There are just two people present: me and the person who is reading my book.

Q. Who is that person?

Fowles. It's a . . . you see, I can't describe it because it's the sum of all the many letters, the many thousands by now, I have received from readers. I would say in general they are people who like narrative, they're at the university level in education (although I've had very touching letters from people far below that), and I'd say they usually share my concerns about the bad social values in the U.S., or whatever. And I think most of them have a sense of humor. They enjoy the kind of games I like to play with readers. I think this is a mistake that some novelists make: they sound as if they're addressing huge crowds. You know, Ronald Reagan talking about the state of the union, when in fact the experience is always one person—one person.

Q. How do you deal with the feeling that your reader has expectations of you—that you tell a story, that you end a book, and so on?

Fowles. I hope they'll follow me in that department. No writer is in control of how people read his books, and this, in some moods, is the delicious thing about the book; because, no matter how precisely and fully you describe something, you never, never know how the reader's going to read it. Your first reader, and your most important reader, is always yourself, in fact. So I basically write what I know is going to please *me*, what *I* am going to enjoy. Sometimes I'm right, and sometimes, as I generally was with *Mantissa*, I'm wrong. This is the risk. You can't go through life—even gamblers don't go through life—betting always on the favorite, the obvious choice. There has to be an outsider principle. You must say, well, probably most people won't like this book, but to hell with it.

Q. Do you feel the same way about making concessions to the reader's understanding? That is to say, your novels are very complex; are you ever afraid that you're being too obscure?

Fowles. No, because another thing that is very important for me in a novel and in the cinema, for that matter, is the gaps in understanding and narrative. Reading a novel is an equally creative experience, and the one thing the fiction reader does not want to be given is something where every question is answered; surely one of the most important functions of the novel is to create, not exactly a sense of mystery, but to leave spaces which the reader has got to fill in. It's . . . it's a kind of discipline—not a discipline so much as—it's a kind of joyous experience, a kind of *jouissance,* in Barthes's terms, that I think the reader deserves, you know. Only a very elementary kind of reading mind complains when it doesn't fully understand a novel. That doesn't mean I like willful obscurity, but I think ambiguity is a very important part of the experience. That's why I like nature. There's so much of it we just cannot understand; we can only guess at the possibilities. Nature is full of gaps and is very bizarrely and asymmetrically designed. This is rather like all those Americans who write to me and say, how dare you use foreign words. They often will send very odd, pathetic pleas: "I had to leave school at the age of thirteen"; "I never had a good education, so how dare you use French words or Latin words." I'm a socialist, but I have no truck with that at all. Language is primary. Nothing must . . . nothing must attack or diminish language. Oh, occasionally, perhaps, if a passage is too obscure, or perhaps a highly unusual word is a bit much, or perhaps I am suffering from, as I tend to (as I'm half brought up in the French culture), the French flu, then I will alter things. But I'm all for richness in language, and if people can't understand then they can bloody well go elsewhere. Buy a dictionary or something.

Q. When you write, are you more conscious of form or idea?

Fowles. Oh, idea. Idea and feeling, I should think.

Q. Will the idea and feeling control the details of the book?

Fowles. Yes. Much more so than the other way around. I try to be very careful about fitting details in with the general mood, or certainly in giving things like dress color or speech patterns a symbolic value. Another great problem in novel writing is names. I think most novelists find that. It's very mysterious the trouble you have with names—when perfectly plausible names for some mysterious reason sound slightly wrong. That's always been a mystery to me. Some complicated little computer in one's unconscious will reject what seem perfectly good names on all other grounds, and then it will suddenly click and you find you've got the right one.

Q. So the idea will control the details almost autonomically?

Fowles. I don't know if I would call it the idea, it's much more than that. It's a very general gestalt kind of feeling about what the mood ought to be. This usually comes up naturally and unconsciously in the writing, I find. All passages of narrative are set in a kind of musical key, and usually you won't put in accidentals unless they have some special reason, they seem to work. It's mood.

Q. You've said that Raymond Chandler occasionally writes perfect prose. What is perfect prose? What does a writer look for in another writer's work?

Fowles. Well, perfect in the context of what he is trying to do. It's certainly *le mot juste* in part, but it is sensitivity to what we've just been talking about. And absolutely accurate choice of words is important. I'm against Hemingway for many reasons but I do admire many of those short stories he wrote—I think they're an example of that. And Flaubert is a great master of this. With most novelists I can read a page and see hundreds of things I would change. In some of Hemingway's stories you can't change a word. Evelyn Waugh was able to do that; Greene also, I suppose. I don't know if it's really terribly important. I think many very good writers didn't have that accuracy. Dickens, for example. There's something to be said for sometimes being dull and boring—it's actually rather an important part of the reading process. In my opinion Jane Austen is an awful bore—very often. A very second-rate writer. Then suddenly she'll get one page, out of dozens of pages, where every word is perfect, and you couldn't in a million years improve it. It's that sudden rise from a very flat, normal level to these superb passages, I think, that's part of her achievement. I like that.

Q. How do you feel about writing in the modern literary climate—if you believe there is such a thing? Do you imagine that it's any different now than it's ever been, given the impact on literature of such things as television or burgeoning academic criticism?

Fowles. I don't think so, really. I used to think so at one time, but I don't now. Literary people, whether academics or writers, are extremely jealous, envious, and back-biting. They've always gone overboard for new theories. I see literature much more in natural history terms, with a whole natural order of genera and species, if you like; and I don't like the idea that you must despise this genus or admire that. You know, there's a parity between them all.

Q. There's nothing inherent in the times that affects the way you write?

Fowles. I think obviously one's influenced by the ideas from outside, often in a very positive way. I think you can very often pick up ideas which intrigue you. In a way, all novelists are information-gathering machines, and all this makes your stock in trade richer. I wouldn't call myself an existentialist now, but certainly that was very fruitful for me at the time. And I find structuralism and all its children quite interesting, inasmuch as I understand it.

Q. How do you feel about experimental writing?

Fowles. First of all, I think what used to be called the avant garde, when I was a student, is dead now. The theory then was if it was avant garde, it must be good. That's an absurd viewpoint. I don't mean I reject experimental writing, but I think the same law applies as to every other kind of writing. A tiny fraction of it will be good, and the great part will be bad. I've watched too many highly praised experimental writers sink beneath the waves. That all good resides in being experimental—that belief now seems thoroughly provincial to me. Some academics still set such great store in experimental writing. I should have thought the interest now is how you can restructure traditional modes.

Q. How do you feel about critics?

Fowles. You can get briefly hurt by critics, if you're talking about adverse reviews.

Q. Not so much reviews, but serious academic criticism. For example, do you think that writers will sometimes write for critics?

Fowles. I think this is a perceptible fault. I find it in reading the occasional American university literary review. I do detect it in some of the short stories and in the poetry. You get the impression that they're not really writing out of their true selves, but writing

out of a campus ambiance; or writing to their creative writing teachers. I think that is a danger, and this is why I am highly suspicious of
creative writing classes.

Q. I've heard you mention that several times. Have you ever sat in
a creative writing class?

Fowles. No, no, I'm like most critics. I'm speaking absolutely
from an armchair view. Actually, a very good friend of mine, Malcolm Bradbury, has really had quite considerable success at the University of East Anglia here. He's produced rather an impressive list of
good young writers. I enjoy most academic papers. I've got stacks
upstairs, but I haven't read all of them by any means. But those I
have read I've practically always enjoyed. There's a certain narcissistic and masochistic enjoyment: how nice of this person to take
me to bits. But what I dislike, more in the English than in the American critics, is the old sort of paradigm which is the curse of this
country; that is, that every critic feels he must be a schoolmaster.
And his subject must in some sense be a rough, backward, and far-
from-perfect pupil. This awful—I may be wrong—but this awful image of the schoolroom haunts literature on this side of the ocean. It
haunts reviewing also. So the poor writer always feels he is somewhere at the back of the class. And there's this weird feeling that I
have disobeyed authority, and that the true basis of authority must
lie in the analyzing academic. Now that I hate; that I hate. And I get
a sense, certainly from reviews in America, that even when an
American reviewer doesn't like your work, at least he treats you like
another adult. You never get this in England. No, you always get put
down as somebody who belongs to an inferior order in reason. It's a
weird part, I think, of the English class system.

Q. You're on the record as having a very disdainful attitude toward
critics. I know you've said the whole lot of British critics should be
thrown into the sea, but . . .

Fowles. No, no. I find certain kinds of academic activity incredibly wasteful and jargon-ridden. I mean, I've had many things written
on me which really make me vomit in a literary sense, because
they're so badly written and all the rest of it. And in the sense that
it's become a kind of campus industry, I'm hostile. If we're talking
about really serious critics of literature, from I. A. Richards or F. R.

Leavis right up through Roland Barthes, I certainly don't have a scorn for them. I do have a certain scorn for some of the French because they are so appallingly obscure. I don't mind obscurity in the novel, but I find obscurity in writing about the novel intolerable, and I think there's no excuse for it.

Q. What should good criticism be?

Fowles. Well, I get lots of letters also from students who write to me for help because they are doing a thesis or an end-of-term paper. And I always write back and say, far more important than what *I* think it means is what *you* think it means, because if criticism of literature or any art is not self-learning, then it is nothing. It's wrongly conceived. So, I would really rather read the silliest paper about me, which at least shows self-thought and gives personal reactions, than the cleverest paper full of all the current theories and the right jargon. For me, good criticism must induce a feeling of greater knowledge of himself or herself in the reader. I must say that is far and away the most important thing.

Q. Have there been good things written on your work?

Fowles. Oh, there's so much of it that I haven't read, really. I think I'm overstudied. It sounds rude to say that to you, but a lot of it is repetitive, that I have read. You get the same ideas coming up again and again. On the other hand, its breadth, in treatment terms, is quite interesting. People do see so many different things, some of which I never imagined. I've just had a paper yesterday on the influence of Chaucer's "Miller's Tale" on *The Magus*. A very good case, truly. Nicholas and Alison— very good case, an excellent case. But I didn't read Chaucer at all till about six years ago. Who was the first man to write a book on me? William Palmer. He sent me the proof to criticize before it was published, and there was a whole lot about the influence of J. S. Mill in it. I wrote back and said, sorry, but I hadn't to my knowledge ever read a word of J. S. Mill. Then I sent this back thinking, well, he'll have to drop all this. Damn me! Then the finished copy comes and it's all still in there! I write to him and say, "What the hell are you doing?" His answer was, "I thought you *ought* to have been influenced by J. S. Mill"! I've had a great deal of "ought to have been influenced." I have very peculiar reading knowledge, I'm afraid. The classics I haven't read—the list is disgraceful.

Q. Does it bother you when your books are misunderstood, given the prodigious amount of thought and care you put into them?

Fowles. No, no. I don't think so. I was hurt because this was a common thing when *The Collector* first came out. A lot of English critics said Miranda deserved everything she got, she was such a young prig. I had intended to show she had the faults of that age: idealism and a certain amount of priggishness. That's still the worst wrong reaction I can remember. But I realized later that it was something to do with the England of that time, which had an absolute horror both of the priggish and of idealism. It didn't happen in America; none of the American reviewers felt that. *The Collector* was reviewed universally in England in the thriller column. That sort of mistake is one of the hazards of the literary life.

Q. Is freedom still your largest concern?

Fowles. No one is free, really, except in some very minimal way.

Q. What in your background has made you so concerned about freedom?

Fowles. I think it probably was a personal thing—being brought up in very cramped suburban surroundings as a child and adolescent. I hate suburbia all through the world with a passion I can't describe to you. You know, I hate same streets, same houses. They bore me to death. And the kinds of minds they produce, too. And certainly the notion of escape from what you seem destined to be has always fascinated me. In a sense, I suppose, becoming a novelist (because, heaven knows, nobody ever thought that was likely), that is the freedom I've got. But, of course, all you do really when you come to be what you've always wanted to be is to find yourself in a new series of chains. The actual experience of writing a novel is a very imprisoning thing. It's also busy writing you as you write it, biting back at you.

Q. Your books are full of the existential individual. They show an individual finding himself through deconstructive and reconstructive processes. You know, being taken apart, then putting himself back together again through remembering, usually as a result of some fantastic godgame. Since we all don't have access to magi, how do ordinary people go about the same process?

Fowles. The basic idea that lay behind *The Magus* was that we are all in fact in a godgame and we're always in close contact with a kind of super-Conchis. This is the very basis of human existence, for me. There are mysteries, there are weird lessons being taught to us by ordinary life itself. I don't think that I ever got that idea across. I know most people read it as a sort of unique, peculiar experience that could only happen to one person in one particular place. But the idea behind it was that whatever first principle one puts behind human existence, it really does have some of the features of a Conchis, which always teaches slightly ambiguous lessons, and at best we don't know what it's trying to do or "say." And that was an existential proposition. Certainly that was, as I was writing it, the major idea behind it. And I still feel this is true but, of course, it's difficult to see, for most people.

Q. How do you go about discovering the lessons?

Fowles. I suppose by examining events, learning to read other people's motives, above all learning to read yourself, realizing there's a huge component of hazard and very real mystery in *everyone's* life. Life does condition us so frightfully that it's terribly difficult to sense this—to sense the underlying nature of existence. You know, we are caged more and more by present society in roles, and I think being able to see through the roles is most important. I once suggested it was as if we were all acting players. What we've lost the trick of is seeing through these public roles and discovering the actor's true self underneath—the experience every real actor has to deal with.

Q. Have you done that yourself?

Fowles. I hope so, yes. You know, one can never do it completely. I think, yes, I play roles, but I don't really believe them, except in the sense the actor has to believe.

Q. Are you interested in political freedom? Your novels suggest that if more people were free, in the existential sense, there would be far fewer problems. Is that true?

Fowles. Well, you have to define freedom very carefully. The first thing, if you do have a sense of freedom, is that in a way it is a very limiting thing. That is, if you gain a sense of freedom and you believe in it and wish to act on it, then you realize it puts appalling limitations on you. In a strange way, freedom is one of the least free things in the world; and so that is the political sense in which I use it. By freedom I don't mean that I think everyone should have the freedom to be as rich as they like or to behave as they like. That is an awful capitalist misunderstanding of freedom.

Q. You seem to assume that there is some sort of innate goodness or right sense about people that will guide their freedom. For example, you suggest in *The Magus* that if more German people had been true to their selves, World War II would not have happened. That implies a tremendous social side to existentialism.

Fowles. Freedom for me is inalienably bound up with self-knowledge. I would say the two words are almost synonymous in this context. And so it's really *that*, you know, the ability to withstand the appalling brainwashing that we all get now through the media, to think of yourself and know yourself. I must see that as a vital kind of freedom. And, honestly, it's an unhappy freedom at the moment because it doesn't exist very much. That's certainly how I see political freedom. It's more self-knowledge, and thus knowledge of others, too, and that's why I'm definitely on the socialist side.

Q. Existentialism, then, could be a strategy for effecting social evolution?

Fowles. Yes. Well, Sartre more or less argued that. I wasn't in agreement with his complete conversion to Marxism, but I certainly think existentialism is an argument for socialism.

Q. Since we're not a society of existential selves and free people, how does the existential individual get along with the rest of his fellows?

Fowles. Badly. In exile from them. Most people like to be conditioned. Unfortunately, it's a fallacy that everybody wants to be freer in the sense we're talking about. They're much happier, I think, having fixed routines and a limited way of life. I haven't really changed from what I said in *The Aristos*. I see no hope for change unless our educational system is changed very extensively.

Q. How do you do that?

Fowles. Well, all state systems pursue—it may not be complete chauvinism—they pursue notions which will bias the individual toward society; so that they will create a "good" or obedient social being out of a child. But that so often becomes merely chauvinistic and merely advantageous to society, to help society run more smoothly. I mean, we don't actually educate to create awkward cusses and bloody-minded people. I'd rather see more of that. I think one can do it by (again I'm slightly tainted by the general English situation) allowing far more free discussion among students and showing them, if one can simplify it enough, the sort of thing that deconstruction is trying to do—you know, the implicit contradictions in texts or social institutions. And certainly by putting far more stress on self-knowledge and less stress, I think, on just feeding absolutely useless external knowledge. There still is a bad split between science and the arts. I suppose I'm lucky because I've always been interested in the scientific side of my interests. It's teaching people to resist fixed ideas which is becoming the urgent problem, and this is because of the enormous power the media now have. The last election in England was very interesting because it was our first media election. It was the first time the country had been swung by clever media manipulation. It's also been called the first American election. It's all very mild, actually, compared to your system. But one must really start teaching societies the danger of all this. So in that sense I'm antisocial, antisociety, as in one or two other things. I'm not sure this should be a right function for a politician but I think it is an eminently right function for a novelist to do this, to be like this. So I don't care if I am quoted as liking birds more than human beings or having peculiar political views. I think this is our function. We must, in a way, try to be different from other people.

Q. I know mystery is very important to you, but what is it exactly that is mysterious? What is the great mystery?

Fowles. There's a lot of the occult in *The Magus*, but I regard all that as parody. I have no, absolutely no interest in the supernatural or mysticism or gurus or all these new Californian occult therapies, all that stuff. It bores me into the ground. A mystery lies at the base of all that is in nature. I see countless mysteries: Why do things behave as they do? Why do things happen as they do? All sorts of things like that. Why is death so important? And in literary terms I think the inexplicable, the gaps, are also very rich. This is partly because of the nature of the writing-reading process. I don't think of mystery in the now-bracketed sense of the mystery book or "the mystery." Mystery really lies in things the author doesn't say and in gaps in the story; that has much more to do with it. I regard all that in books as symbolic of the general mystery in cosmic, existential terms. I rather like stories that begin with an impossible situation or fact that you can make plausible. I'm also interested in brain surgery and in what they are discovering about the nervous system or the brain. There is some extraordinary work going on, especially in America, about brain lobe function. And it begins to seem very likely that one might be able to classify or even predict writers, because they have a reverse lobe domination from the normal. Brain surgery made a gigantic leap in the last world war when they suddenly realized that the two lobes are not one superior, one inferior—specialized, but capable of supplanting each other—they are, in effect, equivalent. They had various cases where a whole lobe had gone and then somehow, mysteriously, the supposed different lobe began to assume all the functions of the other. The Russians have also done some work. It's things like that I begin to find rather fascinating to write about. In a way, such ideas seem absurd, almost gothic, but I feel a fertility in them. Rather like Ray Bradbury, whom I rather admire. I was delighted when I heard he couldn't drive.

Q. You don't drive?

Fowles. I don't drive.

Q. Never?

Fowles. No, I'm too absentminded to be safe on the road. I'm also like every naturalist—I adore watching hedges and looking for plants and birds. That's not helpful.

Q. In your love of mystery you seem to be going against the grain of the major intellectual trend of this century—a structuralist kind of trend that seeks to demystify. Do you feel a tension between your love of having things unanswered and an intellectual current that demands answers?

Fowles. Yes. Yes, I do. That doesn't mean it isn't enjoyable when you're writing to try to explain or make some shrewd comment on something in society. But I would hate a world where everything was explained. You see, this is missing out, as I explained in *The Tree*. It seems to me that there's an art of living and of knowing, and this is what the scientists really won't accept. They won't accept that there's an art of knowing. It's all rational or logical, or not. And I feel this completely betrays the actuality of what goes on in one's head during any few moments of existence. One's mind is full of an indescribable complex of feelings and reactions and past influences and all the rest of it. I think it's bound up with the reader's notion of such presentness, you know. That's how he or she reads.

Q. It's obvious that you do object to a scientific attitude toward life, and yet you are a scientist yourself. How do you explain that?

Fowles. I greatly admire good science, and I recognize that what I know about things as an amateur scientist does help in the actual enjoyment of them outside. But the enjoyment of them always seems to me a whole world which hasn't really been explored. Sometimes the scientific side of it will be dominant. You see some completely new species, and the thing uppermost in your mind when you've looked it up is probably a Latin name and what the scientific handbooks will say about it. But that tends to exclude all familiar species, you know. Scientifically you know them, so nothing is learned. But I have taught myself over the years that this is completely wrong. I can go and look at the flowers in my garden. I've seen them a hundred thousand times, but I can still . . . something is there beyond all the science. It's made up of, most obviously, all my past seeings of it. And there's a kind of "thing in itself." I was rather hooked on Zen for a time and this is a very useful trick. I don't regard it as anything mystical, but simply being able to float without an identity yourself and to have all sense of identity in the thing you are looking at. It just needs practice. I don't regard it as anything transcendental, something you have to pay a thousand dollars for on some California ranch. Anyone can do it.

Q. There's nothing contemptible about science itself, then. Only science that excludes these other feelings?

Fowles. There's nothing contemptible about science which acknowledges it is working within the context of science. No, that is admirable. But what worries me is when the scientific view of life is applied to everything else; then I get upset and very often angry. It's because I think existence itself is not scientific. Even the purest scientist can't actually live his own existence that way. It's not possible.

Q. Are you still very interested in psychology?

Fowles. If you mean, do I keep up with the movements, the journals, and so on, no, unless somebody sends me something. But I owe a great deal to Freud and Jung. I've often said that if I felt I needed psychiatry I would certainly go to a Freudian. Freudian theory does interest me. I still find it a very satisfying kind of symbolism. Whether it's actually true or not, I don't know, but I like its mechanical structure. I think for a writer, Jung is actually the best person to read. He's very fertile and fruitful.

Q. Why is there so much stress on anima in your works?

Fowles. Anima . . . it's very difficult for me to say where it came from originally. I'd have to be analyzed to do that. But it's the idea of the female ghost inside one that's always been very attractive to me. Perhaps it's bound up with my general liking for mystery—the idea that there is a ghost like that inside one. In historical or social terms I've always had great sympathy for, I won't quite say feminism in the modern sense, but for a female principle in life. It doesn't always tie in with modern feminism. My wife would deny point blank that I'm a proper feminist. But I do, more for obscure personal reasons, hate the macho viewpoint. This is the one thing I can't swallow in America, both North and South. I find it detestable.

Q. What do you think is the function of fiction today? Is it any different than it's ever been? The real question is, why do you publish books? Not why do you write them, but why do you publish them?

Fowles. Well, I suppose in a way I am a good test case because I really don't have to publish for economic reasons any more. I think you must presume that there is a kind of devil in you that always enjoys going on show, even though an outward part of me dislikes much of the publishing side very much. But one does think of the future and, you know, it's nice to think this book will be on the cheap shelf in a hundred years' time, in some obscure bookshop. And I also hope there is something good in it. You hope to bring a certain amount of instruction and a certain amount of pleasure, too, because one cannot remove the pleasure principle, I think, from the novel. It must be an entertainment. I was delighted, I remember, in Cairo, to see the old professional oral storytellers still at work.

Q. Are you after any kind of proselytization?

Fowles. I think all I would attempt to do is to try to help people to see primarily themselves and then the world slightly differently. I had a letter from a young man the other day who said *The Magus* had made him—he had been in a seminary—it had made him drop the priesthood. He had read somewhere that I'd said novels can't change lives. He said that in this particular case it had very deeply changed his life. But I had to write back and disclaim most of this because, I think, as I pointed out, all the time he was already on a certain road. He did admit that he'd had grave theological doubts. All *The Magus* was was a signpost which happened to hit him at a certain point and which probably in retrospect he sees as more important than it really was. But I've actually had quite a lot of letters from various people like that, and it's tempting to be very vain and say, "Great, I'm superman." But I'm very suspicious of such claims. I think all a novel can do is, if people are inclining in a certain direction, then push them slightly more quickly towards it. But in general I want to propagate, I suppose, humanism.

Q. Are you happy with *The Magus* now?

Fowles. I'm happy with it now. I've always been fond of it.

Q. Is it your favorite novel?

Fowles. In the sense that one might love a crippled child more than normal children.

Q. Do you really believe it's the product of a retarded adolescent, written for adolescents?

Fowles. Well, as I put the phrase, it is pejorative. I have a very firm belief that writers have to have another kind of animus inside them that is still charmed by existence—under its charm, still adolescent, still a young man, and so on. This is another thing that puts us in exile. All my contemporaries seem much older than I. They don't see it, but I feel it. All the time. They're now getting a dignity and a sort of maturity which I shall never have.

Q. Were you happy with the film of *The French Lieutenant's Woman?*

Fowles. Yes. Well, I could fault it on one or two minor things, but I thought it was a very interesting experiment. And it's been much, much better discussed in France than anywhere else. They, on the whole, really loved the film and some very good stuff has been written on it. I was happy with that.

Q. I am curious about the background of *The Book of Ebenezer Lepage.*

· **Fowles.** Yes, I know. I'm the world's greatest living authority on that!

Q. What were the circumstances behind your bringing that out?

Fowles. I didn't bring it out. I only came in when the publishers got the manuscript and decided to publish it. If I'm honest with you, I didn't altogether admire it, but I felt it was categorically a book that ought to be published. I thought it was rather extraordinary in terms of the circumstances in which it was written. I never thought and I don't think it's an undiscovered masterpiece. I don't think it's anywhere near that. I would have cut it by at least a quarter. But I did feel it was definitely a literary curiosity. We've since learned a good deal more about him, G. B. Edwards.

Q. Where did *Mantissa* come from? Are the Muses really so cruel to you?

Fowles. Another side of me has to regard most of writing as a game. I've always had this, I suppose, half-unconscious feeling that when you're writing there's a tease element: that something is always teasing you and making you have pratfalls. There's some mysterious enemy who one knows also helps, but who can cause all kinds of problems and give you all kinds of misinformation. *Mantissa* came partly from that sense; partly, I suppose, from the sense that I think modern literary criticism has altogether got too serious and pious. I get this from so many of the papers I read—that there's really no fun in writing, it's all got to be taken with seriousness. I suppose I'm a paradoxical person. I do love realism on the surface, but I also love the enormous artifice writing involves. In many ways it is a kind of natural thing, engaging in it is a natural process. But once you're engaged it becomes highly artificial. I get a kind of pleasure out of that. If there were such a thing as a Muse, I can't imagine she would be that dreadful, wishy-washy figure of legend. I think it would be . . . it's your anima, obviously. And extremely naughty and unhelpful a lot of the time. That really is the literal feeling you get, on the page—that whatever inspires you can also be a terrible obstacle, a confounded nuisance. And also, I suppose, I wrote the book because I knew it was a book most people would disapprove of. Really, I wanted to give people an opportunity to kick me—which they duly did.

Notes

1 *The Magus*

1 Boston: Little, Brown, 1977. All quoted passages refer to this edition.

2 For a detailed analysis of the differences between the two drafts, see either Wade, "Mystery Enough at Noon," 717–22, or Binns, "A New Version of *The Magus*," 79–84.

3 Berets, "*The Magus*," 97.

4 Introduction to *The Book of Ebenezer LePage*, by G. B. Edwards, p. ix. See also Fowles's treatise *Islands*.

5 Holmes, "Art, Truth, and John Fowles's *The Magus*," 52.

6 Fowles, *The Aristos*, 217.

7 Dwight Eddins has written an excellent article on Fowles's existential theme. He feels that the masque is designed to teach Nicholas "the provisional nature of his own constructs, and the vagaries of hazard." Eddins, "John Fowles: Existence as Authorship," 212.

8 Fleishman, "*The Magus* of the Wizard of the West," 305.

9 Roberta Rubenstein suggests that Nicholas's journey to and return from the underworld parallels the myth of Orpheus. In Fowles's version of the myth, however, Orpheus rescues his Eurydice. See Rubenstein, "Myth, Mystery, and Irony," 328–39. Delma Presley agrees and says that the name "Urfe" is probably meant to suggest Orpheus. Presley, "The Quest of the Bourgeois Hero: An Approach to Fowles's *The Magus*," *Journal of Popular Culture* 6, no. 2 (1972): 396.

10 Binns, "John Fowles: Radical Romancer," 320. In a new article, however, Janet E. Lewis and Barry Olshen protest that Fowles uses the romance tradition straightforwardly: "The more one works on Fowles's writing, the more convincing it becomes that medieval romance constitutes, consciously and unconsciously, the

very roots of his fiction and his thought." Lewis and Olshen, "John Fowles and the Medieval Romance Tradition," 15.

11   In an article published in 1985 Frank G. Novak, Jr., protests that "the final synthesis asserts a view of life that is both empty and terrifying. The view the book propounds is a compound of nihilism and narcissism; it is the response of impotent, insignificant man attempting to cope with immense, threatening, and often mysterious forces he can neither understand nor control." Novak, "The Dialectics of Debasement," 72. Novak's reading recalls an early review of the original version of *The Magus* by the London *Times*. They called the book "unhealthy."

12   Martin Price, "The Irrelevant Detail and the Emergence of Form," in *Aspects of Narrative*, ed. J. Hillis Miller (New York: Columbia University Press, 1971), 83.

13   Robert Huffaker has the most sustained and coherent discussion of Jung's influence on Fowles. See Huffaker, *John Fowles*.

14   Henry James, Preface to *The American*, in *The Art of the Novel* (New York: Scribner's, 1934), 31.

15   Fowles, *The Aristos*, 20.

2   *The Collector*

1   Boston: Little, Brown, 1963. All references are to this edition of the text.

2   Palmer, "John Fowles and the Crickets," 11.

3   Dwight Eddins adds that Clegg creates a masque which, like Conchis's masque, produces a temporary autonomous existence for its participants. But while Conchis's production encourages hazard, Clegg's denies hazard. Eddins, "John Fowles: Existence as Authorship," 204–22.

4   Kermode, *The Sense of an Ending*, 30.

5   Rackham, "John Fowles: The Existential Labyrinth," 91.

6   Ronald Binns shows how Fowles first uses the attributes of romance (as in freeing Clegg from normal social interaction by taking him outside of society, and by using English society as a mythic battleground), and then undercuts them (as in letting the persecuted maiden die). Binns, "John Fowles: Radical Romancer," 317–34. This expectation and denial is a familiar pattern in Fowles.

7   Fowles describes the nemo as "the state of being nobody—'nobodiness.' In short, just as physicists now postulate an anti-matter, so must we consider the possibility that there exists in the human psyche an anti-ego. This is the nemo" (*The Aristos*, 47). Fowles believes that the nemo is a fourth division of the mind, after ego, id, and libido. Hence, Clegg's disease may be understood as an imbalance of the mind's constituents, with the nemo overrunning the others.

8   Bellamy, "John Fowles' Version of the Pastoral," 72–84. Bellamy further reads much of *The Collector* as Clegg's abuse of the pastoral.

9   Kermode, *The Sense of an Ending*, 160.

10   Jeff Rackham feels that Fowles creates an "allegory of existence" in describing the contradictory nature of Miranda's professed identity and her real identity. He

says *The Collector* is "an extended metaphor that is more vivid and perceptive than works by Sartre or Simone de Beauvoir, for Fowles illustrates, perhaps with an ironical jab at himself, that even those (or especially those) who think they have the key to life wrapped up in existential jargon are actually trapped by their own smugness." Rackham, "John Fowles: The Existential Labyrinth," 94.

11   Fowles, *The Aristos*, 215.

12   Jung, *Modern Man in Search of a Soul*, 102.

13   Booth, *The Rhetoric of Fiction*, 99.

14   Booth, *The Rhetoric of Fiction*, 92.

3   *The French Lieutenant's Woman*

1   Fowles, "Notes on Writing a Novel," 88–97.

2   Boston: Little, Brown, 1969. All page references are to this edition of the text.

3   Brantlinger, Adam, and Rothblatt, "*The French Lieutenant's Woman*: A Discussion," 340.

4   Allen, "The Achievement of John Fowles," 66.

5   A. A. DeVitis and William Palmer say, for example, that *The French Lieutenant's Woman* echoes Hardy's *A Pair of Blue Eyes*. They demonstrate how closely related the two novels are in such areas as image patterns, characters, and existential theme. DeVitis and Palmer, "*A Pair of Blue Eyes* Flash at *The French Lieutenant's Woman*," 90–101. Phyllis Grosskurth has argued that the novel's inspiration comes from a novella by James Anthony Froude, *The Lieutenant's Daughter*. Grosskurth, "*The French Lieutenant's Woman*," 130. George Eliot's *Adam Bede* has frequently been cited as an influence, as has Dickens's *Great Expectations* (especially in regard to the double ending). Ruth Christiani Brown has recently published a new study in which she names Melville's *Pierre* as a primary influence. Brown, "*The French Lieutenant's Woman* and *Pierre*," 115–32.

6   Fowles, "Notes on Writing a Novel," 94. Jeff Rackham sees this quasi anachronism as one of the novel's strong points, because "by setting his scene in the middle of the nineteenth century, Fowles can ignore the whole problem of the existential cliche which concerns him so much in his first two novels." In other words, Fowles purifies his ideas of jargon by regressing a century. Rackham, "John Fowles: The Existential Labyrinth," 99.

7   Jung, *Modern Man in Search of a Soul*, 236.

8   Sarah's indeterminate identity has elicited much critical controversy. Most critics like Charles himself) try to identify and explain her rather than to see her in what I believe is her proper role: as a mirror for Charles. John Hagopian says, for example, "There are three possible ways of regarding Sarah: (1) The narrator tells the truth when he says, 'modern women like Sarah exist and I have never understood them.' . . . (2) She is, as Dr. Grogan diagnoses her, a psychopathic personality. (3) She is . . . an intelligent woman who uses whatever tactics she feels

necessary to liberate herself from a society and a culture that oppress, constrain, and stifle her." Hagopian, "Bad Faith in *The French Lieutenant's Woman*," 198.

9 Jung. *The Undiscovered Self*, 102.

10 Cf. Roland Barthes, whom Fowles thinks is one of the finest modern literary theorists: "In the process of communication the course of the 'I' is not homogeneous. For example, when I use the sign 'I' I refer to myself inasmuch as I am talking: here there is an act which is always new, even if it is repeated, an act whose sense is always new. However, arriving at its destination, this sign is received by my interlocutor as a stable sign, product of a complete code whose contents are recurrent. In other words, the 'I' of the one who writes 'I' is not the same as the 'I' which is read by thou. This fundamental dissymmetry of language, linguistically explained by Jesperson and then by Jakobson under the name of 'shifter' or an overlapping of message and code, seems to be finally troubling literature in showing it that intersubjectivity, or rather interlocution, cannot be accomplished simply by wishing, but only by a deep, patient, and often circuitous descent into the labyrinths of meaning." Barthes, "To Write: An Intransitive Verb?" P. 163.

11 Binns, "John Fowles: Radical Romancer," 330.

12 McDaniel, "Games and Godgames," 37.

13 Jung, *The Undiscovered Self*, 56.

14 Adam, in Brantlinger et al., "*The French Lieutenant's Woman*: A Discussion," 347.

15 Evarts, "Fowles's *The French Lieutenant's Woman* as Tragedy," 58.

16 I am indebted for this phrase to Frederick N. Smith, who has used the four drafts of this novel to examine it as a book being written. He concludes that "the author's reactions to what he has himself written become part of the text he is composing." Smith, "Revision and the Style of Revision," 90.

17 A. J. B. Johnson argues that these details constitute Fowles's vigorous claim for his setting to be real and that because he deliberately overdoes the realism, "he achieves its undoing." Fowles, he says, argues for a "reassessment of those habitual *un*surprised responses to more conventional forms of representational writing." Johnson, "Realism in *The French Lieutenant's Woman*," 293–94.

18 Conradi, "*The French Lieutenant's Woman*: Novel, Screenplay, Film," 41. He goes on to say that "Fowles's fiction habitually addresses the ways in which the novel traditionally turns sex into discourse" (42).

19 Scholes, "The Orgastic Fiction of John Fowles," 1.

20 Scholes, "The Orgastic Fiction of John Fowles," 2.

21 The double ending of this novel has generated more critical discussion than any other single aspect. Most critics feel that the reader is offered a choice between the two. (See especially Palmer, *The Fiction of John Fowles*, 74.) The feeling also prevails that a competent reading of the novel will inevitably lead the reader to choose the second, bleak ending. Frederick M. Holmes expresses this popular attitude: "The final ending is both a logical resolution of the novel's themes and

the only one not vitiated by the narrator's irony." (He feels that the first ending is a parody of the closure of most Victorian novels.) Holmes, "The Novel, Illusion, and Reality," 190. Cf. Elizabeth Rankin, who uses "To Marguerite" to show that Fowles preferred the second ending. Rankin, "Cryptic Coloration in *The French Lieutenant's Woman*," 205.

Elizabeth Mansfield uses the endings very imaginatively to examine the "general process" of Fowles's writing "through a study of the artifacts of composition" (276). She uses the four drafts as well as Elizabeth Fowles's five typed pages of commentary on her husband's novel to show how the endings evolved. See Mansfield, "A Sequence of Endings," 275–86. And, most recently, Charles Scruggs offers a new approach to the endings: "All three endings are authentic in that each reflects a fictional universe intimately tied to a specific historical period and the characters' relationship to it." Scruggs, "The Two Endings of *The French Lieutenant's Woman*," 97.

22 Kermode, *The Sense of an Ending*.

4 *Daniel Martin*

1 Boston: Little, Brown, 1977. All quoted passages refer to this edition of the text.

2 In "Dickens, Griffith, and the Film Today," Sergei Eisenstein speaks about film having learned everything from novels. He goes on to give an imaginative analysis of the cinematic qualities of Dickens's work. In Eisenstein, *Film Form* (New York: Harcourt, Brace, 1949).

3 The first chapter of this novel, like the double ending of *The French Lieutenant's Woman*, is a favorite subject for critical contention. The most exhaustive treatment of this chapter has been done by Simon Loveday, who does a close, word-by-word examination of the text. See Loveday, "The Style of John Fowles," 198–204.

4 In an interview with Daniel Halpern, Fowles says, "There are hundreds of things a novel can do that cinema can never do. The cinema can't describe the past very accurately, it can't digress, above all, it can't exclude. . . . You don't have to 'set up' the whole screen [in a novel]. The delight of writing novels is that you can leave out on each page, in each sentence. The novel is an astounding freedom to choose. It will last just as long as artists want to be free to choose." Halpern, "A Sort of Exile in Lyme Regis," 45.

5 Leon Edel, "Fiction and Cinematography: Novel and Camera," in *Theory of the Novel*, ed. Daniel Halpern (New York: Oxford University Press, 1968).

6 Docherty, "A Constant Reality," 127.

7 The great amount of this kind of dialogue led many of Fowles's countrymen (Americans gave the book ovations) to condemn his novel. Kerry McSweeney, for example, calls it a "quite disappointing novel," full of "inert prose," with "lifeless and unfocused characters"; middle-brow best-seller fiction." McSweeney, "Withering into Truth," 37.

8 Ina Ferris suggests that the middle portion of that epigraph, about a woman who

has gone to the nether world, establishes Jane as Eurydice and Dan as Orpheus. She feels that in all Fowles's novels "a woman is the elusive Eurydice who abandons the hero and draws him into the underworld." Ferris, "Realist Intention and Mythic Impulse in *Daniel Martin*," 150.

9   Alter, "*Daniel Martin* and the Mimetic Task," 70.

10   Fowles's Afterword to *Le Grand Meaulnes (The Wanderer)* underlines his interest in a person telling the story of his life by reconstructing his past. Fowles painstakingly demonstrates the great degree to which the story of Meaulnes is also the story of Alain-Fournier. He calls the reconstruction a "unique piece of alchemized memory." Alain-Fournier, *The Wanderer.*

11   Fowles says in *The Aristos*, "The more absolute death seems, the more authentic life becomes" (34).

12   Several critics are now beginning to read *Daniel Martin* as a system of parallels. Susan Strehle Klemtner was the first to write about a pattern of what she calls counterpoles in the novel. She discovered that "the novel's landscapes form a centrally significant contrast between the sacred combe (*la bonne vaux*) and the end of the world." Klemtner, "The Counterpoles of John Fowles's *Daniel Martin*," 63. In a recent essay Sue Park traces the symbol of ruins through the novel and finds that the three visits to ruins are "integral parts of the 'whole sight' search" (159). She says the three settings develop a "progression of mounting force. . . . This incremental pattern parallels movement from innocence and youth toward knowledge and age" (161). Park, "Time and Ruins," 157–63.

13   The ghost motif is so insistent that it led John Bernstein to make a connection between *Daniel Martin* and Ibsen's *Ghosts*. Bernstein, "John Fowles's Use of Ibsen in *Daniel Martin*," 10.

14   Gardner, "Moral Fiction," 23. He goes on to laud Fowles for using "the symbolism that arises out of life itself, not the symbolism imposed by the dogmatist. . . . *Daniel Martin* is a masterpiece of symbolically charged realism: every symbol rises or is made to seem to rise, out of the story."

15   Robert Arlett reads *Daniel Martin* as a "contemporary epic," because both its subject ("the interaction of public and private worlds") and its structure (the flashing backward and forward form a central point of tension) "approximate the Aristotelian notion of epic." Arlett, "*Daniel Martin* and the Contemporary Epic Novel," 176.

16   Park, "John Fowles, Daniel Martin, and Simon Wolfe," 167. In her essay Park uses the mirror motif to show how Fowles identifies with his protagonist.

5   *Mantissa*

1   Boston: Little, Brown, 1982. All quoted passages refer to this edition of the text.

2   New York: New American Library, 1966. The name Miles probably comes from another of O'Brien's (né Brian O'Nolan) pseudonyms—Myles na gCopaleen. The

name Green is probably a reference to the fact that the narrator of O'Brien's novel could only read green books.

3   Fugal inversion occurs when an interval is transposed so that the bass becomes the upper voice. In this particular argument Miles is searching for the "upper hand" after Erato has had it for so long. He is trying to seduce her out of a pique. Erato is introduced in a kind of inverse canonical form. She plays a scale in the Lydian mode, becomes Erato the Muse, then plays the same scale in reverse after the metamorphosis.

4   Robert Scholes, "Towards a Semiotics of Literature," in *What Is Literature?* ed. Paul Hernadi (Bloomington: University of Indiana Press, 1978), 236.

5   Fowles, "Notes on Writing a Novel," 92.

6   Fowles mentioned this connection in conversation, June 1983.

6 *A Maggot*

1   Boston: Little, Brown, 1985. All quoted passages refer to this edition.

2   Carl Jung, *Synchronicity: An Acausal Connecting Principle* (Bollingen Series 51. New York: Pantheon, 1955), 28.

3   "Beyond the fact of his [Bartholomew's] existence nothing is certainly known of him." Herbert Thurston, S.J., and Donald Attwater, eds. *Butler's Lives of the Saints* (New York: P. J. Kenedy and Sons, 1963), 391. Interestingly, many Biblical scholars suggest that Bartholomew and Nathaneal were the same person. Perhaps the dual identity of the Apostle is reflected in the ambiguity of Dick and Bartholomew.

4   Carl Jung, "The Principal Archetypes," in *The Modern Tradition*, ed. Richard Ellmann and Charles Feidelson, Jr. (New York: Oxford University Press, 1965), 657.

5   From "The Republic," in *Great Dialogues of Plato*, ed. Eric H. Warmington and Philip G. Rouse. Trans. W. H. D. Rouse (New York: New American Library, 1956), 313.

6   The ratio between any two Fibonacci numbers approaches phi as a limit. James Newman says, "This number is no other but the ratio known as the *aurea secto*, which has played such a role in attempts to reduce beauty of proportion to a mathematical formula." Newman, *The World of Mathematics*, vol. 1 (New York: Simon and Schuster, 1956), 718.

7   H. E. Huntley, a modern mathematician, echoes Bartholomew's theory: "One craves to understand why phi, which permeates the pentagram and is at home in platonic polyhedra, should also be the limit of a ratio initiated so casually. . . . The conviction grows stronger that we have chanced on an unexplored world which, like the universe around us, appears to have no boundaries. . . . Are we to regard phi as a 'constant of nature'?" Huntley, *The Divine Proportion: A Study in Mathematical Beauty* (New York: Dover, 1970), 36. He goes on to say that phi

appears in the configuration of the hydrogen atom, in the honeycomb, the sun-flower, the fir cone, the pineapple, the spira mirabilis, the wavelengths between the twelve semitones of the chromatic scale, and in phyllotaxis, the spiral arrangement—a helical form common in all living things—of leaves on a stem.

8 Jung, *Synchronicity,* 58. Jung goes on to say, "Numbers were as much found as invented, and . . . in consequence they possess a relative autonomy analogous to that of the archetypes."

9 From "The Shaker Adventure," in *The Shakers and the World's People,* by Flo Morse. (New York: Dodd, Mead, 1980), 114–15.

10 "Every Good and Simple Gift," in Morse, *The Shakers and the World's People,* 115.

11 The collected sayings of Mother Ann Lee are found in *Testimonies of the Life, Character, Revelations, and Doctrines of Mother Ann Lee and the Elders with Her* (Albany: Weed, Parsons, 1888).

12 Henri Desroche, *The American Shakers from Neo-Christianity to Presocialism,* trans. John K. Savacool (Amherst: University of Massachusetts Press, 1971), 149.

13 "Life in the Christ Spirit," in Morse, *The Shakers and the World's People,* 72.

14 Edward Deming Andrews, *The People Called Shakers* (New York: Dover, 1963), 12.

Bibliography

Works by John Fowles

Novels, Translations, and Nonfiction

The Aristos: A Self-portrait in Ideas. Boston: Little, Brown, 1964. Revised edition, 1970.
Cinderella, by Charles Perrault. 1697. Translated by John Fowles. Boston: Little, Brown, 1976.
The Collector. Boston: Little, Brown, 1963.
Daniel Martin. Boston: Little, Brown, 1977.
The Ebony Tower. Boston: Little, Brown, 1974.
The Enigma of Stonehenge. London: Jonathan Cape, 1980.
The French Lieutenant's Woman. Boston: Little, Brown, 1969.
Islands. Boston: Little, Brown, 1978.
A Maggot. Boston: Little, Brown, 1985.
The Magus. Boston: Little, Brown, 1965. Revised edition, 1977.
Mantissa. Boston: Little, Brown, 1982.
Ourika, by Claire de Durfort. 1824. Translated by John Fowles. Austin, Texas: W. Thomas Taylor, 1977.
Poems. New York: Ecco, 1973.
Shipwreck. Boston: Little, Brown, 1975.
Steep Holm—A Case History in the Study of Evolution. With Rodney Legg. London: Kenneth Allsop Memorial Trust, 1978.
The Tree. Boston: Little, Brown, 1980.

Essays and Articles

Afterword to *The Wanderer (Le Grand Meaulnes)*, by Henri Alain-Fournier. Translated by Lowell Bair. New York: New American Library, 1971.

Foreword and Afterword to *The Hound of the Baskervilles*, by Sir Arthur Conan Doyle. 1902. Reprint edition, London: John Murray and Jonathan Cape, 1974.

Foreword to *The Lais of Marie de France*, by Marie de France. Translated and introduced by Robert Hanning and Joan Ferrante. New York: E. P. Dutton, 1978.

Introduction, Glossary, and Appendix to *Mehalah: A Story of the Salt Marshes*, by Sabine Baring-Gould. 1880. Reprint edition, London: Chatto and Windus, 1969.

Introduction and Glossary to *The Book of Ebenezer LePage*, by G. B. Edwards. New York: Alfred A. Knopf, 1981.

"Hardy and the Hag." In *Thomas Hardy After Fifty Years*. Edited by Lance St. John Butler, pp. 28–42. London: Macmillan, 1977.

"Is the Novel Dead?" *Books* 1 (1970): 2–5.

"I Write Therefore I Am." *Evergreen Review* 8 (1964): 16–17, 89–90.

"Jacqueline Kennedy Onassis and Other First (and Last) Ladies." *Cosmopolitan*, October 1970, 144–49.

"*The Magus* Revisited." London *Times* 28 May 1977, 7.

"Making a Pitch for Cricket." *Sports Illustrated*, 21 May 1973, 100–103.

"Marriage, Passion, and Love: My Side of the Dialogue." *Vogue*, 15 November 1964, 114–15.

"*My Recollection of Kafka*." *Mosaic* 3 (1970): 31–41.

"Notes on Writing a Novel." *Harper's Magazine* 237 (1968): 88–97.

"On Being English But Not British." *Texas Quarterly* 7 (1964): 154–62.

"Remembering Cruikshank." *Library Chronicle* 35 (1973): xiii–xvi.

"Seeing Nature Whole." *Harper's Magazine* 259 (1979): 49–68.

"The Trouble with Starlets." *Holiday* (June 1966): 12–20.

"Weeds, Bugs, Americans." *Sports Illustrated*, 21 December 1970, 84–88.

Untitled Essay in *Bookmarks*. Edited by Fredrick Raphael, pp. 53–57. London: Jonathan Cape, 1975.

Book Reviews of Nonfiction

"All Too Human." Review of *Birds, Beasts, and Men*, by H. R. Hays. *New Statesman*, 20 July 1973, 90–91.

"Aperitifs." Review of *Companion Guide to Devon and Cornwall*, by Darrell Bates. *New Statesman*, 11 June 1976, 785–86.

"Bleeding Hearts." Review of *The Akenham Burial Case*, by Ronald Fletcher. *New Statesman*, 14 June 1974, 842–43.

"Come to Britain?" Review of *Circles and Standing Stones*, by Evan Hadingham. *New Statesman*, 5 December 1975, 728–29.

"Confined Species." Review of *The Ark in the Park*, by Wilfred Blunt; *London's Zoo*, by Gwynne Vevers; *Golden Days*, by Lord Zuckerman. *New Statesman*, 7 May 1976, 612–14.

"Country Matters." Review of *Finches*, by Ian Newton; *The Pollination of Flowers*, by Michael Proctor and Peter Yeo. *New Statesman*, 27 April 1973, 620–21.

"Death on the Ocean Wave." Review of *Supership*, by Noel Mostert; *Death Raft*, by Alexander McKee. *New Statesman*, 4 July 1975, 22–24.

"For the Dark." Review of *The Death of Narcissus*, by Morris Fraser. *New Statesman*, 18 February 1977, 221–22.

Review of *From Cliche to Archetype*, by Marshall McLuhan, with Wilfred Watson. *Saturday Review*, 21 November 1970, 32–33.

"Gory Details." Review of *Blood: The Paramount Humour*, by Earl Hackett. *New Statesman*, 9 March 1973, 345–46.

"Guide to a Man-Made Planet." Review of *The World of Charles Dickens*, by Angus Wilson. *Life*, 4 September 1970, 8–9.

"Horse Magic." Review of *The Days That We Have Seen*, by George Evart Evans. *New Statesman*, 1 August 1975, 148.

"Ivory Towers." Review of *Lighthouse*, by Tony Parker. *New Statesman*, 9 May 1975, 628–29.

"Late Harvest." Review of *The Worm Forgives the Plough*, by John Stewart Collis. *New Statesman*, 26 October 1973, 612–13.

"A Lost World." Review of *Lark Rise to Candleford*, by Flora Thompson. *New Statesman*. 3 August 1973, 154–55.

"Menhirs Maketh Men." Review of *Beyond Stonehenge*, by Gerald S. Hawkins; *The Old Stones of Land's End*, by John Michell. *New Statesman*, 22 March 1974, 412–13.

"Missing Beats." Review of *Autobiography*, by Margiad Evans, *New Statesman*, 13 September 1974, 352.

"The Most Secretive of Victorian Writers, a Kind of Giant Mouse." Review of *Thomas Hardy: Distance and Desire*, by J. Hillis Miller. *New York Times Book Review*, 21 June 1970, 4.

"Other Edens." Review of *Landscapes and Seasons of the Medieval World*, by Derek Pearsall and Elizabeth Salter. *New Statesman*, 12 October 1973, 524–25.

"Outlook Unsettled." Review of *Times of Feast, Times of Famine*, by Emmanuel LeRoy Ladurie. *New Statesman*, 26 January 1973, 130–31.

"The Rambler." Review of *The Naturalist in Britain*, by David Elliston Allen. *New Statesman*, 6 August 1976, 183–84.

"Royal Stews." Review of *The Cleveland Street Scandal*, by H. Montgomery Hyde. *New Statesman*, 19 March 1976, 362–64.

"Softer than Beef." Review of *Alive*, by Piers Paul Read. *New Statesman*, 10 May 1974, 664–65.

"A Study in Scarlet." Review of *The Adventures of Conan Doyle*, by Charles Higham. *New Statesman*, 26 November 1976, 751–52.

"Unnatural Habitats." Review of *The Unofficial Countryside*, by Richard Mabey; *In-*

sects of Britain and Northern Europe, by Michael Chinery; *The Book of Flowers,*
by Alice M. Coats. *New Statesman,* 14 December 1973, 912.

"Voices of the Deep." Review of *Whales, Dolphins, and Seals,* by D. E. Gaskin; *Man's
Place,* by Karl-Erik Fichtelius and Sverre Sjolander. *New Statesman,* 15 June
1973, 892–93.

Reviews of Irish Fiction in The Irish Press, *as guest reviewer for the Thursday
"Book Page," edited by David Marcus.*

"On Target." Review of *Out of Focus,* by Alf Maclochlainn. 12 January 1978.

"Downandoutdom." Review of *Four Novellas,* by Samuel Beckett. 16 February 1978.

"The Nature of Irishness." Review of *Selected Stories of Sean O'Faolain,* by Sean
O' Faolain. 13 April 1978.

"Sidesteps." Review of *The Destinies of Darcy Dancer, Gentleman,* by J. P. Donleavy.
1 June 1978.

"Irish Keys." Review of *Getting Through,* by John McGahern; *Mrs. Reinhardt and
Other Stories,* by Edna O'Brien. 15 June 1978.

"Central Values." Review of *Lovers of Their Time,* by William Trevor. 28 September
1978.

"Crime and Punishment." Review of *Bogmail,* by Patrick McGinley. 19 October 1978.

"Mainstream and Sidestream." Review of *Paddy No More: Modern Irish Short Stories,* edited by William Vorm. 28 December 1978.

Secondary Sources

Alain-Fournier, Henri. *The Wanderer.* Translated by Lowell Bair. New York: New
American Library, 1971.

Allen, Walter. "The Achievement of John Fowles." *Encounter* 35 (1970): 64–67.

Alter, Robert. "*Daniel Martin* and the Mimetic Task." *Genre* 14, no. 1 (1981): 65–78.

Arlett, Robert. "*Daniel Martin* and the Contemporary Epic Novel." *Modern Fiction
Studies* 31, no. 1 (1985): 173–87.

Barnum, Carol. "John Fowles's *Daniel Martin:* A Vision of Whole Sight." *Literary
Review* 25, no. 1 (1981): 64–79.

Barthes, Roland. "To Write: An Intransitive Verb?" in *The Structuralists.* Edited by
Richard DeGeorge and Fernande DeGeorge, pp. 155–67. Garden City: Doubleday,
1972.

Bellamy, Michael O. "John Fowles' Version of the Pastoral: Private Valleys and the
Parity of Existence." *Critique Studies in Modern Fiction* 21, no. 2 (1979): 72–84.

Berets, Ralph. "*The Magus:* A Study in the Creation of a Personal Myth." *Twentieth
Century Literature* 19 (1973): 89–98.

Bernstein, John. "John Fowles' Use of Ibsen in *Daniel Martin.*" *Notes on Contemporary Literature* 9 (1979): 10.

Billy, Ted. "Homo Solitarus: Isolation and Estrangement in *The Magus.*" *Research Studies* 48 (1980): 129–41.

Binns, Ronald. "John Fowles: Radical Romancer." *Critical Quarterly* 15 (1973): 317–34.

_____. "A New Version of *The Magus.*" *Critical Quarterly* 19, no. 4 (1977): 79–84.

Boomsma, Patricia J. "Whole Sight: Fowles, Lukács, and *Daniel Martin.*" *Journal of Modern Literature* 8 (1980–81): 325–36.

Booth, Wayne. *The Rhetoric of Fiction.* Chicago: University of Chicago Press, 1961.

Bradbury, Malcolm. "John Fowles's *The Magus.*" In *Sense and Sensibility in Twentieth-century Writing.* Edited by Brom Weber, pp. 26–38. Carbondale: Southern Illinois University Press, 1970.

Brantlinger, Patrick; Ian Adam; and Sheldon Rothblatt. "*The French Lieutenant's Woman:* A Discussion." *Victorian Studies* 15 (1972): 339–56.

Brown, Ruth Christiani. "*The French Lieutenant's Woman* and *Pierre:* Echo and Answer." *Modern Fiction Studies* 31, no. 1 (1985): 115–32.

Churchill, Thomas. "Waterhouse, Storey, and Fowles: Which Way out of the Room?" *Critique* 10 (1968): 72–87.

Conradi, Peter J. "*The French Lieutenant's Woman:* Novel, Screenplay, Film." *Critical Quarterly* 24, no. 1 (1982): 41–57.

_____. *John Fowles.* Contemporary Author Series. New York: Methuen, 1982.

Corbett, Thomas. "The Film and the Book: A Case Study of *The Collector.*" *English Journal* 57 (1968): 328–33.

Costa, Richard Hauer. "Trickery's Mixed Bag: The Perils of Fowles' *The French Lieutenant's Woman.*" *Rocky Mountain Review of Language and Literature* 29, no. 1 (1975): 1–9.

Detweiler, Robert. "The Unity of John Fowles' Fiction." *Notes on Contemporary Literature* 1 (1971): 3–4.

DeVitis, A. A., and William J. Palmer. "*A Pair of Blue Eyes* Flash at *The French Lieutenant's Woman.*" *Contemporary Literature* 15 (1974): 90–101.

D'Haen, Theo. "Fowles, Lodge, and the Problematic Novel." *Dutch Quarterly Review* 9 (1979): 162–75.

Dixon, Terrell F. "Expostulation and Reply: The Character of Clegg in Fowles and Sillitoe." *Notes on Contemporary Literature* 4, no. 2 (1974): 7–9.

Docherty, Thomas. "A Constant Reality: The Presentation of Character in the Fiction of John Fowles." *Novel* 14 (1981): 118–34.

Eddins, Dwight. "John Fowles: Existence as Authorship." *Contemporary Literature* 17 (1976): 204–22.

Evarts, Prescott, Jr. "Fowles' *The French Lieutenant's Woman* as Tragedy." *Critique* 13 (1972): 57–69.

_____. "John Fowles: A Checklist." *Critique* 13 (1972): 105–7.

Ferris, Ina. "Realist Intention and Mythic Impulse in *Daniel Martin.*" *Journal of Narrative Technique* 12 (1982): 146–53.

Fleishman, Avrom. "*The Magus* of the Wizard of the West." *Journal of Modern Literature* 5 (1976): 297–314.

Franklyn, A. Fredric. "The Hand in the Fist (A Study of William Wyler's *The Collector*)." *Trace* (Spring 1966): 22–27, 101–7.

Gardner, John. "Moral Fiction." *Saturday Review*, 1 April 1978, 30–33.

Glaserfeld, Ernst von. "Reflections on John Fowles's *The Magus* and the Construction of Reality." *Georgia Review* 33 (1979): 444–48.

Gramsci, Antonio. *Selections from the Prison Notebooks of Antonio Gramsci*. Edited by Quintin Hoare and Geoffrey Nowell-Smith. London: Lawrence and Wishart, 1971.

Gross, David. "Historical Consciousness and the Modern Novel: The Uses of History in the Fiction of John Fowles." *Studies in the Humanities* 7, no. 1 (1978): 19–27.

Grosskurth, Phyllis. "*The French Lieutenant's Woman*." *Victorian Studies* 16 (September 1972): 130–31.

Hagopian, John V. "Bad Faith in *The French Lieutenant's Woman*." *Contemporary Literature* 23 (1982): 191–201.

Halpern, Daniel. "A Sort of Exile in Lyme Regis." *London Magazine* n.s. 10, no. 12 (1971): 34–46.

Holmes, Frederick M. "Art, Truth, and John Fowles: *The Magus*." *Modern Fiction Studies* 31, no. 1 (1985): 45–56.

————. "The Novel, Illusion, and Reality: The Paradox of Omniscience in *The French Lieutenant's Woman*." *Journal of Narrative Technique* 11 (1981): 184–98.

Huffaker, Robert. *John Fowles*. Twayne's English Author Series 292. Boston: Twayne, 1980.

Johnson, A. J. B. "Realism in *The French Lieutenant's Woman*." *Journal of Modern Literature* 8 (1980–81): 287–302.

Jung, Carl. *Modern Man in Search of a Soul*. New York: Harcourt, Brace, 1933.

————. *The Undiscovered Self*. Boston: Little, Brown, 1957.

Kane, Patricia. "The Fallen Woman as Free-Thinker in *The French Lieutenant's Woman*." *Notes on Contemporary Literature* 2 (1972): 8–10.

Kaplan, Fred. "Victorian Modernists: Fowles and Nabokov." *Journal of Narrative Technique* 3 (1973): 108–20.

Karl, Frederick. *A Reader's Guide to the Contemporary English Novel*. Revised edition. New York: Farrar, Straus and Giroux, 1972.

Kermode, Frank. *The Sense of an Ending*. London: Oxford University Press, 1966.

Klemtner, Susan Strehle. "The Counterpoles of John Fowles's *Daniel Martin*." *Critique* 21, no. 2 (1979): 59–71.

Laughlin, Rosemary. "Faces of Power in the Novels of John Fowles." *Critique* 13 (1972): 71–80.

Lever, Karen M. "The Education of John Fowles." *Critique* 21 (1979): 85–99.

Lewis, Janet E., and Barry N. Olshen. "Fowles and the Medieval Romance Tradition." *Modern Fiction Studies* 31, no. 1 (1985): 15–30.

Loveday, Simon. "Magus or Midas?" *Oxford Literary Review* 2, no. 3 (1977): 34–35.

———. "The Style of John Fowles: Tense and Person in the First Chapter of *Daniel Martin*." *Journal of Narrative Technique* 10 (1980): 198–204.

Lukács, Georg. *The Historical Novel*. Translated by Hannah Mitchell and Stanley Mitchell. London: Merlin Press, 1962.

———. *The Meaning of Contemporary Realism*. Translated by John and Necke Mander. London: Merlin Press, 1963.

McDaniel, Ellen. "Games and Godgames in *The Magus* and *The French Lieutenant's Woman*." *Modern Fiction Studies* 31, no. 1 (1985): 31–42.

———. "*The Magus*: Fowles's Tarot Quest." *Journal of Modern Literature* 8 (1980–81): 247–60.

McSweeney, Kerry. "Withering into Truth; John Fowles and *Daniel Martin*." *Critical Quarterly* 20, no. 4 (1978): 31–38.

Magalaner, Marvin. "The Fool's Journey: John Fowles's *The Magus*." In *Old Lines, New Forces: Essays on the Contemporary English Novel, 1960–1970*. Edited by Robert K. Morris, pp. 81–92. Cranbury, N.J.: Fairleigh Dickinson University Press, 1976.

Mansfield, Elizabeth. "A Sequence of Endings: The Manuscripts of *The French Lieutenant's Woman*." *Journal of Modern Literature* 8 (1980–81): 275–86.

Mathews, James W. "Fowles's Artistic Freedom: Another Stone from James's House." *Notes on Contemporary Literature* 4, no. 2 (1974): 2–3.

Mellors, John. "Collectors and Creators: The Novels of John Fowles." *London Magazine* n.s. 14, no. 6 (1975): 65–72.

Mills, John. "Fowles' Indeterminacy: An Art of Alternatives." *West Coast Review* 10 (1972): 32–36.

Novak, Frank, Jr. "The Dialectics of Debasement in *The Magus*." *Modern Fiction Studies* 31, no. 1 (1985): 71–82.

O'Brien, Flann. *At Swim-Two-Birds*. New York: New American Library, 1976.

Olshen, Barry N. *John Fowles*. Ungar Modern Literature Series. New York: Ungar, 1980.

Palmer, William J. *The Fiction of John Fowles: Tradition, Art and the Loneliness of Self-hood*. Columbia: University of Missouri Press, 1974.

———. "John Fowles and the Crickets." *Modern Fiction Studies* 31, no. 1 (1985): 3–13.

Park, Sue. "John Fowles, Daniel Martin, and Simon Wolfe." *Modern Fiction Studies* 31, no. 1 (1985): 165–71.

———. "Time and Ruins in John Fowles's *Daniel Martin*." *Modern Fiction Studies* 31, no. 1 (1985): 157–63.

Pinter, Harold. *The French Lieutenant's Woman: A Screenplay*. Boston: Little, Brown, 1981.

Rackham, Jeff. "John Fowles: The Existential Labyrinth." *Critique* 13, no. 3 (1972): 89–103.

Rankin, Elizabeth D. "Cryptic Coloration in *The French Lieutenant's Woman*." *Journal of Narrative Technique* 3 (1973): 193–207.

Rose, Gilbert J. "*The French Lieutenant's Woman:* The Unconscious Significance of a Novel to Its Author." *American Imago* 29 (1972): 165–76.

Rubenstein, Roberta. "Myth, Mystery, and Irony: John Fowles' *The Magus*." *Contemporary Literature* 16 (1975): 328–39.

Scholes, Robert. "The Illiberal Imagination." *New Literary History* 4 (1973): 521–40.

————. "The Orgastic Fiction of John Fowles." *Hollins Critic* 6 (1969): 1–12.

Scruggs, Charles. "The Two Endings of *The French Lieutenant's Woman*." *Modern Fiction Studies* 31, no. 1 (1985): 95–113.

Seferis, George. *George Seferis: Collected Poems 1924–1955.* Translated by Edmund Keeley and Philip Sherrard. Princeton: Princeton University Press, 1967.

Smith, Frederick N. "Revision and Style of Revision in *The French Lieutenant's Woman*." *Modern Fiction Studies* 31, no. 1 (1985): 85–94.

Tatham, Michael. "Two Novels: Notes on the Works of John Fowles." *New Blackfriars* 52 (1971): 404–11.

Wade, Cory. "Mystery Enough at Noon: John Fowles's Revision of *The Magus*." *Southern Review* 15 (1979): 717–23.

Walker, David H. "Subversion of Narrative in the Work of Andre Gide and John Fowles." *Comparative Criticism: A Yearbook.* Edited by Elinor Shaffer, pp. 187–212. Cambridge: Cambridge University Press, 1980.

Wolfe, Peter. *John Fowles: Magus and Moralist.* 2d ed. Lewisburg, Penn.: Bucknell University Press, 1979.

Wymard, Eleanor B. "'A New Version of the Midas Touch': *Daniel Martin* and *The World According to Garp*." *Modern Fiction Studies* 27 (1981): 284–86.

Index

Alain-Fournier, Henri, 19, 118; *Le Grand Meaulnes*, 110, 198 (n. 10)
Attis, 145
Austen, Jane, 178

Barthes, Roland, 177, 181, 196 (n. 10)
Bartholomew (Apostle), 146
Beckett, Samuel, 125
Bergman, Ingmar, 152
Bloom, Leopold, 121
Booth, Wayne, 55, 57, 82
Bradbury, Malcolm, 180
Bradbury, Ray, 186
Browning, Robert: "Childe Roland to the Dark Tower Came," 147; "Porphyria's Lover," 46
Bunyan, John: *Pilgrim's Progress*, 147

Carroll, Lewis, 107
Chandler, Raymond, 178
Chaucer, Geoffrey: *The Canterbury Tales*, 147
Citizen Kane, 94
Conrad, Joseph, 34, 66
Cybele, 145

Dedalus, Stephen, 90
de la Bretonne, Restif, 110

Descartes, René, 120
Dickens, Charles, 84, 178

Edel, Leon, 90
Edwards, G. B.: *The Book of Ebenezer Lepage*, 190
Eisenstein, Sergei, 197 (n. 2)
Eleusinian mysteries, 28
Eliot, T. S., 101, 112; "Journey of the Magi," 147; *The Waste Land*, 147
Escher, M. C., 106

Faulkner, William, 63; *The Sound and the Fury*, 55
Faustus, 146
Fibonacci series, 157, 199 (nn. 6, 7)
Flaubert, Gustave, 178
Fowles, John: *The Aristos*, 12, 15, 37, 78, 85, 170, 184; *The Collector*, 2, 12, 39–58, 62, 82, 88, 114, 130, 171, 175, 182; *Daniel Martin*, 87–118, 125, 128, 136, 147; *The Ebony Tower*, 2, 88, 114, 115; *The Enigma of Stonehenge*, 142; *The French Lieutenant's Woman*, 5, 7, 9, 57, 59–85, 88, 97, 102, 113, 114, 116, 118, 127, 129; *Islands*, 170; *A Maggot*, 2, 5, 135–68; *The Magus*, 2, 9, 11–37, 40, 44, 46, 48, 57, 62, 73, 75,

Fowles, John (*continued*)
  83, 88, 107, 113, 114, 143, 172, 182,
  184, 185, 189; *Mantissa*, 7, 114, 119–
  33, 176, 190–91; *The Tree*, 170, 186
Freud, Sigmund, 30, 35, 67, 97, 111, 188
Frye, Northrop, 118

Greene, Graham, 178

Hardy, Thomas, 84, 113
Hawthorne, Nathaniel, 41
Hemingway, Ernest, 178
Heraclitus, 27, 54
Hitchcock, Alfred, 41, 48, 82
Hitler, Adolf, 9, 82

Ibsen, Henrik: *Ghosts*, 198 (n. 13)

James, Henry, 37, 41; *The Turn of the
  Screw*, 125
John the Baptist, 146
Jung, Carl, 9, 35, 54, 64, 65, 77, 143,
  148, 159, 188

Kafka, Franz, 123
Kepler, Johannes, 157
Kermode, Frank, 41, 48, 84–85

Lawrence, D. H., 104
Leavis, F. R., 180–81
Lemprière, John, 121
Lukács, Georg, 128

Marx, Karl, 81
Mary Magdalene, 147
Merlin, 124
Mill, John Stuart, 181

Miller, J. Hillis, 175
Morgan LeFay, 124
Muses, 114

Nabokov, Vladimir, 81
Narcissus, 21
Nazism, 9, 46, 62
Newton, Sir Isaac, 142

O'Brien, Flann, 198 (n. 2); *At Swim-
  Two-Birds*, 122, 129–30

Pandora, 146
Persephone, 28
Plato: allegory of the cave, 155
Poe, Edgar Allan, 41
Pynchon, Thomas, 173

Richards, I. A., 180
Robbe-Grillet, Alain, 81
Rossetti, Dante Gabriel, 66

Salinger, J. D., 173
Sartre, Jean-Paul, 184
Scholes, Robert, 83, 84, 127
Seferis, George, 94, 96, 101, 102
Shakers, 158–67
Sterne, Laurence, 81
Stonehenge, 159, 162

Tate, Allen, 84
Thackeray, William Makepeace, 174
Thomas, Dylan, 90
Twin myths: Winnebago, 146

Walpurgisnacht, 148
Waugh, Evelyn, 172, 178